Far from Rome, Near to God

Far from Rome, Near to God

The Testimonies of Fifty Converted Roman Catholic Priests

Edited by
Richard Bennett and Martin Buckingham

THE BANNER OF TRUTH TRUST

THE BANNER OF TRUTH TRUST
3 Murrayfield Road, Edinburgh EH12 6EL
P.O. Box 621, Carlisle, Pennsylvania 17013, USA

*

© Richard Bennett & Martin Buckingham
First Published 1994
First Banner of Truth Trust Edition 1997
ISBN 0 85151 7331

*

Typeset at The Spartan Press Ltd,
Lymington, Hants
Printed in Finland by WSOY

Contents

Foreword

It has been a great joy and a sadness to read this book. A joy because we have here, in every chapter, a reminder of what real Christianity is. The Apostle Paul in 1 Corinthians 15:3–4 sets down as fundamental truths of the faith the death and resurrection of the Lord Jesus Christ. A Christian, then, is one who understands the meaning of the death which Christ suffered in his place, but also one who has entered into the experience of knowing Christ as the living Saviour. The kingdom of God is not something which we are to enter at death, but, as Christ teaches in John 3, the moment we are born again we enter into that kingdom and we begin for the first time to 'see' spiritual things. This book recounts the testimonies of many men, most of them unknown to each other and living in different places, who came by God's grace into this living knowledge of Christ. Their concern in making their experience known in these pages is not to draw others to themselves or to any organization, or even to any particular church. Their desire is that Christ himself should be known and that men and women everywhere should be brought into the same joy which they have found.

But this is also a sad book, for it is proof that some may

believe that they are actually Christians and may even be engaged as workers in professing churches, and yet all the time, like Nicodemus in John 3, know nothing of a real salvation. Here are men who found that the Church of Rome, far from being a safe guide to Christ, was actually leading them away from him. When Cardinal Heenan was dying he declared, 'The Church has given me everything.' The testimony of these men will cause readers to ask whether what the Church of Rome professes to impart to people is actually true. That is a question that can only be settled by taking the Bible as a rule and, wherever that is done with true prayer to God for light and help, the consequence will be the same as was found in the lives of all these writers. But we must remember that it is not only in the Church of Rome that people can be so misled. Any church which does not teach people to put no confidence in man, but to put trust in Christ alone, is in equal blindness.

I believe that the testimonies found in these pages will be used of God to his glory because they are not the words of those seeking to advance themselves. They simply reflect the desire of men whose controlling passion has been to honour Christ and his Word. A Christian is a poor redeemed sinner for whom *Christ* has given everything. May this book be used to increase this testimony in all the world!

IAIN H. MURRAY

Is the only purpose of those selected to provide testimonies with the reader with insight?

Editorial Comment

We have endeavoured to select testimonies which reflect the biblical principles that salvation is by grace alone, through faith alone, in Christ alone, on the authority of the Bible alone, so that God alone should have the glory. This has been done with a pastoral purpose: the salvation of souls. We have not produced a theological manual, nor is it the intention of the editors or those who have assisted in compiling the book to endorse every doctrinal statement made in the testimonies. We do however truly praise the Lord for the unity of faith expressed among us.

For further information or assistance please contact:

The Converted Catholic Mission
P.O. Box 515
Leicester
LE3 6GY
UK
Director: Martin Buckingham

Berean Beacon of Oregon
P.O. Box 55353
Portland
OR 97238–5353
USA
Telephone and FAX: (503) 257–5995
E-mail: bereanbennett@juno.com
Director: Richard Bennett

MARTIN BUCKINGHAM
RICHARD BENNETT

Acknowledgements

The testimonies themselves give thanks and praise to God for his sovereign grace that made the account of each life possible.

While thanking the Lord, we wish also to express heartfelt thanks to his faithful servants who have made this collection possible. First is Janice Buckingham, Martin's wife, who has been the greatest encouragement to Martin since he initiated the work some years ago. Without her untiring work we simply would not have a book. The publishing, business and financial acumen behind the first edition of the book was that of J.A. Tony Tosti. We truly appreciate him.

For translations from other languages we are deeply grateful to Michael and Chris Reynolds of the UK for their devout and much needed work. In the USA, when the stack of typewritten material was first transferred to computer, the Lord provided the devoted and untiring help of John and Bonnie Tantanella. The dedicated work of Sylvia Thompson and Denise Hiller was invaluable. May the Lord truly bless them. Word-by-word proofreading for the first edition was carefully done by Pastor Ed Bauer, to whom we express deep thanks.

For the testimony of John Preston we wish to thank *The Reformer*, a publication of the Protestant Alliance of Bedford, UK, and the Protestant Truth Society of London.

Henry Gregory Adams was a real blessing to us in giving us permission to use his testimony and also in making known to us other testimonies in the magazine *The Convert*. We are very grateful to the Metropolitan Tabernacle, London, for permission to reproduce testimonies from their publication *How Real Is Your Religion?*

We are thankful to Roland Hall and the Italian Missionary Fellowship, London, for communicating with Salvatore Gargiulo and Edoardo Labanchi for us, and for obtaining permission for their testimonies and others to be published.

We extend thanks to the Rev. Donald Maconaghie of The Conversion Center, Havertown, Pennsylvania, USA, for permission to use the testimony of Jose A. Fernandez.

Frank Eberhardt and his Gospel Outreach have been truly a blessing to us. We express deep gratitude to him for permission to reproduce the testimonies of Charles Bolton.

It has been a great joy to meet Sandy Carson in person. We thank him for rewriting his story, *Free Indeed*, and his publisher for granting permission to publish it. We also acknowledge the invaluable help of Herman J. Hegger of Velp in the Netherlands who supplied several of the testimonies. Cornelius Bas has been a great joy to us in our work. His minute care in the translation of the testimonies of our Dutch brothers has been very valuable.

Our eleventh hour help for the first edition was Mike Stevens. May the Lord truly reward him, and all who have toiled from start to finish.

1

Henry Gregory Adams

Christ Alone Is the Way

I was born of Roman Catholic parents in Wolseley, Saskatchewan, Canada and brought up strictly in the Roman Catholic faith. From early youth I was trying to be good, yet falling progressively into sin. With the rest of the crowd I was heading to perdition. I was told that by becoming a monk and priest I could avoid sin and be more certain of my salvation. Because I was sincerely seeking salvation, I entered the Basilian Order of monks, received the long black robe and an adopted monastic name of 'Saint Hilarion the Great' and made my vows. As a monk-student I was called 'Brother Hilarion' and after ordination 'Father Hilarion'.

I Whip Myself

How eager I was to serve the Lord Jesus Christ! By leading a monastic life I thought I was doing just that. I performed all my monastic duties to the last rule. I whipped myself every Wednesday and Friday evening till at times my back bled; in penance I often kissed the floor; often I ate my meagre meal kneeling down on the floor, or completely deprived myself of food. I did many forms of penance for I was truly seeking salvation. I was taught that I could eventually merit heaven. I did not know that the Word of God says, 'For by grace are ye saved through faith; and that not of yourselves: it is the gift of God: not of works, lest any man should boast' (*Eph.* 2:8–9).

A Priest at Last

After years of studies and manual labour in the monastery I was ordained a priest. I served five parishes in the Lamont, Alberta, area, said Mass every day, heard confession, recited the rosary to Mary, had devotions to many saints, recited the breviary of formula prayers every day, and, as a monk, performed my penances more fervently than ever. Yet these did not satisfy my weary soul. I was heading into even deeper distress of soul than when I was a boy, but Christ was faithful in his care for me.

God's Book and My Church

Among the studies for the priesthood we had three textbooks on the Bible but not the Bible. After I was ordained a priest, I became acquainted with the Roman Catholic version of the Bible and in it were striking

[handwritten annotation: Religious organizations are manmade and suffer from man. ego which can not be always said to be righteous or a true reflection of God nature?]

verses that contradicted my very beliefs and practices. God's Book said one thing, my Church another. Who was right, the Roman Church or God? I eventually believed God's Word.

The monastic life and the sacraments prescribed by the Roman Catholic Church did not help me to come to know Christ personally and find salvation. After twelve and a half long years I escaped from the monastery, a lost sinner, without peace in my soul. In me there was still only the nature of the 'the old man, which is corrupt according to the deceitful lusts'. I needed a new nature, a new heart. Scripture tells me, 'Be renewed in the spirit of your mind . . . put on the new man, which after God is created in righteousness and true holiness' (*Eph.* 4:21–24). That can only be brought about by being born again of the Spirit of God by faith alone in Jesus Christ, and not by monotonous repetition of prayers, penances, sacrifices and good works. 'Except a man be born again, he cannot see the kingdom of God' (*John* 3:3). 'Believe on the Lord Jesus Christ, and thou shalt be saved, and thy house' (*Acts* 16:31).

I Trust Christ Alone

I realized that the man-made sacraments of my Church and my good works were in vain for salvation. They led to a false security. Soon afterwards I believed that Christ died for me because I could not save my soul, and I trusted him alone for my salvation. When I repented of my sins and received him into my heart, believing that on the cross he paid the complete penalty for my condemnation, I knew that my sins were not only forgiven but forgotten and that I was justified before God. 'For all have sinned, and come short of the glory of God' (*Rom.* 3:23). 'For the wages of sin is death; but the

gift of God is eternal life through Jesus Christ our Lord'
(*Rom.* 6:23). The blood of Christ cleansed me from all
my sins. 'The blood of Jesus Christ his Son cleanseth us
from all sin' (*1 John* 1:7). And now I have God's peace.
'Therefore being justified by faith, we have peace with
God through our Lord Jesus Christ' (*Rom.* 5:1).

My Word to You

Friend, if you too are trying to reach heaven on your
own, may I impress upon you that it is 'not of works, lest
any man should boast'. Heaven can never be earned.
Christ alone is the way and the answer. 'For there is one
God, and one mediator between God and men, the man
Christ Jesus; who gave himself a ransom for all, to be
testified in due time' (*1 Tim.* 2:5–6). Come to him now
just as you are, admitting your sins. Ask his pardon and
receive him as your own Saviour and Lord. Begin to rely
on him for your eternal welfare for he bought salvation
for you. He calls you now: 'Come unto me, all ye that
labour and are heavy laden, and I will give you rest'
(*Matt.* 11:28).

Then you too can rejoice with me in your new-found
Saviour, the living Christ.

2

Joseph Tremblay

A Priest, but a Stranger to God

I was born in Quebec, Canada, in 1924. From childhood my parents inculcated in me a great respect for God. I desired intensely to serve him to the best of my ability and to consecrate myself totally to him in order to please him, according to the words of the apostle Paul: 'I beseech you therefore, brethren, by the mercies of God, that ye present your bodies a living sacrifice, holy, acceptable unto God, which is your reasonable service' (*Rom.* 12:1). It was this desire to please him that motivated my decision to take the holy orders of the Roman Catholic Church.

A Missionary to Bolivia

After several years of study I was ordained a priest in Rome, Italy. One year later I was sent to Bolivia and Chile, where I served for more than thirteen years as a missionary in the Congregation of the Oblate Fathers of Mary Immaculate. I liked the life very much and tried to discharge my responsibilities as best I could. I enjoyed the friendship of all of my co-workers, and even if they looked with a certain irony upon my taste for the study of the Bible, their invitations to share with them the results of my studies evidenced their approval. When they called me 'Joe the Bible', I knew that, in spite of the sarcastic expression, they envied me. My parishioners also appreciated the ministry of the Word of God, so much so that they organized a club for home Bible studies. I was compelled to give myself to earnest study of the Bible, as much to prepare myself for the improvised home meetings as to prepare my Sunday sermons.

Serious Bible Study

The study of the Bible, which, until that time, had been just a hobby, quickly became a professional obligation. I became aware of the clarity with which certain truths were taught, and on the other hand I discovered that nothing at all was written about many dogmas that I had studied. My Bible study revealed that I did not know the Bible. I suggested to my superiors that I should go for further studies in the Bible when my turn for vacation arrived. In the meantime the Jesuits at Antofagasta invited me to teach the Bible at the Normal School of the university which they directed. I do not know how they learned of my interest in the Bible. Notwithstanding my lack of preparation, I accepted the invitation, knowing that this new responsibility would necessitate even more serious study of the Word of God.

The Gospel via Radio

Many hours, days and nights were consecrated to the preparation of my classes, my meetings, and my sermons. To maintain a good morale during my readings and studies I had the habit of listening to music. I had a little transistor radio on which I could listen to beautiful background music without the bother of changing records. One day I became aware that it was religious songs and hymns that were coming through to me on the little radio. I heard the word 'Jesus' from time to time while I was reading the Bible or commentaries. Then followed a short Bible reading. The last verse that was read caught my attention: 'For he hath made him to be sin for us, who knew no sin; that we might be made the righteousness of God in him' (2 *Cor.* 5:21). The sermon which followed was based on this verse. At first I was tempted to change the station, because it was too distracting to listen to someone speaking while trying to study. In addition, I thought to myself, What could this ministry add to me, after all? Me, with all my degrees. I could teach him a thing or two. After a moment's hesitation I decided to listen to what the speaker had to say. And, truly, I learned some of the most wonderful things concerning the person of Jesus Christ. I was even filled with shame, knowing without a doubt that I could not have done as well as the one who had preached. It had seemed to me that it was Jesus himself who had been speaking to me, who was there before me. And how little I knew him, this Jesus, who nevertheless was the subject of my thoughts, and of my studies. I felt that he was far from me. It was the first time that such a feeling concerning Jesus Christ had ever presented itself to me. He seemed to be a stranger. It was as if all of my being were but emptiness, around which I had erected a structure of principles and theological dogmas, very beautiful, well-constructed, well-illustrated, but which had not touched my soul, which had not changed my being. I felt as if there were a great emptiness in me. And even though I continued to study, pray and meditate, this emptiness became even greater with each day that passed.

I Learn Salvation by Grace

I went on listening to this same radio station, tuning in to every programme that I could. I learned that the station was in Quito, Ecuador, and was known as HCJB. I learned also that it was a radio station consecrated exclusively to the preaching of the gospel to the whole world. Sometimes I was very much touched by all that I heard, and on such occasions I wrote directly to the station to thank them and to ask for information.

What struck me most in all that I heard was the insistence with which they spoke of salvation by grace, that all the credit for the salvation of man was given, not to the one who was saved, but to the Lord Jesus Christ, the only Saviour; that man could boast of nothing, that his works were but filthy rags, that eternal life could be received within the heart only as a free gift, that it was not a reward in exchange for merits that had been acquired but was an unmerited gift given by God to whoever repents of his sins and receives Jesus Christ into his heart and life. All of this was new to me. It was contrary to the theology I had been taught: that heaven and eternal life are gained by means of one's merit, faithfulness, charity and sacrifices. And this is what I had been working at for so many years. But what was the result of my efforts?

As I considered this question I said to myself, I'm not any further ahead. If I commit a mortal sin, I'll go to hell if I die in that state. My theology has taught me that salvation is by works and sacrifices. I discover in the Bible a free salvation. My theology gives me no assurance of salvation; the Bible offers me that assurance. I'm confused. Perhaps I should stop listening to those evangelical programmes.

My inner battle was taking on alarming proportions. I suffered in my body and in my heart, with headaches, insomnia, fear of hell. I had no desire to celebrate Mass nor to listen to confessions. My soul had greater need of pardon and consolation than all the other souls with which I was in contact. I avoided everybody. But God continued to speak to me in the solitude of my anguished heart. So many questions came up in my spirit; so many misgivings smouldered in my heart. The Word of God came to my rescue, spreading a refreshing balm upon my fevered emotions. 'God so loved the world, that he gave his only begotten Son, that whosoever believeth in him should not perish, but have everlasting life' (John 3:16). 'For all have sinned, and come short of the glory of God; being justified freely by his grace through the redemption that is in Christ Jesus' (*Rom.* 3:23–24). 'For the wages of sin is death; but the gift of God is eternal life through Jesus Christ our Lord' (*Rom.* 6:23). Many other texts came to mind, texts that I now knew because I had heard them often on the radio over station HCJB.

Holy Mother Church

I decided to talk to my superior. A very wise man and a real father to everyone, he had already noticed my attitude. I had changed, he commented; something was wrong. I told him why I had changed. He let me talk. In concluding my confession I said to him, 'I would like not only to read and study the Bible, but also to try to adapt my life to it, to live according to what is written in it without impositions of men.' The reply was very vague. He did not want to offend me. He counselled me to continue reading the Bible, but reminded me that I must maintain my faithfulness to the teachings of Holy Mother Church, to whom one must submit even in the things one does not understand. I listened to my superior with all the respect that I owed him. He was not himself sure of his salvation. But in my heart I had lost faith in my Church because it did not teach the assurance of salvation.

The light dawned in my heart at the moment that I least expected it. It was my turn to preach in my parish. For that Sunday I had chosen as my theme 'Religious Hypocrisy' from the text: 'Not every one that saith unto me, Lord, Lord, shall enter into the kingdom of heaven; but he that doeth the will of my Father which is in heaven. Many will say to me in that day, Lord, Lord, have we not prophesied in thy name? and in thy name have cast out devils? and in thy name done many wonderful works? And then will I profess unto them, I never knew you: depart from me, ye that work iniquity' (*Matt.* 7:21–23).

The Holy Spirit Works

As I delivered my message, I was conscious that the Word of God was coming back to me. Someone else was speaking in my heart and preaching a sermon to me that was precisely adapted to my personal needs. I tried to tell God all that I had done in his service, but the same condemnation rang in my ears, 'I never knew you: depart from me'.

I broke down and could not continue my sermon. I took refuge in my office. There, on my knees, I waited until calm returned. I could do no more; I was in a state of complete exhaustion, depressed and discouraged. This was God's moment to give me his grace. He opened my eyes to see the meaning of the death of Christ. It was here that I understood my error and the reason for God's rejection. I had been trying to save myself by my works. God wanted to save me by grace. Someone else had already taken care of my sins and of the judgment attached to them. This someone was Jesus Christ. It was for this that he died on the cross. It was for the sins of another that he died, for he himself had never sinned. For whose sins, then, did he die? Could it be mine? Yes, mine. I remembered the words of Jesus: 'Come unto me, all ye that labour and are heavy laden, and I will give you rest' (*Matt.* 11:28). I understood that I must go to Jesus if I wanted to have the assurance of salvation and peace of soul. I remembered another word that I had heard: 'Behold, I stand at the door, and knock: if any man hear my voice, and open the door, I will come in to him, and will sup with him, and he with me' (*Rev.* 3:20). I hurried to invite him to enter into my heart, without taking the time to ask permission of any man. At that moment I knew that I was freed from the punishment that had menaced me for such a long time. I was saved, pardoned. I had eternal life. God had begun his work in me. Now I understood the word that I had heard so often and which had become real to me: 'For he hath made him to be sin for us, who knew no sin; that we might be made the righteousness of God in him' (*2 Cor.* 5:21).

My Struggle to Continue

What happened after that? At first I continued my
priestly service as best I could. But little by little I began
to feel like a stranger in that position. I realized that the
grace that had saved me, that had made me a child of
God, was going to enter into conflict with the 'works' of
the position in which I was trying to live. I was happy
because I had the assurance of my salvation. But I was
stifled in a setting in which I was pushed to do good
works to merit my salvation. Salvation I had; therefore
all of these works began to be put aside, one after the
other. All that interested me was Jesus Christ, who he
was and what he had done. I abandoned the subjects
prepared in advance by the liturgical organization of the
diocese, to devote all of my efforts to the person and
work of my beloved Saviour, presenting him as such to
my bewildered parishioners, who were confused but
often edified. I asked to be released from my functions
as a parish priest, since I could no longer preach that
which contradicted the Word of God. My superiors
accepted my resignation, though they could not understand why I wanted to leave. They had, in fact, treated
me very well, indulged me in many ways; as far as they
were concerned I lacked nothing. This was true, as far as
food, clothing, housing and so on were concerned. But
now I had the assurance of my salvation. Christ was now
my Saviour. I had nothing more to do to gain my
salvation. It had been gained by Another.

Christians Visit Me

I returned to Quebec in 1965, for an extended period of
rest. Shortly after, I was visited by evangelical Christians
to whom my name had been given by the personnel of

HCJB. However, even if I found their conversation very edifying, I did not give myself wholly to them. I did not want to fall into another theological system, having been suppressed for years by the system into which I had been born and in which I had grown up and lived for some forty years. Nevertheless I prayed to the Lord to find for me brothers and sisters to whom I could join myself, so that I would not feel so alone. I knew the experience of the first Christians, according to the report given in Acts, 'And they continued steadfastly in the apostles' doctrine and fellowship, and in breaking of bread, and in prayers' (*Acts* 2:42). Was it possible that Christians still met together in our day to remember the Lord, while awaiting his return? God, who had provided for the salvation of my soul, would provide again, in order to disclose to me the existence of his children.

New Duty

My superiors in Montreal invited me to replace a professor of theology in a college in Rouyn. The subject I was given to teach was 'The Church'. I was given access to all the books that would be necessary for the preparation of my classes.

I began my preparations using only the Bible. I explained to the students what the church is, according to the Bible. I admit that I had difficulty myself in understanding what I was teaching. It was such a contrast to the hierarchical church in which I still found myself. I very much enjoyed the study of this subject. I used a little tape recorder to illustrate the lessons, playing for the students certain interviews that I held with the general public in different places of the city.

One day I learned from the newspaper that a television programme was to be presented having as its subject: 'The Church'. I recorded the programme in order to use it in my classes and discovered that the subject was treated from the point of view of what the Bible taught. I was so impressed by the similarity between the presentation by this unknown person, whom I later learned was an evangelical Christian, and my own, that I sent a note of thanks to the preacher, inviting him to come to see me. He came, and I recognized in him someone who knew the Lord. After several visits he invited me to his home to spend Sunday with him and his family. On the occasion of that visit I attended a service at the church to which he belonged.

God Answers Prayer

I recognized in this service that which was described in 1 Corinthians 11 and realized that God had answered my prayer, having led me to my brothers and sisters in the Lord, and having shown me that Christians in our day do indeed meet together as a local church to remember the Lord while awaiting his return. 'For as often as ye eat this bread, and drink this cup, ye do shew the Lord's death till he come' (*1 Cor.* 11:26).

Shortly afterwards, I wrote to my superiors in Montreal, announcing to them the news that I had found my family and requesting that they obtain for me a dispensation from all the vows I had made to the Roman Catholic Church, since I no longer considered myself a member. My life now belonged to the Lord and its direction was henceforth under his control.

New Life in the Lord

It was thus that the Lord liberated me, not only from my sins, not only from his condemnation, but also from every system of man which burdens and suppresses. 'There is therefore now no condemnation to them which are in Christ Jesus, who walk not after the flesh, but after the Spirit. For the law of the Spirit of life in Christ Jesus hath made me free from the law of sin and death' (*Rom.* 8:1–2).

3

Bartholomew F. Brewer

Pilgrimage from Rome

Millions of Roman Catholics are Roman Catholic by name, by culture, or by inertia. Our family, however, was Roman Catholic by conviction. We understood and practised the teachings of our religion. Our Church we believed to be 'the one true Church' founded by Jesus Christ. Because of this we accepted without question everything our priests taught. In those days before Vatican II the common belief was that 'outside the Roman Catholic Church there is no salvation'. This brought us a feeling of security, of being right. We were somehow safe in the arms of 'Holy Mother Church'.

From the time my father died (I was almost ten), my mother attended daily Mass, not missing even one day for over twenty-four years. Our family faithfully recited the rosary every evening. We were encouraged to make regular visits to the 'blessed sacrament'. In addition to the teaching at home, all of our schooling was Roman Catholic. Monsignor Hubert Cartwright and the other priests at our home parish, the Cathedral of Saints Peter and Paul in Philadelphia, Pennsylvania, used to say that our family was more Roman Catholic than Rome.

It was no wonder that as I approached high school age, I felt called to prepare for the Roman Catholic priesthood. Rather than the secular priesthood, which serves parishes, I chose to apply to the Discalced Carmelites, one of the more strict and ancient monastic orders.

Motivated by Love

From the first day at Holy Hill, Wisconsin, I loved the religious life, and this love was the motivation I needed to get through all the Latin and other studies, which I found very difficult. The dedication and self-sacrifice of the priests who taught our classes were a continual reminder of the value of making any sacrifice to reach the goal of ordination.

The training I received in four years of the high school seminary, two years in the novitiate, three years of philosophy, and four years of theology (the last after ordination) was thorough. I was sincere in practising the various mortifications and other disciplines and never once doubted my calling or anything I was taught. Taking the vows of poverty, chastity and obedience represented my lifetime commitment to God. For me the voice of the Church was the voice of God.

Another Christ

My ordination to the Roman Catholic priesthood was at the Shrine of the Immaculate Conception of Mary in Washington, D.C., the seventh largest church in the world. When Bishop John M. McNamara imposed his hands on my head and repeated the words from Psalm 110:4: 'Thou art a priest for ever after the order of Melchizedek', I was overwhelmed with the belief that I was now a mediator between God and the people. The anointing and binding of my hands with special cloths signified that they were now consecrated to changing bread and wine into the real (literal) flesh and blood of Jesus Christ, to perpetuate the sacrifice of Calvary through the Mass, and to dispense saving grace through the other Roman Catholic sacraments of baptism, confession, confirmation, marriage and the last rites. At ordination a Roman Catholic priest is said to receive an 'indelible' mark: to experience an unending interchange of his personality with that of Christ, that he may perform his priestly duties as 'another Christ' or in the place of Christ. People actually knelt and kissed our newly consecrated hands, so sincere was this belief.

After completing the last year of theology, which was principally a final preparation for preaching and hearing confession (involving giving absolution or forgiveness of sin), I was granted my long-expressed desire to be a missionary priest in the Philippines.

Finding New Freedom in Missionary Life

The change from a regimented, monastic life to the simplicity and freedom of a missionary life proved a challenge for which I had not been prepared. I loved travelling to some of the eighty or more primitive *barrios* assigned to our parish and I also cherished teaching my religion class at the Carmelite high school in our small town. Until then my life had been almost exclusively among men. I enjoyed watching the girls as they giggled and flirted with boys. After a while, though, my attention was drawn to one of the more diligent students, who thoroughly captivated my interest. This young lady was mature beyond her years because of the responsibilities that had fallen to her after her mother had died. She was lovely and shyly responded as we stole moments talking alone after class. This was a new adventure, and I soon interpreted our newly discovered affection as love.

It is not surprising that soon the bishop learned of this, though he was many miles away, and he quickly sent me back to the States before any serious relationship could develop. The embarrassment of this discipline was difficult for both of us, but life always moves on.

After the adventure and freedom of the Philippines, I had no motivation to return to monastic living, so the Father Provincial granted permission for me to work as a Discalced Carmelite parish priest in Arizona. I enjoyed my responsibilities in that parish, but my next assignment was not so fulfilling. Soon I was granted a dispensation from Rome to leave the Carmelite Order to serve as a secular (diocesan) priest. While serving a large parish in San Diego, California, I requested and was granted permission to enter the United States Navy as a Roman Catholic chaplain. There new goals, rank and travel served as an escape from what had gradually become a sterile parochial life of ritualism and sacramentalism.

My religious life broadened quickly as I mixed with non-Catholic chaplains. For the first time, I was living outside my Roman Catholic culture. Amid the ecumenical

atmosphere I gradually became neutralized. Then as
Vatican II opened the windows of rigid tradition to let in
fresh air, I took in a deep and delightfully refreshing
breath. Change was in. Some wanted it to be radical;
others wanted only a little modernization.

Questioning Rome's Authority

For many, the Roman Catholic faith was failing to give
answers to common, modern-day problems. Many felt
alienated and misunderstood. This was especially true of
priests. With all the change, the priesthood was losing its
glamour. No longer was the priest's education considered far superior to that of the parishioner. No longer
was the priest cultured above the majority of his people.
To experience an identity crisis was more common
among priests than any were willing to acknowledge,
even among the chaplains.

At first I was scandalized to realize that some of the
Roman Catholic chaplains were actually dating. I
listened with interest as some openly discussed the
impractical nature of mandatory celibacy. Soon I also
gained the courage to question the authorities of our
Church who persisted in retaining such traditions,
especially when the law of celibacy was the source of so
many moral problems among priests. For the first time
in my life I doubted the authority of my religion, not
because of intellectual pride, but as a matter of conscience.

As students for the priesthood we were well informed
regarding the ancient tradition that binds the Roman
Catholic priest to celibacy. We well knew that the few
who are granted permission from the Vatican to marry
may never again function as priests. But times were
changing. Questions never before voiced were being

raised at the Vatican Council in Rome. Many thought that priests with wives could, like the Protestants, bring greater sensitivity and understanding to marital and family issues. Discussions about such things were commonplace wherever priests got together, such as when my fellow priests visited the apartment that mother and I shared off base.

Mother was not shy in joining the discussions. She was a well-informed and intelligent person, and I greatly valued her opinions. I recall how appalled she was that evolution was being taught in Roman Catholic schools and that Rome had established dialogue with the Communists. She had long been disturbed over some of the conflicts she had observed between principles taught in Scripture and the lack of principles among many of the religious leaders of our own Church. Many years before Monsignor Cartwright had comforted mother with the reminder that though there were many problems in our Church, Jesus promised that 'the gates of hell shall not prevail against it'. Mother always expressed a tremendous respect for the Bible. Though she had read it faithfully through the years, she was now becoming an avid student of Scripture. As I observed a liberal trend grow among my colleagues, mother was leaning in another direction. It was a mystery to me. While others discussed a relaxation and loosening of traditional rules and rituals, mother expressed her desire to see a more biblical emphasis in the Church – more attention to the spiritual aspects of life and a greater emphasis upon Jesus, even a personal relationship with him.

Questioning Rome's Beliefs

At first I did not understand, but gradually I observed a wonderful change in mother. Her influence helped me

realize the importance of the Bible in determining what
we believe. We often discussed subjects such as the
primacy of Peter, papal infallibility, the priesthood,
infant baptism, confession, the Mass, purgatory, the
immaculate conception of Mary, and the bodily assumption of Mary into heaven. In time I realized that not only
are these beliefs not in the Bible, they are actually
contrary to the clear teaching of Scripture. Finally the
barrier against having personal convictions was broken.
There was no doubt in my mind about the biblical view
on these subjects, but what effect would all this have on
my life as a priest?

I truly believed that God had called me to serve him.
An ethical dilemma was staring me in the face. What was
I to do? Yes, there were priests who did not believe all
the dogmas of Rome. Yes, there were priests who
secretly had wives and families. Yes, I could remain a
Roman Catholic chaplain and continue serving without
voicing my disagreements. I could continue receiving
the pay and the privileges of military rank. I could
continue receiving the benefits for my mother. There
were many reasons to stay, both professional and
material, but to do so would have been hypocritical and
unethical. From my youth I always tried to do right, and
that is what I chose to do now.

Breaking Ties with Roman Catholicism

Though my bishop had recently granted approval for me
to pursue twenty years in the military, I resigned after
only four. Mother and I simply and quietly moved near
my brother, Paul, and his wife, in the San Francisco Bay
area. Shortly before we moved, mother cut her ties with
Roman Catholicism by being baptized in a Seventh-Day
Adventist church. I knew she had been studying the

Bible with one of their workers, but she did not tell me
about the baptism until I had already decided to leave
the priesthood.

The decision to leave was anything but easy. Rome's
claim that there are no objective reasons for leaving 'the
one true Church' was something to be considered
carefully. Traditional Catholics would still brand me a
'Judas priest', to be damned, excommunicated, and
avoided. Yes, there were many difficulties involved in
leaving the security of the Roman Catholic fold, but I
have found that Jesus never fails.

The Authority of the Bible

After shaking the Roman Catholic dust off my shoes, I
faced a momentous issue: where was ultimate authority
to be found? Through a process of elimination, I
gradually concluded that the Bible is the only authority
that cannot be shaken. Many systems, including Roman
Catholicism, have attempted without success to under-
mine its sufficiency, its efficiency, its perfection, even its
authorship by holy men of God as they were moved by
the Holy Spirit. 'The prophecy came not in old time by
the will of man: but holy men of God spake as they were
moved by the Holy Ghost' (2 *Pet.* 1:21). Oh, happy day
when all who name the name of Jesus Christ understand
that the Bible is the only source of authority and that it
does not change. It is the final authority because of its
complete identification with its unchanging Author,
God. Perhaps the reason many regard the Bible as
insufficient is that they have not thoroughly studied it.
My transcripts from thirteen years of formal study in the
Discalced Carmelite Order show that I had only twelve
semester hours of Bible. This alone is evidence that
Scripture is not the basis of Roman Catholic teaching.

Premature Decision to Join a Church

After leaving Roman Catholicism I wanted to study the Bible. After investigating some of the Protestant churches, I sadly concluded that in their ecumenical folly they were Rome-ward bound at the expense of biblical truth. The variety of churches can be discouraging and even dangerous for the former Roman Catholic in his search for truth.

Mother's Adventist friends were enthusiastic about their faith, and their love of the Scriptures echoed my desire to study the Bible. This resulted in a somewhat premature decision to join the Seventh-Day Adventist denomination. The pastor who baptized me arranged for the Southern California Conference to send me to seminary at Andrews University for a year.

While making plans for a year of study I met Ruth. For about a year I had been hoping and praying to find a wife. From the first time Ruth visited our church I knew she would be my life companion. We were married shortly before leaving for the seminary. She was a convert to Adventism and like everyone else had assumed that since I wanted to enter the seminary I was a Christian.

Born of the Spirit

Realizing that I never mentioned anything about being 'born again', one day my wife asked me, 'Bart, when did you become a Christian?' My unbelievable reply was, 'I was born a Christian.' In the conversations that followed, she tried to help me understand that man, being born in sin, must at some point be born again spiritually and trust only in Jesus Christ to save him from the consequences of sin. When I responded that I had

always believed in God, she quoted James 2:19: 'Thou
believest that there is one God; thou doest well: the
devils also believe, and tremble.'

Through these conversations and through reading the
Epistles to the Romans, Galatians and Hebrews, I
finally understood that I had been relying on my own
righteousness and religious efforts and not upon the
completed and sufficient sacrifice of Jesus Christ. The
Roman Catholic religion had never taught me that our
own righteousness is fleshly and not acceptable to God,
nor that we need to trust in his righteousness alone. He
has already done everything that needs to be done on
behalf of the believer. Then one day during chapel the
Holy Spirit convicted me of my need to repent and
receive the 'gift' of God.

During all those years of monastic life I had relied on
the sacraments of Rome to give me grace, to save me,
but now by God's grace I was born spiritually: I was
saved. Being ignorant of God's righteousness, like the
Jews of Paul's day, I had gone about establishing my
own righteousness, not submitting to the righteousness
of God (*Rom*. 10:2–3).

Some Would Pervert the Gospel of Christ

I was ordained as a Seventh-day Adventist minister, but
not long after I heard a lecturer say that the writings of
Ellen G. White (one of the founders of Adventism) were
as inspired as those of the Gospel writers. This so
troubled me that I knew I could not continue as an
Adventist minister. Later, for a time, Ruth and I were
influenced by the charismatic movement but we left it
because of its ecumenical involvement. We are now
members of an evangelical Baptist church.

A Mission to Roman Catholics

Prayerfully and deliberately I decided to return to San Diego, where I had once served as a parish priest. Aware that Vatican II had brought many Roman Catholics into confusion and disillusionment, I felt led to begin a ministry to help them in the transition from the Roman Catholic Church. Mission to Catholics International was founded and has since distributed millions of tracts, books and tapes exposing the contradictions between Roman Catholicism and the Bible and presenting biblical salvation. A monthly newsletter is available to any contributors requesting it. The Lord has allowed us some radio and television time and we are pleased that my autobiography *Pilgrimage from Rome* has been published and is well received in both English and Spanish. We have held meetings and taken literature into many foreign countries, and mail orders are sent out five days a week from our home office in San Diego.

Meetings keep us busy, as we travel throughout the USA and other countries. A School of Roman Catholic Evangelism provides a week or more of intense training for pastors and key workers who desire to establish specialized ministries for effectively reaching the Roman Catholic community through their churches. Missionaries and ex-Roman Catholics are also encouraged to attend, especially ex-priests and ex-nuns, so that they may be prepared to minister in biblical churches.

At Mission to Catholics we are convinced that it is not love to withhold the truth from those in darkness. Roman Catholics need to be challenged to think about what they believe and to study the Bible, comparing their religion with the truth of Scripture. Only then can they experience the freedom and light of God's truth. 'And ye shall know the truth, and the truth shall make you free' (*John* 8:32).

4

Hugh Farrell

From Friar to Freedom in Christus

'*There is therefore now no condemnation to them which are in Christ Jesus, who walk not after the flesh, but after the Spirit' (Rom.* 8:1).

Many years ago, when I decided to become a priest in the Roman Catholic Church, I wanted to walk with Christ. However, because I was born a Roman Catholic, I believed that the Roman Catholic Church was the only true church and that outside of that faith it was almost impossible to be saved. Popes have repeatedly declared this dogma. Pope Innocent III, Boniface VIII, Clement VI, Benedict XIV, Leo XIII, Pius IX and Pius XII plainly state it thus: 'By faith it is firmly to be held that outside of the Apostolic Roman Church none can

achieve salvation.' Hence, I never for a moment thought
of looking for salvation elsewhere.

From early boyhood I wanted to be a priest. I was
born on 2 April 1911 in Denver, Colorado, USA.
Our neighbourhood was made up of Irish, Scots and
Slav families, most of whom were Roman Catholic.
Naturally, in such an environment, I could not help
noticing the immense power exercised by the local
priests and the high esteem in which they were held. But
it was not only the power and esteem they enjoyed that
led me to decide to study for the priesthood but the
sacerdotal dignity claimed for them by the Roman
Church which determined my vocation for me.

The priest, according to the teaching of the Roman
Catholic Church, has the power to take ordinary bread
and wine, and, by pronouncing the words of the
consecration prayer in the sacrifice of the Mass, to
change it into the actual body and blood and soul and
divinity of Jesus Christ. Hence, since one cannot
separate the human nature of Christ from his divinity,
the bread and wine, after being changed into the body
and blood of Jesus Christ, are entitled to the worship of
adoration.

Also, Roman Catholics are taught that in the confessional, after the penitents have told their sins to the
priest, the confessor has the power to forgive their sins.
The Council of Trent, which met after the Reformation,
declared in 1545: 'Whosoever says that the priests are
not the only ministers of absolution (forgiveness), let
him be condemned.' Since I began to go to confession at
the age of seven years, I soon realized that this power
gave the priests a tremendous hold over the lives of their
people and that it made them superior to any secular
authority on the face of the earth.

However, it was not only the power and dignity of the

priesthood that motivated me. It was also a sincere desire to save my soul. I knew from the teachings of the priests and nuns that I could not hope to go directly to heaven after my death. My Roman Catholic catechism taught me that after death I had to pay for the temporal punishment due to my sins. The Roman Catholic Church teaches that 'the souls of the just which, in the moment of death, are burdened with venial sins or temporal punishment due to sins, enter purgatory'. I therefore realized that since I committed venial sins daily, and sometimes even mortal sins, I must spend a very long time in purgatory. Now the Roman Church is rather vague in its official teaching concerning the pains of purgatory, but the fertile imagination of the Irish Roman Catholic priests and nuns helped them to invent such sufferings and pain that our childish lives were filled with fear and we would have done anything to avoid purgatory if possible. Consequently, as a boy, I reasoned that if a priest had the power through the offering of the sacrifice of the Mass to obtain the release of souls from purgatory I would help my own soul by becoming a priest, for after my death those souls who had been aided by my Masses would be obligated to pray for my soul before the throne of the Queen of Heaven (the Blessed Virgin Mary), and she in turn would intercede for me before the throne of her Son. This was the teaching of the Church for it declared that 'the poor souls in purgatory can be helped, above all, by the sacrifice of the Mass which is pleasing to God', and 'the souls in purgatory can intercede for other members of the Mystical Body (the Church)'. I determined to become a priest and in due time made known my decision to the proper authorities.

The Role the Bible Played

It would take too long for me to tell you all about the
many years of preparation for the priesthood in the
Roman Catholic Church. It will suffice for me to relate
those incidents that mark the turning points in my life.
For me there was to be no short road to the assurance of
salvation. That road would be beset with many trials and
temptations. Often I am asked if I did not know the
Bible, or if it was forbidden to me. Actually, I had in my
possession a New Testament during all of my years of
preparation and the years spent in the monastery. When
I left for the junior seminary I carried besides my missal
and prayer books three other books: *The Glories of
Mary* by Alphonse de Liguori, *The Imitation of Christ*
by Thomas à Kempis, and the Roman Catholic New
Testament. The latter bore the following notation: 'An
indulgence of three years is granted to all the faithful
who read the Holy Scriptures at least a quarter of an
hour with the veneration due to the Divine Word and as
spiritual reading.' Roman Catholics should be moved to
read the Bible since most are eager to gain indulgences.
However, you will note that the indulgence is granted
only when the Bible is read as spiritual reading and not
for study or interpretation. Since Roman Catholics
know that they can gain indulgences in other, easier
ways, such as making the sign of the cross (seven years
each time that it is made with holy water) etc., most do
not bother with the reading of the Scriptures. Then, too,
many are fearful of interpreting the Word of God
contrary to the teaching of the Roman Church. In my
own case, when, many years later, I left the monastery, I
still had these three books. *The Glories of Mary* no
longer had a cover – it had worn out. The cover of *The
Imitation of Christ* hung by several threads. The New

Testament, however, was still new. I had only read it
when I wished to compare a translation from the Latin
with the English.

Constant Indoctrination

The routine of the seminary is so arranged that one
seldom has time for real reflection. True, there is a
period each morning set aside for meditation. But points
are read out for consideration, and if the mind is allowed
to wander, one is in danger of committing venial sin.

The daily programme of life is so well thought out by
the Roman Church that individuality is gradually destroyed and one's personality is so shaped that one
conforms to a pattern designed by the Roman Church as
being best for their purpose – the complete renunciation
of self. Despite the great esteem in which a priest is held
by the laity of the Roman Church, the authorities regard
him as a mere cipher in their plan for the Roman
Catholic conquest of the world. Hence, if he is to serve
their purpose, he must be thoroughly brainwashed. This
they achieve much in the same way as the Communists.
In seminary training, they never permit sufficient sleep,
require frequent fasting, and use every means and form
of indoctrination. When a doubt arises concerning any
major doctrine taught by the Roman Church, it must be
rejected immediately because to entertain such a doubt
(willingly) is a sign that God may be removing one's
priestly vocation and thus jeopardizing one's eternal
salvation.

Near the end of my minor seminary training I had to
make up my mind whether I wanted to be a secular priest
(under the authority of a bishop as a parish priest or a
chaplain in an institution) or a religious priest (one
who has taken the three vows of poverty, chastity and

obedience and who lives in a monastery or house of a
religious order).

Choosing a Monastic Order

I felt that secular priests had too many temptations and
consequently had a difficult time in obtaining salvation.
I also knew that in past centuries the Roman Catholic
Church had canonized only one secular priest, the Curé
of Ars, John Mary Vianney. Logically, therefore, I
reasoned, if it was so difficult for a person to be saved as
a secular priest, it was safer to become a monk or friar (a
member of a religious order). I therefore spent my final
year in the seminary deciding what order appealed to me
and where I would best fit.

I was well acquainted with the better known Orders,
such as the Benedictines, Dominicans, Servites, Fran-
ciscans, Trappists and the Society of Jesus (Jesuits).
None of these appealed to me. I wanted a very strict
order in which I could find every assurance possible of
obtaining salvation. I thought I had found this in the
Order of our Lady of Mount Carmel, commonly called
Discalced Carmelite Fathers.

The Carmelite Order had been founded by Crusaders
and others in the Holy Land. They remained behind
after the Crusades and occupied the caves of the sons of
the prophets on Mount Carmel. The Patriarch Albert of
Jerusalem gave them a simple rule of life and they
followed it until the middle of the thirteenth century
when they were driven out of the Holy Land by the
Muslims. Some of the exiles settled at Mantua in Italy,
and others in England. The first prior general in England
was a man called Simon Stock. It is claimed that the
Blessed Virgin Mary appeared to him in a vision and
made the famous so-called brown scapular promise, that

is, that anyone wearing this scapular should not suffer eternal fire. The scapular may be made by anyone. All that is required is brown (or nearly black) woven wool cloth made into two squares or oblongs of reasonable size joined by strings. The first scapular worn must be blessed by a priest authorized to confer such a blessing.

Monastery Routine

My first year as a Discalced Carmelite was spent in the house of novices in preparation for my simple profession of vows. It was a year devoted to prayer and meditation. In addition to the regular daily schedule observed by all Discalced Carmelite Fathers, novices have extra prayer time, increased penances and more mortifications. The silence observed in the novitiate is very strictly observed. Apart from half an hour of daily recreation the novices are forbidden to speak to each other, and during the Lenten and Advent seasons total silence is observed. In those seasons the novices walk about during recreation in silence, making rosaries, and disciplines, etc.

The day begins in the novitiate at midnight. The community is called by the bell-ringer and assembles in the chapel. At the last stroke of the bell, the divine office begins. Matins, consisting of nine psalms and nine lessons from the Old and New Testaments, with a commentary from one of the early Fathers of the Church, is sung, or recited, and this is followed by the five psalms of praise with the *Benedictus*, which portion of the office is called Lauds. The monks then retire again to their beds and await the next rising bell at 4.45 in the morning.

When I speak of beds do not think of soft feather beds, or even comfortable beds. The bed of a Carmelite consists of three planks laid over two trestles and covered by a thin pallet and three blankets. Everything in the monk's room is in keeping with the austerity of his bed. Besides the latter there is a small table and a stool. No other furnishing is permitted.

Many Hours of Prayer

On rising, the community goes to the chapel and recites Prime and Terce, each of which consists of three psalms followed by a short lesson and a short written prayer. At the conclusion of this portion of the divine office, the community spends an hour together in silent prayer upon their knees.

After mental prayer the Masses of the day follow. If a monk is a priest, he celebrates a private Mass at one of the many altars in the monastery, usually assisted by another monk, called the server. If the monk is still studying for the priesthood, he attends the community Mass, which is celebrated by the priest assigned for the week. The lay-brothers who do the manual labour in the monastery also attend this Mass. All are expected to receive Holy Communion. These exercises, divine office, mental prayer and Mass, take about three hours and so it is usually eight o'clock before the monks have breakfast. This consists of bread and coffee and must be taken standing, since in the primitive rule of the order no allowance is made for breakfast, which is a modern concession to man's weakness.

The morning is devoted to study, classes and private prayer. In the year of novitiate one is not permitted to study anything but spiritual subjects and, of course, the rule, customs and discipline of the Carmelite Order. After profession of vows the monk studies theology and the other necessary subjects for ordination to the priesthood.

Shortly before noon the community goes to the chapel where they recite the last two little hours of the morning office, Sext and None. They, like Prime and Terce, consist of three psalms each followed by a short lesson from the Holy Scripture and the prayer of the day. At the conclusion of the office, the remainder of time until the Angelus is devoted to the examination of conscience. During the examination one recalls any sins that one may have committed since the previous night and asks God's forgiveness. However, if one has committed a mortal sin it is necessary to go to confession at the first opportunity. For a venial sin it suffices to say the act of contrition. After the recitation of the Angelus the monks go to the dining room for the main meal of the day.

The Monastic Meals

All meals are taken in silence. The only exceptions are at Easter, Pentecost, the Feast of our Lady of Mount Carmel, the Assumption of the Blessed Virgin Mary, the Feast of St Teresa of Avila, the Feast of St John of the Cross, All Saints, the Immaculate Conception, Christmas and some other days. However, while the community eats in silence, one of the monks, assigned weekly, reads from a spiritual book or from the rule and customs of the order.

The food is simple and usually consists of soup, fish or eggs, two vegetables and fruit. The Discalced Carmelite rule forbids the eating of meat unless a doctor prescribes it. This rarely occurs as most medical men feel that the eggs and fish are sufficient. When a monk must eat meat he is placed in the lower part of the refectory and shielded from the gaze of the other monks by a screen. This area is jokingly referred to as 'hell'.

As each monk finishes his meal he looks around to see if he may be of assistance in the refectory. One will relieve the reader, others the waiters, so they may eat. Several more perform public penances and humiliations. These penances consist of standing with the arms outstretched to form a cross, kissing the sandalled feet of the monks, receiving a blow upon the face from the monks, and, at the end of the meal, lying prostrate before the entrance to the refectory so that the departing monks must step over one's body. These, and other penances, are supposed to gain one merit in heaven and increase one's 'spiritual bank account.' After the noon meal, in most monasteries of the Discalced Carmelite Fathers, the recreational period of the day provides time for a fraternal exchange of spiritual ideas in order to encourage one another in the observance of the religious life. However, it very often becomes a strain and most uncharitable acts are committed at this time. One cannot confine twenty or more healthy men in the unnatural environment of a monastery without resultant psychological repercussions. It is usually with evident relief that the monks welcome the end of the daily recreational period and retire to their cells for the afternoon rest time.

The Constant Repetition of Psalms

Vespers and Compline follow the afternoon siesta. The former consists of five psalms, the *Magnificat* and the prayer of the day, and the latter three psalms, the *Nunc Dimittis* and a closing prayer. This concludes the divine office of the day. It was divided into seven parts by the early Benedictine abbeys in keeping with Psalm 119:164: 'Seven times a day do I praise thee because of thy righteous judgments.' Very often I am asked how it is that, in view of our daily recitation or singing of about thirty psalms (we were supposed to cover the entire Psalter weekly), we did not thereby come to know of God's plan of salvation. The answer is very evident to a Roman Catholic. Whenever we heard a particular passage that seemed to be in conflict with the teaching of the Roman Church, we would decide that we were not interpreting it properly. For example, in Psalm 18:2: 'The LORD is my rock', and in Psalm 62:6: 'He only is my rock', we would either ignore the implication that Peter was not *the* Rock, or come to the conclusion that we did not possess sufficient knowledge of the Scriptures to understand the passage. It was the same when we heard passages read from the Old and New Testaments during the recitation of the Divine Office. As to Romans 5:1, 'Therefore being justified by faith', we would understand it as reading: 'Therefore being justified by faith in the Roman Catholic Church.'

The afternoon, after Vespers, is generally spent in one's cell. There in the solitude of his chamber the monk tries to achieve 'union with God' through spiritual reading, private meditation and prayer. The Carmelite rule stresses this part of the monk's life and states, 'Remain in your cell, day and night, meditating on the law of the Lord.' Actually, a great deal of time is frittered away in idleness and boredom.

Mortifying the Flesh

Another hour of silent meditation in the choir, collation (a simple supper consisting of bread and tea), evening prayers and the discipline bring to an end the monastic day.

The discipline is a public scourging. All the monks return to the dormitory and each friar places himself in front of the door of his cell. At a signal from the superior the lights are extinguished, and the monks partially disrobe themselves and proceed to scourge their naked thighs, while singing Psalm 51 very slowly in Latin. The scourge, or discipline as it is called, is made of three lengths of rope passed through a woven handle in such a fashion as to form a whip of six ends, each about fifteen inches in length. The tips of the ropes are dipped in beeswax to harden them. The application of this scourge depends, of course, on the fervour of the friar. But the individual usually draws blood. At the end of the singing of the psalm, the superior, the Father Prior, recites several prayers and the monks rearrange their clothing. When the lights have been turned on, the monks kneel, each one in his own doorway, and the Father Prior passes down the corridor, blessing each monk who in turn kisses the scapular (an apron-like garment which hangs at the front and back) of the superior. The monks retire and thus ends the monastic day.

The Profession of Vows

In 1935, at the end of my novitiate, I made my first profession of vows, and then in 1938, on the Feast of the Ascension, I made my solemn profession of vows. A copy of my profession follows so that you may see how binding the profession is to a Roman Catholic:

'I, Fr Hugh of St Thérése Margaret, make my profession of solemn vows, and promise obedience, chastity and poverty to God, and the most blessed Virgin Mary of Mount Carmel, and to our Reverend Father, Fr Peter Thomas of the Virgin of Carmel, Prior General of the Order of the Discalced Carmelite Brethren, and to his successors, according to the primitive Rule of the above mentioned Order even until death.'

In 1938, when I made my solemn and final profession of vows, I was completing my theological studies for my ordination to the priesthood. I had received tonsure, minor orders and the sacred order of the subdiaconate from the hands of Bishop Francis Clement Kelley of Oklahoma City. As I now recall, I had not really been bothered by any serious doubts concerning the official teaching of the Roman Catholic Church. It looked as if I were set for life. However, God had other plans for me. 'And we know that all things work together for good to them that love God, to them who are the called according to his purpose. For whom he did foreknow, he also did predestinate to be conformed to the image of his Son' (*Rom.* 8:28–29).

Doubting the Power of the Priest

During this period of my training I was practising how to celebrate Mass. It takes months to learn the rubrics and ritual of the Mass. Many times while practising I would ask myself if I believed that after my final ordination to the priesthood I would have the power to command God to come down upon the altar. According to the teaching of the Roman Church the priest, no matter how unworthy he may personally be, even if he has just made a pact with the devil for his soul, has the power to change the elements of bread and wine into the actual body and blood, soul and divinity, of Jesus Christ. Provided he pronounces the words of consecration properly and has the intention of consecrating, God must come down on the altar and enter and take over the elements. The more I thought about this power claimed by the Roman Church for the priests, the less I believed in such a power. Repeatedly I went to my Father Confessor and told him about my doubts. His only answer was that I must have patience. He told me that even if I did not believe in anything that the Roman Church taught, it would be all right for me to be a priest, provided that I would faithfully teach what they wanted me to teach. He said: 'Your own personal faith has nothing to do with it. You are merely a tool in the hands of Mother Church for the propagation of the faith. Be loyal to the Roman Catholic faith and all will come out well in the end.' However, that was not to be the case. Daily my doubts increased. The superiors noticed my attitude and surmised that I had problems, but did nothing about it. As a matter of fact, the high superior, the Father Provincial, hated me. He realized that I knew that he was not a learned man. He pretended to great learning and sanctity and possessed neither. He was determined to break and destroy me, if possible.

Fortunately, the local prior, Father Edward, was my friend and protected me, even at the cost of incurring the wrath of the Provincial. Finally, I lost faith completely in the Roman Church and its invented dogmas. I ceased to care whether the superiors found out about my loss of faith or not.

During the months that followed I many times considered leaving the order. But I knew that if I stepped out of the Order I would, in conscience, have to leave the Roman Catholic Church. I knew very little of the claims of Protestantism. The only books that I had been allowed to study were those written by Roman Catholic authors, and these had so perverted and distorted the teachings of God and the Protestant theologians as to paint them to be tools of Satan. I did not know where to turn, but I placed my faith in God. I knew that he would not desert me in my time of trial.

Decision to Escape

At length, on 2 August 1940, I realized that for a long time I had not believed in the peculiar doctrines of the Roman Church such as transubstantiation, auricular confession (confession to a priest to be forgiven by him personally), and the infallibility of the Pope (that when he is speaking in his official capacity concerning faith and morals he cannot err). I knew that to remain in the monastery would be impossible. The life is difficult enough when one believes all that the Roman Church teaches. When that belief is lost, life as a friar monk becomes intolerable.

I had completed my theological education and I knew that I could never again hold the faith of a Roman Catholic. Therefore, without letting anyone know, I resolved to leave the monastery and to do it that very afternoon. I was very careful. The Father Provincial, my enemy, was visiting the monastery to which I was attached. I knew that if he became suspicious and thought that I intended to leave, he would have a Roman Catholic medical doctor sign commitment papers and place me in a mental institution under the control of the Roman Church. This may sound far-fetched to those who know kindly Roman Catholics, but I can assure you that in America, Ireland and many other countries there are hundreds of priests and monks in mental hospitals who are there simply because they lost faith in the Pope and the Roman Catholic Church and wanted to leave.

While the Fathers were taking their afternoon siesta I quietly slipped out by the back door and fled to the YMCA in San Antonio for protection. I knew that the Provincial and his religious associates would not risk bringing this matter to the Protestant ministers of Texas

by trying to seize me. After contacting a number of
ministers and discussing my plight with them, I moved
to Houston, a more Protestant dominated city than
San Antonio, which is about sixty per cent Roman
Catholic.

Entering the Protestant Ministry without Christ

At this time I was not really converted. I considered it to
be enough for one's spiritual welfare to accept the
theological opinion of the church to which one belonged. Consequently, I entered the Protestant ministry
and for the next fifteen years of my life served in various
capacities without being assured of my salvation.

However, God's grace kept working. 'It is the
spirit that quickeneth; the flesh profiteth nothing . . .
Therefore said I unto you, that no man can come unto
me, except it were given to him of my Father' (*John*
6:63, 65). Finally the turning point in my spiritual life
came. One trial yet awaited me. I began to believe
that I had made a mistake in leaving the Roman
Church, and so in 1955 I returned. They sent me to a
Trappist monastery for penance. I was quite willing. I
wanted to do anything within my power to bring about
some assurance as to my eternal destiny. I opened my
mind to all they tried to teach me, but it was useless. I
not only found out that I did not believe in the
doctrines of the Roman Church, but I also realized
that they could not have the truth since most of their
doctrines were man-made. Again I left the Roman
Church – of course, without their knowing that I intended to do so. I then set out for the east coast and
prayed that God would show me his will. My prayers
were quickly answered, and in such a fashion that I
could not any longer doubt his will.

Steps towards My Conversion

I was speaking before a group of business men on the political implications of a Roman Catholic for the presidency when, after the meeting, a large man approached me and congratulated me on my knowledge of the Roman Church and its teachings. I, as usual, was puffed up with pride. Then he said, 'However, my friend, I must tell you that you have the lowest spiritual temperature I have ever taken.' I was thoroughly offended and turned from him with as much rudeness as I could summon. I dismissed him in my mind as being a 'crack-pot'. However, he was too much of a soul-winner to let me off his hook so easily. He belonged to that very dedicated group of 'Fishermen for Christ' who do not cease in their pursuit of souls, no matter how badly they are rebuffed or even insulted. He kept after me, and finally the Spirit of God brought me under conviction.

At first I refused his solution to my spiritual problems. He told me I merely had to receive Christ, place all my trust in him, 'believe on him', and I would have eternal life. He constantly reminded me of Christ's words: 'Verily, verily, I say unto you, he that believeth on me hath everlasting life' (*John* 6:47). It all seemed too easy to be true. Why, I asked myself, would all of the teachings of the various faiths be promulgated when it was as easy as that? But then I realized that it was not easy. One had to acknowledge humbly that one was a sinner. 'For all have sinned, and come short of the glory of God' (*Rom.* 3:23). Furthermore, one was saved by the blood of Christ shed on Calvary, and not by one's own merit. So I acknowledged that I was a sinner, and said with the psalmist, 'Behold I was shapen in iniquity, and in sin did my mother conceive me.' Then I received Christ as my only Saviour, counting on no one else – not even the Blessed Virgin Mary. 'But to him that worketh not, but believeth on him that justifieth the ungodly, his faith is counted for righteousness' (*Rom.* 4:5).

After My Conversion

From that day I have never had any doubts about my salvation. 'Whosoever shall confess me before men, him will I confess also before my Father which is in heaven' (*Matt.* 10:32).

When I was first saved by God's grace, I worked with an organization which helped priests to understand the gospel. However, I soon realized that God was calling me to a unique ministry – that of teaching Christians how to win Roman Catholics for the Lord. Therefore in 1959 I went out in faith, as we say in the United States of America, trusting in him to provide for all of my needs. This he has done. Lack of space prevents me from telling of all of the great blessings and mercies that I have enjoyed. I have travelled many times throughout the USA and Canada and have been on preaching tours across Europe several times. Everywhere I have preached with love and authority and have been well received.

It is not my purpose to sow the seeds of hatred and bitterness, but rather to show by the gospel how to win Roman Catholics for Christ. I constantly remind people of those wonderful words in the first chapter of John which form part of the last Gospel read at the end of every Mass in the Roman Catholic Church: 'He came unto his own, and his own received him not. But as many as received him, to them gave he power to become the sons of God, even to them that believe on his name' (*John* 1:11–12). Praise be to that holy Name forever. Amen.

5

Robert V. Julien

Saved by the Free Grace of God

I chose to become not only a Roman Catholic priest but more than that, a Roman Catholic missionary priest. The reason was that I wanted to do great exploits for God. I thought that being a missionary in some far-away land and learning a strange language and strange customs would indeed be a great adventure, and I even entertained the thought that perhaps I might be chosen by God to suffer and die a martyr's death for the cause of Christ. Such were my thoughts during the long years of study in the seminary as I prepared myself to become a missionary father of the Roman Catholic Foreign Missions Society of America.

I Sought a High Grade with God

Looking back upon those years, I can now recognize the real motive behind it all. What I was really seeking was God's approval and an assurance in my heart that I would make the grade and be worthy to enter God's heaven when I died. I had no real peace in my heart all those years, even during my ten years as a missionary priest in Tanzania, East Africa. Just as Adam hid his nakedness behind fig leaves (*Gen.* 3:7), so did I constantly strive to hide my spiritual nakedness behind fig leaves of religious and missionary activities.

A Missionary but Lost

It gives me no pleasure to recall the years of my past. It was so very shameful. I was such a sinful person and so hypocritical. Some might say that I did much good for those African people, building schools for their children, providing medicines for their sicknesses, and teaching them religion; but today I know that all those so-called 'good deeds' were but 'filthy rags' in God's sight (*Isa.* 64:6). I was a poor, lost sinner in deep need of God's salvation, and did not realize it. I thought I was somehow already saved by the fact that I was a Roman Catholic, for I truly believed that all Roman Catholics were saved the moment they received the sacrament of baptism.

I Thought My Good Deeds Would Get Me to Heaven

How I regret those wasted years, years in which I did not know the true God, nor his Son, the true Lord and

Saviour Jesus Christ! How deceived I was to believe that I could merit heaven by my good deeds and my priestly and missionary labours! I was thirty-seven years old when the God of the Bible revealed himself to me. How free and how bountiful were his grace and mercy towards me! He pardoned all my sins, and he gave me a peace in my heart that truly satisfied my every longing. In a moment of time, I was changed, radically changed, inside my being. Indeed, I was born anew, born of the God of heaven himself. 'Verily, verily, I say unto thee, except a man be born again, he cannot see the kingdom of God' (*John* 3:3).

God's Plan

From all eternity God had chosen me to be his. That is why he intervened the way he did in my life and put a stop to my headlong plunge towards hell. Yes, that is exactly where I was headed, even as a missionary priest. I was on my way to a fiery hell, forever separated from a loving God. He showed me what I was under my pious exterior: I was a vile sinner! 'For all have sinned and come short of the glory of God' (*Rom.* 3:23).

'But God, who is rich in mercy, for his great love wherewith he loved us,' saved me by his grace. 'For by grace are ye saved through faith, and that not of yourselves: it is the gift of God: not of works, lest any man should boast' (*Eph.* 2:4, 8–9). I was so happy to discover that God's salvation is a gift. I thank God every day for 'his unspeakable gift' (*2 Cor.* 9:15).

In November 1966 I left the Roman Catholic Church and her priesthood for good. Some have said that I left because I wanted to get married, but that is absolutely false. I did not want to get married. I was too proud to think of marriage. Somehow I held marriage in very low esteem, thinking it was something below my dignity. Nevertheless, the God who saved me by his grace in due time made it clear to me that it was his will that I get married. His Word is plain enough: 'Marriage is honourable in all, and the bed undefiled: but whoremongers and adulterers God will judge' (*Heb*. 13:4). Also, 'Nevertheless, to avoid fornication, let every man have his own wife, and let every woman have her own husband . . . but if they cannot contain, let them marry: for it is better to marry than to burn' (*1 Cor*. 7:2, 9). God did provide me with a Christian wife, one who knows and loves the Lord Jesus Christ as I do, and at the time of writing we have recently celebrated our twenty-fifth wedding anniversary.

God Speaks through His Word

But why did I leave the Roman Catholic Church and her priesthood? People have asked me that question and I have answered, 'Because God told me to leave it.' I tell no lie. God did not speak to me in an audible voice. He spoke to me through his written Word in the book of Revelation where he says very distinctly 'Come out of her, my people' (*Rev*. 18:4). The true Christ is calling his people to come out of Roman Catholicism. Of course, those who are not of his people, that is, not his sheep, cannot receive that command. 'My sheep hear my voice, and I know them, and they follow me' (*John* 10:27). Before God saved me by his grace, no man could have persuaded me to come out of Romanism. But when he saved me and revealed his great love for me, and I heard his kind, gentle voice for the first time, it was easy for me to obey his command to come out and to follow him. I love him so, because he first loved me.

At one time I did believe the Church of Rome to be the one and only true Church of Jesus Christ on earth. Whenever a Protestant would say to me, 'Oh, one religion is as good as another,' I would answer, 'Yes, it is true, one religion may be as good as another, but only one religion is the true one, and that is the Roman Catholic religion.'

Believers 'See' Christ in the Scriptures

Believers do not need visible signs such as the Mass and sacraments because their salvation is wrought by the power of the Holy Spirit as they place their total trust in Jesus Christ alone as their personal Saviour. Nor do they require visible successors of the apostles because they know from the Bible that it is God who raises up the spiritual leaders he wants, when he wants them to feed his church with the precious Word of God. Finally they do not need images or statues to remind them of God because they see the true image of Christ in the written Word, the Bible. Besides, God has condemned both the making and the veneration of images and statues as idolatry (*Exod.* 20:3–5).

My Present Work

At the present time I am employed, and have been for the past twenty-three years, in the commercial printing trade. I teach an adult Bible class in a local evangelical church. In this church there are a number of former Roman Catholics who, like myself, have been saved by God's amazing grace and know and love the true Jesus Christ of the Holy Bible.

'And this is life eternal, that they might know thee the only true God, and Jesus Christ, whom thou hast sent' (*John* 17:3).

6

Alexander Carson

Free Indeed

I was baptized into the Roman Catholic Church as an infant in 1928. When I was just over a year old my family moved from New York State to New Milford, Connecticut, where I was raised in the Roman Catholic faith. I thoroughly believed in all Roman Catholic practices and beliefs, and I took my relationship to the Church, and therefore to God, very seriously. My first communion and confirmation were important events to me. After high school I went to Tufts College in Boston to undertake pre-medical studies, hoping one day to become a medical doctor like my revered uncle. However, at the end of two years of study I really desired to become a priest. I felt it was more important to help people spiritually than to aid them medically.

The Seminary

In September 1948, I began studies for the priesthood at
St John's Seminary, Brighton, Massachusetts. How I
loved the seminary! Everything was so 'holy' there.
Nevertheless, at the end of my first year in the seminary,
I withdrew. I felt I could never measure up to being a
priest, being convinced at the time that it was the highest
possible call on a young man's life. I attended Boston
College (Jesuit) and served Mass almost every morning
at a local Roman Catholic monastery. At this time,
during the fall of 1949, God saved me by his grace (the
only way!) even though I did not know a lot about the
Bible. Jesus saves believing sinners even though they
walk in a measure of confusion and darkness. I had come
to a place where I was uncertain about my relationship
with God, and I wanted to be sure about that above
everything else.

A Confession Absolutely Different

One night I knelt in a confessional booth and confessed
every sin of my life that I could bring to mind. At
confession I always really confessed my sins to God first,
though it was in the presence of the priest who would
give 'absolution'. 'If we confess our sins, he is faithful
and just to forgive us our sins, and to cleanse us from all
unrighteousness' (1 John 1:9). After I expressed my
repentance and while the priest was giving the ritual
'absolution', I cried out to God with my heart, saying,
'God, if you'll forgive all my sins, I take you as Lord of
my heart and I'll serve you the rest of my life!' 'For
whosoever shall call upon the name of the Lord shall be
saved' (Rom. 10:13). Leaving that confessional box and
walking across the transept of the church, I felt a great

peace and 'Abba, Father!' rang in my heart. I knew that I had a relationship with God! This did not happen because of the presence of a priest and liturgical absolution. It happened because of the presence of Jesus Christ, our great High Priest who made intercession for me and who made me the object of his grace, mercy and compassion. 'In whom we have redemption through his blood, the forgiveness of sins, according to the riches of his grace ... For by grace are ye saved through faith; and that not of yourselves: it is the gift of God: not of works, lest any man should boast' (*Eph.* 1:7, 2:8–9).

The next year I re-entered the seminary to complete studies for the priesthood, the best way I knew to serve God at the time. I was ordained by Bishop Lawrence Shehan of Bridgeport, Connecticut on 2 February 1955 and began ministry as a diocesan, or secular, priest in the diocese of Alexandria, Louisiana. The great excitement and joy I felt about my unique position of service began to wane after a few years and, try as I might to do everything right, it became empty, meaningless ritual.

The Bible – A New Standard

In 1971, after several years of crying out to God for something more meaningful, my great hunger began to be satisfied. Jesus and the Word of God (the Scriptures) became very real to me. Because 'the love of God is shed abroad in our hearts' (*Rom.* 5:5), the Holy Spirit led me to judge Roman Catholic theology by the standard of the Bible. Previously, I had always judged the Bible by Roman Catholic doctrine and theology. It was a reversal of authority in my life.

On a Sunday night in July 1972, while I was pastor of Sacred Heart Catholic Church, Rayville, Louisiana, I began to read the book of Hebrews in the New

Testament. This letter exalts Jesus, his priesthood, and his sacrifice over all the Old Covenant or Testament. This is some of what I read: 'Who needeth not daily, as those high priests, to offer up sacrifice, first for his own sins, and then for the people's: for this he did once, when he offered up himself' (*Heb.* 7:27). This startled me, and I began to feel very uneasy. I understood for the first time that Jesus' sacrifice was a one-time sacrificial offering at Calvary, in itself effectual to reconcile me and believing penitents of all ages to God. I saw at this time that the 'Holy Sacrifice of the Mass' offered by me and thousands of other Roman Catholic priests daily throughout the world was a fallacy and completely irrelevant. If the 'sacrifice' I daily offered as a priest was meaningless, then my 'priesthood' which existed for the purpose of offering that 'sacrifice' was likewise without meaning. These realizations were soon clearly confirmed as I continued to read in Hebrews chapter 10: 'But this man, (Jesus) after he had offered one sacrifice for sins for ever, sat down on the right hand of God; from henceforth expecting till his enemies be made his footstool. For by one offering he hath perfected for ever them that are sanctified' (verses 12–14). 'Now where remission of these is, there is no more offering for sin' (verse 18).

Saved by God's Grace Alone

That night the Roman Catholic Church lost credibility for me, since it had taught as truth what was clearly contrary to the Scriptures. I then chose the Scriptures as my standard of truth, no longer accepting the 'Magisterium', or teaching authority of the Roman Catholic Church as my standard. Like the Jewish priests of Acts 6:7, I became 'obedient to the faith'. In my letter of resignation from the Roman Catholic Church and ministry, I stated to the bishop that I was leaving the priesthood because I could no longer offer the Mass, as it was contrary to the Word of God and to my conscience. This was in 1972. It was not long before I was baptized by immersion, began biblical studies and was ordained to the gospel ministry. For over twenty years I have walked in the freedom of which Jesus spoke: 'Then said Jesus to those Jews which believed on him, If ye continue in my word, then are ye my disciples indeed; and ye shall know the truth, and the truth shall make you free' (*John* 8:31–32), and 'If the Son therefore shall make you free, ye shall be free indeed' (*John* 8:36).

7

Charles Berry

A Priest Asks God for Grace

As practising Roman Catholics, our family dedicated half an hour each Sunday to attending Mass, but religion really played a minor part in our life. As a teenager I was ashamed of my Roman Catholic beliefs, avoiding going to church whenever I could. Then something happened that changed the direction of my life.

Suffering to Get to Heaven

While baby-sitting for a Protestant neighbour I chanced to read a booklet on the subject of hell and eternal punishment. I was convinced, as I am at this moment, of the terrible reality of hell. Determined that my first obligation was to find a way of drawing closer to God, I entered deeply into Roman Catholic practices. I began attending Mass and saying the rosary every day, wearing the brown scapular and various medals. I was told that if I really wanted to find out how to get to heaven I should read the lives of the Roman Catholic saints and discover how they managed it. Thus I determined that the surest way to heaven was to cause myself to suffer. Pain became my constant companion, yet I was careful never to betray by my expression how much I was suffering. Then at the age of nineteen, I entered the Order of Hermits of St Augustine and for the next seventeen years lived under the rule of St Augustine, progressing from postulant to novice, to 'professed', and finally to priest.

During the first ten of those pre-Vatican II years, I did not even see the inside of a monastery nor have the opportunity of association or frank discussion with regular monks or priests. Students for the priesthood never mixed with their superiors and teachers. The hardships were many, but were gradually relaxed a little as we advanced and approached ordination. Few of us complained if the food was poor, the time for rest insufficient or the discipline degrading or inhuman, because we felt that this was the price that we had to pay to become men of God. Obedience to authority was the one theme which dominated our lives. Not only did we surrender the right to our own possessions, ambitions and private lives, we surrendered even our minds and intellects and private thoughts. We were told that God spoke to us directly through the mouths of our superiors and that any doubt or hesitation in accepting their complete control was a grave sin against God.

'Be Ye Holy for I Am Holy'

My first assignment as an ordained Roman Catholic
priest was somewhat different from the average. Instead of being sent to some monastery to assist in
parochial work or to teach, I was given orders to
continue studying until I achieved a Ph.D. in chemistry,
so that I could teach in a Roman Catholic University.
The new monastery where I was sent was luxuriously
furnished with every convenience, boasting of the finest
foods that money could buy. But I had not sacrificed
for so many years to be able finally to live in luxury, but
rather to become a true man of God, a saint. What was
disappointing and disillusioning to find upon entering
the inner circles of the clergy was how very un-
important God was to those who were expected to have
extraordinary holiness and love of God. The part of
each day which was concerned with doing the Lord's
work was regarded as the unpleasant part. I noticed
(not only there but wherever I have been in the world)
that the only clergymen who would get up for services
in the church would be those appointed to conduct
them, and then they would feel sorry for themselves
that it was their turn. After asking to be sent somewhere else, I was delighted to be transferred to the
headquarters of the Augustinian Order in the United
States. But instead of discovering it to be a spiritual
powerhouse I found it to be where many priests were
brought when their lives became so scandalous as to
hurt the reputation of the Church. Where was this
Church which had been described to me, to which I had
given my life because of her purity and beauty? Could
it be, I wondered, that it did not exist in the United
States because of contamination by Protestantism?
Could it be that it only existed in its full purity in

Roman Catholic countries where it had full liberty of expression and freedom from constraints?

At this time I heard of a Roman Catholic university in a Roman Catholic country that needed a scientist to build up its programme in science and engineering. Eagerly I volunteered and soon became Director of the School of Chemical Engineering. Needless to say, I did not find there the Church which I had expected to find. Any American Roman Catholic who travels to a Roman Catholic country is embarrassed and shocked by what he sees. In the United States the Roman Catholic Church is on its best behaviour, putting its best foot forward because of its critics and opponents. In a Roman Catholic country, where it has few opponents or critics, it is a very different matter. Ignorance and superstition and idolatry are everywhere, and little effort, if any, is made to change the situation. Instead of following the Christianity taught in the Bible the people concentrate on the worship of statues of their local patron saints.

'Thou Shalt Not Make Unto Thee Any Graven Image'

For many years I had maintained the idea that Roman Catholics do not worship idols, but now I saw with my own eyes that there was no difference between the Roman Catholics with their images and the pagans with theirs. When I met in Cuba a genuine pagan who worshipped idols (a religion transplanted from Africa by his ancestors), I asked how he could believe that a plaster idol could help him. He replied that the idol was not expected to help him; it only represented the power in heaven which could. What horrified me about his reply was that it was almost word-for-word the explanation Roman Catholics give for rendering honour to the statues of the saints.

Works Without Faith

Little by little, I devoted myself to my work at the university. Under my leadership, we built and equipped a group of large buildings to house schools of chemical engineering, mechanical engineering, architecture, pharmacy and psychology. As each school developed, I turned it over to a qualified dean, while I became assistant to the rector in charge of science and a member of the four-man executive committee governing the entire university. Probably the most outstanding success I had was the formation of a Bureau of Quality Standards, under which industries voluntarily agreed to accept minimum standards and contracted with our laboratories so that we might continually test their products to insure uniform high quality. The most powerful and wealthy people, from the president down, showered me with honours and gifts so that I might be their friend and support their projects and ambitions. Yet deep in my heart I knew that whatever honour I had achieved, I had not gained the real goal for which I had set out. Augustine said it so well centuries ago, 'Thou hast made our hearts for thee, O God, and they are restless until they rest in thee'.

Many doubts assailed me. I knew that so many of the things which we preached, so many of the glib answers we gave the people, were hotly disputed among theologians and laughed at or disregarded by many of the clergy. I was ashamed of the priests who had for centuries robbed the people, ignored the poor, supported rich oppressors and lived scandalous lives.

Determined to rescue the few remaining years of my life, I decided that as soon as I received my doctorate in physics and chemistry, I would leave the priesthood and the Church. I am sure that every priest faces such a decision some time in his life. The Church had promised to make us men of God, but sooner or later after ordination, each one must face his conscience to 'balance up the books'. That is when he realizes that he is worse off than the day he began, in spite of using all the means which the Church had offered.

The Cost of Leaving the Church

To decide to leave means to be cut off from most, if not all, of those who have loved, honoured and respected us and, what is more important, those whom we have loved and served. Every priest must know several companions who attempted the break and were forced, for one reason or another, to return. I did. They told me how they returned, not out of love for the Church but, among other reasons, so that they could get 'three square meals a day and a decent burial'.

I planned my break carefully, requesting from my superiors permission to take a vacation in Europe. Then, after receiving my doctorate degree, I bought a used car in Miami with the idea of disappearing in some small town where I was unknown. I felt none of that joy of liberation and freedom which might have been expected. Everyone I had ever known was now cut off from me by their bondage to the Church. I was a stranger and foreigner to the whole world, and more of a stranger to God than ever before.

In casting about for somebody who might help me find employment, I turned to a certain chemist who had worked for me in the Bureau of Quality Standards, but who was now living in Mexico. After receiving assurance that there were friends there who would come to my assistance, I packed my things and headed south of the Rio Grande.

Martha, a friend, was living with an aunt from Spain. Both women were very kind to me and, as a close circle of friendship developed, little did I guess how much each one would influence my life. Eventually Martha and I were married. Her aunt then sought to be reunited with her errant husband, but not long after he returned she was found dead in bed. There was a great deal of circumstantial evidence against him, and we became involved in one of the most sensational murder cases in the history of Mexico. Because of the resulting publicity, my name was recognized and several Roman Catholic reporters of leading newspapers began attacking me as a renegade priest. Then, fearing for the stability of his business, my employer fired me.

Facing difficulties all the way, we slowly worked our way to San Diego. After several months working at Convair Astronautics, I was informed that they had a staff position for me with the parent corporation, General Dynamics. Several weeks were taken up in conferences and briefings. Naturally I had to give a detailed account of my life, education and professional work, as well as references. All this I spelled out in great detail, omitting only the fact that I had been a Roman priest. Suddenly, just a day or two before I was to begin my new work, I received a telegram cancelling all arrangements.

I never did have any direct evidence of what led to my dismissal, but after only a few days I received a letter from Church authorities warning me never to try again to obtain recommendations from Church-controlled sources because they would always deny they ever knew me. Never again did I find a position worthy of my training and experience.

The Gift of Salvation

I had been taught all my life to fear and distrust Protestant pastors. We were told that they greedily seized upon ex-priests to use them to promote their own evil ends. In desperation and in spite of these forebodings, I decided to take the risk and thus discovered that all over the world, since the days of Jesus, there have been people who can best be called Bible-believing Christians. Not people who merely believe that the Bible is divinely inspired, but people who consider it a personal message from their loving God and therefore make it the guiding force in their lives.

I borrowed a handbook on Christian teaching from a pastor and found that all the references were texts from Scripture, no logic, no tradition. I noticed for the first time the simple statements of the Bible on how one can attain heaven and avoid hell. I realized that Scripture is not to be approached from a scholarly point of view but from the position of children listening to their father, accepting and believing every word, recognizing that God means what he has said and knows how to say what he means. On page after page of the Bible I saw truths which I had thirsted for all my life. The teaching regarding salvation was clear: 'For by grace are ye saved through faith; and that not of yourselves: it is the gift of God: not of works, lest any man should boast.' (*Eph.* 2:8–9).

Martha and I agreed that I had done more than almost anyone in the world to obtain salvation, but that there was one thing I had never done. I had never asked for it as a gift from God. We decided that we would ask God for his gift of grace. We got down on our knees and prayed together for the first time.

In a spirit of humility and contrition we asked God to

save us, not because of the good we had done nor the good we vowed to do, but because of the good which Jesus did when he made atonement for our sin by his death on the cross.

Little did we realize it, but we were born again, so young that we did not even know who we were in Christ. From that moment on we began noticing changes in our thinking. We began to love the things of God. In one way or another since then, the Lord has kept us busy witnessing and preaching, winning many hundreds of souls for the Lord Jesus Christ and biblical Christianity.

'But ye are come unto mount Sion, and unto the city of the living God, the heavenly Jerusalem, and to an innumerable company of angels, to the general assembly and church of the firstborn, which are written in heaven, and to God the Judge of all, and to the spirits of just men made perfect, And to Jesus the mediator of the new covenant and to the blood of sprinkling, that speaketh better things than that of Abel' (*Heb.* 12:22–24).

8

Bob Bush

Once a Jesuit, Now a Child of God

I began my Roman Catholic journey in a little country town in northern California in the USA. The town was so small that we did not have Mass every Sunday, but a priest used to come once a month if possible to hold Mass in a big public hall.

I have both an older and a younger brother. My father had been trained at the University of Santa Clara. As a result my parents thought it would be a good idea for us to attend a Roman Catholic boarding school. The school was run by the Jesuits and I was a student there for four years. Academically it was a very good school, but the only type of religion to which we were exposed was Roman Catholic theology and tradition with no emphasis on the Bible.

Desire to Serve God and Mankind

As graduation approached I considered what I should do with my life. I thought that becoming a Jesuit priest could be a good way to honour and serve God and help mankind; that was all I knew. At that time, even when I left high school, I had a longing and a hunger in my heart to meet God and to know him. In fact, once when I was a senior (fourth and final year) in high school, I remember going out to the football field and just kneeling there in the dark with my arms up to the sky. I cried out, 'God, God, where are you?' I really had a hunger for God.

Jesuit Seminary

I entered the Jesuit Order in 1953 after graduation from high school. When I entered the order, the first thing that happened was that I was told I had to keep all the rules and regulations, that to do so would be pleasing to God, and that this was what he wanted for me. We were taught the motto, 'Keep the rule and the rule will keep you.'

We read a lot about the lives of the saints, and right from the beginning I was trained to look at them as models to follow, not realizing that they had become saints because they had served the Roman Catholic Church. I did seminary studies for a total of thirteen years, taking course after course and studying one thing after another. It finally ended in a study of theology, culminating in ordination in 1966.

Hunger for God but No Peace

I still had a hunger in my heart for God. I had not met the Lord yet and still did not have peace. In fact, at that time

I used to smoke and I was very nervous. I would pace back and forth in my room puffing one cigarette after another because of my inner unrest.

I entered a post-graduate programme in Rome thinking I would be on top of the mountain, but the hunger in my heart persisted. I even spoke to a priest who was in charge of missionaries to Africa, since I wanted to go there as a missionary. I was aware that if I went to Africa, however, the only thing I could do would be to tell people what I had learned about the Roman Catholic doctrines and what the Roman Catholic Church had to offer, even though it had not satisfied me. I did not see how it could satisfy them either.

I studied during the years of Vatican Council II (1962–5) and was ordained a year after it ended. The documents from Vatican Council II were coming out from Rome and I thought everything would change. It was a time of discovery. I thought I would get to the rock bottom truth, and this would change the world. This idea was the force that drove me. But I was not aware of any changes, as the same Roman Catholic doctrines from the Council of Trent were still in place. So I did not go to Africa but returned to California, where God had a surprise in store for me.

Leading a Prayer Group

While at a retreat house where I said Mass, a lady asked me if I would lead a prayer group in her home. I had never led a prayer meeting in my life and did not know how it worked, but I thought that as I had been trained for all those years I should be qualified to do it and assented. It was held every Thursday from 10.00 a.m. until noon. A group of people would gather and read only the Bible, sing praises to the Lord, and pray for one another's needs. Early on the morning when the prayer meeting was due to take place, I paced back and forth and thought, 'Oh, why did I say I was going to go there?' I was not at all enthusiastic about going, but when noon came, I did not want to leave. The power of the Word of God was beginning to touch my heart and life.

Surprised by God's Grace

The great surprise that the Lord had in store for me happened in this way. One night in August 1970 we went to a retreat house with a group of people from the home prayer meeting. The speaker asked at the end of his address, 'Now if there is anyone here who is hungry for God and has not been touched by God and wants God to touch his life, then come forward and we will pray for you.' This was the moment I prayed that God would change me. I went forward and they laid hands on me and prayed over me. It was not because of any works that either they or I did, but it was truly by God's grace that I was born again. At that moment God changed my life. Jesus became real, the Bible became real. 'Not by works of righteousness which we have done, but according to his mercy he saved us, by the washing of regeneration, and renewing of the Holy Ghost' (*Titus* 3:5).

Our High School Prayer Group

We started a prayer group in a high school and it grew so large we had to move to a gymnasium. Before long we had eight hundred to one thousand people coming every Friday night. We were stressing praise and worshipping and glorifying God. Based in the gymnasium where there were no statues or any other such thing, we had one manual, the Bible.

I had a lot to learn. It took me many years to realize that I was compromising by staying in the Roman Catholic Church. Throughout all of those years I continued to stress that salvation is only in the finished work of Jesus Christ on the cross and not in infant baptism; that there is only one source of authority which is the Bible, the Word of God; and that there is no purgatory but rather that when we die we either go to heaven or hell.

Here is where the conflict came. Seeing people depend upon such false and deceiving beliefs for their salvation was heart-wrenching to me. I felt that maybe God could use me to change things in the Roman Catholic Church. I even had prayer sessions with people who felt the same way. We prayed that God would change the Roman Catholic Church so that we could remain Roman Catholics. But to remain Roman Catholic, I now see, is to be living a compromised life.

Conviction by the Holy Spirit

I finally realized after much conviction of the Holy Spirit that not giving myself totally to him, one hundred per cent, was grieving my Lord, as I was sinning a sin of compromise. I also came to realize that the Roman Catholic Church cannot change. If it did change, there would be no Pope, no rosary, no purgatory, no priests, no Mass, etc. After seventeen years of brainwashing, my brain was washed and cleansed by the Holy Spirit. In a word, what was happening to me over this period is explained in Romans 12:1–2:

'I beseech you therefore, brethren, by the mercies of God, that ye present your bodies a living sacrifice, holy,

acceptable unto God, which is your reasonable service.
And be not conformed to this world: but be ye transformed by the renewing of your mind, that ye may prove
what is that good, and acceptable, and perfect, will of
God'.

Research in India

By this time I had met another priest who has since left
the Church of Rome. He was preaching the same kind of
thing, spending half of the year in India and half in the
United States. Victor Affonso was also a Jesuit, and I
told him I thought it would be wonderful to go to India
and to do some missionary work there.

I went to India in 1986 and spent six months there
doing missionary work. We were also able to spend a
month with a group of people researching Roman
Catholic dogma in the light of the Scriptures. We were
determined to follow what the Bible said; if Roman
Catholic doctrines contradicted that, we would reject
them.

We saw that Jesus said, 'Come unto me', and that in
the Gospels we are told to pray to our Father in Jesus'
name, never to a saint or to Mary. The disciples did not
pray to Stephen, who died very early in the Acts of the
Apostles, or to James, who was killed very early. Why
would they do that when they had the resurrected Jesus
with them? He said, 'For where two or three are
gathered together in my name, there am I in the midst of
them' (*Matt.* 18:20). They prayed to Jesus; they prayed
to the Father; they had the guidance of the Holy Spirit
and obeyed the commandments of God.

In India we discovered that the Roman Catholic
catechism had changed the Ten Commandments from
the way they were in the Bible. In the Roman Catholic

catechism, the first commandment is as it is in Scripture. The second commandment in the catechism is: 'Thou shalt not take the name of the Lord thy God in vain.' This is a complete change from the Bible. The third commandment of the Bible has been moved up to the second. The original second commandment as is found in Scripture has been dropped. Virtually all of the catechisms drop the second commandment of the Bible. For example, the *New Baltimore Catechism*, question 195, answers, 'The commandments of God are these ten: (1) I am the Lord thy God, thou shalt not have strange gods before me; (2) Thou shalt not take the name of the Lord thy God in vain,' etc.

In the Bible, the second commandment declares, 'Thou shalt not make unto thee any graven image, or any likeness of any thing that is in heaven above, or that is in the earth beneath, or that is in the water under the earth: Thou shalt not bow down thyself to them, nor serve them: for I the LORD thy God am a jealous God, visiting the iniquity of the fathers upon the children unto the third and fourth generation of them that hate me; And shewing mercy unto thousands of them that love me, and keep my commandments'(*Exod.* 20:4–6). God forbids us to bow down before these or to serve them, yet there are pictures of the Pope bowing down and kissing statues.

We were concerned that this commandment had been dropped out of the catechism. So now we might well ask, 'How do we get ten commandments?' The catechisms divide the last commandment (formerly the tenth, now split into the ninth and tenth). 'Do not covet thy neighbour's wife' is listed as a separate commandment from that of not coveting his goods. This is quite a distortion of the Bible. I was discovering dogmas and doctrines that directly contradicted the Scriptures.

Mary and the Mass

We also investigated the doctrine of the Immaculate
Conception. This is defined as 'the doctrine that Mary
was conceived without sin; at the first moment of
conception there was no sin there.' This contradicts
Romans 3:23 which says, 'For all have sinned and come
short of the glory of God.' Here we had a doctrine, a
tradition that is passed down and solemnly defined as
infallibly true, and it contradicts what is in the Bible.

Then we came to one of the biggest areas of conflict. It
had to do with the sacrifice of the Mass. The official
Roman Catholic position on the sacrifice of the Mass is
that it is a continuation of the sacrifice of Calvary. The
Council of Trent actually defined it this way:

'And since in this divine sacrifice, which is celebrated
in the Mass, that same Christ is contained and immola-
ted in an unbloody manner, who on the altar of the cross
'once offered himself' in a bloody manner (Hebrews
9:27), the holy Synod teaches that this is truly propitiatory . . . For it is one and the same victim, the same one
now offering by the ministry of the priests as he who then
offered himself on the cross, the manner of offering
alone being different.'

Some people might say the Council of Trent is not
valid any more and that things have changed. But
Cardinal Ratzinger, head of the Congregation for the
Doctrine of the Faith in a book called *The Ratzinger
Report* said, 'It is likewise impossible to decide in favour
of Trent and Vatican I, but against Vatican II. Whoever
denies Vatican II denies the authority that upholds the
other two councils and thereby detaches them from their
foundation.' Catechisms also say that the Mass is the
same sacrifice as that of the cross. For example, the *New
Baltimore Catechism* says, 'The Mass is the same

sacrifice as the sacrifice of the cross because in the Mass the victim is the same, and the principal priest is the same, Jesus Christ.' Yet in Hebrews 10:18 it says, 'Now where remission of these is, there is no more offering for sin'. So Scripture makes it very clear. In fact, eight times in four chapters, beginning in chapter seven of the letter to the Hebrews, it says *'once for all';* there was one offering for sin, once for all.

Finished Sacrifice

Anyone who has attended Mass in the Roman Catholic Church will remember the prayer said by the priest, 'Pray, brethren, that our sacrifice may be acceptable to God, the Almighty Father.' This is a very serious prayer. The people respond saying the same thing, asking that the sacrifice may be acceptable to God. But this is contrary to the Word of God because the sacrifice has already been accepted. When Jesus was on the cross, he said, 'It is finished' (*John* 19:30), and we know that it was completed because Jesus was accepted by the Father and rose from the dead and is now at the right hand of the Father. The good news that we preach is that Jesus has risen from the dead, that his sacrifice is completed, and that he has paid for sin. When by God's grace we accept his work as the finished sacrifice for our sins, we are saved and have everlasting life.

A memorial is a remembrance of something that someone has done for us. Jesus said, 'This do in remembrance of me.' So anyone who is reading this, or any priest who is saying Mass, must seriously consider the error of the prayer, 'Let us pray, my brothers and sisters, that our sacrifice may be acceptable.' The sacrifice has been accepted. We are to have the communion service in memory of what Jesus has done. The

sacrifice that Jesus offered on the cross cannot be added
to or re-enacted.

Can the Mass Atone for Sin?

The Roman Catholic Church says that the Mass is a
propitiatory sacrifice effective to take away the sins of
those on earth and those who have died. That is why, to
this very day, even though some people will say that the
Church in some places does not believe in purgatory,
still virtually every Mass that is said is for someone who
has died. It is believed that the Mass will shorten their
time in purgatory. That is why it is said for dead people.
When a person dies, judgment immediately follows, 'It
is appointed unto men once to die, but after this the
judgment' (*Heb.* 9:27). If they are saved, they go
directly to heaven; if they remain in their sins, they go to
hell. There is nothing to change one from hell to heaven.
The Roman Catholic Church believes that the Mass,
being a propitiatory sacrifice, will decrease the time in
purgatory. But all the suffering and all the atonement
that was ever made for sins was accomplished by Jesus
on the cross, and we need to accept this truth. We need
to receive everlasting life and to be born again while we
are still alive. There is no biblical evidence to support
the idea that after death we can experience any kind of
change.

To Be Right before God

We then began to study what the Roman Catholic
Church teaches on salvation. It is a doctrine of the
Roman Catholic Church that we can be saved by being
baptized as infants. Present-day canon law says,
'Baptism is the gate to the sacraments, necessary for

salvation, in fact, or at least in intention, by which men and women are freed from their sins, reborn as children of God, configured to Christ' (Canon 849). This teaches that when a baby is baptized, it is saved and has everlasting life by virtue of baptism. But that is not true. Jesus never said anything like that, neither is there a word in the Bible about anything like that happening. There is no limbo! Jesus said, 'Suffer the little children to come unto me.' The Bible always says we are saved when we accept that Christ Jesus totally paid the price of our sin so that his right standing with God becomes ours. 'For he hath made him to be sin for us, who knew no sin; that we might be made the righteousness of God in him' (*2 Cor.* 5:21).

Christ's Work or Our Works?

The Roman Catholic Church then goes on to say that in order to be saved you must keep its laws, rules and regulations. And if these laws are violated (for example, laws concerning birth control or fasting or attendance at Mass every Sunday), then you have committed a sin. The Roman Catholic Church says in canon law of the present day that if you commit a serious sin, that sin must be forgiven by confessing to a priest. 'Individual and integral confession and absolution constitute the only ordinary way by which the faithful person who is aware of serious sin can be reconciled with God, and with the Church' (Canon 9609). The Roman Catholic Church says that this is the way sins are forgiven, the ordinary way that sins are forgiven. The Bible says that if we repent in our heart and believe on Christ's finished sacrifice we are saved. We are saved by grace, not by our works. The Roman Catholic Church adds works, in that you have to do these specific things in order to be saved, whereas the Bible says in Ephesians 2:8–9 that it is by grace that we are saved, not by works. The Bible makes it very clear that we are saved by grace. It is a free gift given by God, not because of any works we do. 'For by grace are ye saved through faith; and that not of yourselves; it is the gift of God; not of works, lest any man should boast' (*Eph.* 2:8–9). 'And if by grace then is it no more of works; otherwise grace is no more grace. But if it be of works, then is it no more grace; otherwise work is no more work' (*Rom.* 11:6).

I Leave India and the Roman Catholic Church

We examined these and many other doctrines while we were in India, and as I left, I knew that I could not represent the Roman Catholic Church any longer. I began to see that Roman Catholic dogmas which contradict Scripture are so rooted that they cannot be changed.

The Roman Catholic Church will always insist that the Mass is an ongoing continuation of the sacrifice of Jesus. The Church will not let go of the dogma that babies are reborn and receive eternal life at baptism, nor of all the various requirements that are put upon her people.

Now I do sincerely love Roman Catholics and want to help them. I want to help them find the freedom of salvation and the life and blessing that comes from following the Scriptures. And I have nothing against any Roman Catholic or any priest; it is the dogmas and doctrines that keep them bound. God himself wants to loose them. Jesus said, 'Laying aside the commandments of God, ye hold the tradition of men' (*Mark* 7:8). That is the problem we are facing right here. These traditions destroy the very Word of God because they contradict its truths.

When I left India and came home, I knew that I was facing the biggest change of my life. It was a time of great distress for me because I had totally believed in the Roman Catholic Church and had served it for so much of my life. I knew when I came back I was going to have to leave the Church of Rome.

In 1987 I left the Roman Catholic Church formally by writing a letter of resignation and then corresponding with my former superiors. I ended up writing to Rome before I left. I did it in that manner because I wanted to witness to all of them and give them reasons why I was leaving. I wanted to follow the Bible.

My Parents and My Wife

At that time I was experiencing a great deal of suffering. I came home to my parents, both of whom were over eighty, and one night we had a serious conversation. I told them what I was going to do; I told them that I was saved by God's grace and I was going to leave the Roman Catholic Church for doctrinal reasons. There was a long pause and my father said, speaking very slowly, 'Bob, you know, both your mother and I have been thinking the same thing.' They went to one more Mass and came home and said, 'Do you know that is an altar in front of the church? An altar is a place of sacrifice.' And my father said, 'I see clearly now that there is no more sacrifice.' Both my mother and my father began reading the Bible and following it. In 1989 my mother died reading the Word of God and with the peace and assurance that she had everlasting life and was going to be with the Lord forever. My dad passed away in 1993 with a prayer on his lips for those he left behind. He had written his own testimony to the grace of God, and while quite old had witnessed to others, even in the retirement home. On 6 June 1992 God gave me the greatest gift he can give a person besides salvation, my beautiful wife, Joan.

The Present Day

I am now an ordained minister, in fellowship with others of the biblical faith. I continue to preach the gospel of God's grace through the death of the Lord Jesus Christ alone.

9

Cipriano Valdes Jaimes

An Irresistible Call

I was born in Michoacan, Mexico, to a devout Roman Catholic family. I received my primary education under the watchful eye of those who taught me to observe frequent confession and daily communion. When I reached the age of twelve, I entered the diocesan seminary in Chilapa, in the State of Guerrero. For five long years I studied the Latin of Cicero and Virgil. For three years my mind was filled with the philosophy of the Greek writers. With great care I was given four years of theology where I learned all the dogmas of Romanism. Finally, on 18 October 1951, on the Day of St Luke the Evangelist, I was ordained a priest.

Sincerely Deceived

On that day, through the laying on of hands by the bishop, I was given the incredible, the deceitful, the false powers which the Roman Catholic Church pretends to give to man to delude others. I was granted the ability to forgive men's sins, both inside and outside the horrible confessional box. On that day I received the power to sacrifice Christ over again on an altar at my whim and fancy. I could now release souls from purgatory, a place invented by Rome, through a lying and lucrative ritual. This is the undeniable teaching of the Roman Church, that before going to heaven men's souls must pass through such a lake of fire. How far from the truth! What error! Yet that is what I believed as the result of four years of painstaking, incisive work in dogmatic and moral theology. So when I was told that I had power to forgive the sins of my fellow men, I accepted the fact with all my heart, not realizing that the forgiving of sins is a divine attribute. It cannot be delegated to a man. The Scripture says, 'I, even I, am he that blotteth out thy transgressions for mine own sake, and will not remember thy sins' (*Isa.* 43:25); 'Who can forgive sins but God only?' (*Mark* 2:7). For twenty years in the Roman Catholic priesthood I performed this ridiculous, shameful, anti-scriptural practice of daily listening to the frailties of society, including military men, professionals and politicians. I was the spiritual director in schools. For one year I held the post of assistant parish priest, and for nineteen years I was a parish priest. I had aides and assistant priests who helped me carry out my absurd duties.

Christ Sacrificed Once for All

In order to repeat the bloodless sacrifice of Christ on the altar, I was given the power to convert the bread into his body and the wine into his blood through the words of consecration. With joy and deep respect I accepted this authority. In my hands would be found the very Creator of the universe, the eternal God, made man for us. Is it possible that for twenty years I kept sacrificing Christ? And I did it up to four times on Sundays. What an awful, shameful travesty this was for me and for all who took part in what Rome calls the Mass. Man can never repeat Christ's work on the cross. To think he can is an invention of the devil. The Bible says in Romans 6:9, 'Christ being raised from the dead dieth no more; death hath no more dominion over him.' How then can a priest cause him to die a bloodless death? Hebrews 9:22 states that 'without shedding of blood is no remission'. So what does a Mass accomplish? Does it purify and free souls from purgatory? The Bible states, 'The blood of Jesus Christ his Son cleanseth us from all sin' (*1 John* 1:7).

God is a Spirit

Roman Catholic dogma declares that in every particle of the consecrated bread and in the consecrated wine the body and the blood of Jesus Christ are fully present. What falsehood! Christ said, 'Where two or three are gathered together in my name, there am I in the midst of them' (*Matt.* 18:20). But the sacrilegious lying and deceit reach their climax when the priest, after the so-called consecration, raises the bread and the cup while the people bow and strike their breasts or raise their eyes toward heaven, and exclaim, 'My Lord and my God.' This is idolatry, the worship of created matter. God is not a piece of bread.

'God is a Spirit: and they that worship him must worship him in spirit and in truth' (*John* 4:24).

Tradition versus Truth

But I believed, taught, preached and defended the doctrine of Rome whether or not it agreed with the Word of God. For me, at that time, the Church with its councils and its traditions came before the sacred Scriptures. The voice of the Pope had more authority than that of the Holy Spirit. Was not the Church of Rome the only one which men were bound to believe and obey? For that reason, I, as did Paul, actively persecuted the Church of God (*Gal.* 1:13). In their own places of worship I defied evangelical pastors, Protestants as they were called in official Roman Catholicism. I insulted them, I humiliated them and I forced them out of the parishes where I was lord and master. I do not know how much of their literature I destroyed. I recall a particularly shameful incident. I, along with some supposedly devout men, came upon a young Christian woman surrounded by a group listening intently as she presented God's Word to them. I forced myself into the midst of the crowd and began to ridicule and humiliate her and the work she was doing as a servant of God. I threatened the crowd around her by telling them that they would die without the sacraments of the Holy Mother Church. I ordered those with me to gather up all the Bibles that had been given out because they were false. They did not have the stamp of approval of the true Church, the *nihil obstat,* or the *imprimatur.* They collected sixty-six Bibles, freshly delivered from the press, and with my own hands I tore them up and fed them to the flames. Yet I did it all in ignorance. My Saviour says, 'He that rejecteth me, and receiveth not my words, hath one that judgeth him: the word that I have spoken, the same shall judge him in the last day' (*John* 12:48).

Called by God

Like Paul I can say that, when it pleased him, God 'called me by his grace' (*Gal.* 1:15). I heard within me his voice saying, 'Cipriano, this is not where you belong. Leave all of this.' I simply obeyed and I left. The bishop summoned me and I returned to my parish, offering some of the well-worn excuses. However, the Lord's voice kept insisting. While I listened to confessions he said, 'Don't listen to the weaknesses of others. You can't forgive them anyway.' When I celebrated Mass or baptized babies, his voice interrupted me. I left my position a second time, and the bishop called me back again. And still God's irresistible voice would not leave me alone. At last I could no longer stand it. I went to the bishop's office and announced to him that I was going to leave the Church. He replied, 'What are you saying? You are leaving the Church? If you are not happy with this parish I will get you a better one.' My answer was, 'No, what I am trying to tell you is that I want nothing more to do with the Church.' The bishop reacted with, 'What are you going to do? Where will you go?' And I simply replied, 'I don't know what I'll do, nor where I'll go. All I know is that I have to leave.' Irritated, the bishop stood up and brought me some forms to fill out requesting my release from Rome. His disgust was not so much with me personally as with the fact that he was losing a man with eighteen years of study and twenty years of experience. I was not expelled from the priesthood in the Roman Church; I left because the Lord called me.

Saved by Christ's Work Alone

One month later I was in the city of Tijuana, Baja California, Mexico. There the Lord had a missionary, under the guidance of the Holy Spirit, prepared to show me Christ as the only Saviour. Finally I was able to understand the Scripture that says, 'For God so loved the world, that he gave his only begotten Son, that whosoever believeth in him should not perish, but have everlasting life' (*John* 3:16). I have trusted in Christ; I have received him as my Saviour and as the Lord of my life. And because of this I know that I have eternal life. A man does not enter heaven because of his works or his sacrifices or his virtues, great as these may be. The only way to the Father is through the unlimited merits of Christ. No ceremony, no ritual, no sacrament can save a man.

I have not proclaimed these truths to offend you or anyone else. There is love in my heart and my life now because I am a born-again Christian. Recognize the fact that you are a sinner and confess your sins directly to God just as I did. Ask his forgiveness for your sins. Invite Christ into your heart and life, and he will give you eternal life. I now preach the gospel in churches, in public places, in prisons and in private homes.

10

Dario A. Santamaria

Yesterday, a Priest –
Today, a Missionary

I was born in Bello, Antioquia, Colombia, on 22 June 1942. I first went to school in the Institute Manuel José Caicido, taught by the Christian Brothers, an order whose work is teaching children. Here I studied for six years. After this, I studied in the school of the Salesian Fathers for five years. My last year of high school I studied in Bogota, the capital of Colombia, with the Dominican Fathers.

Climbing the Ecclesiastical Ladder

After leaving high school I received the habit of the Dominican Order and began my novitiate year. I wore

85

the white robe and black cape of the novitiate. My head was shaved, leaving just a fringe of hair. For that year I was studying the constitutional laws, customs, obligations and privileges of the religious life in the Roman Catholic Church.

It was a year of hard work. The restrictive regimen forbade communication with outsiders. We were never allowed to eat meat, except on certain holidays. Every Friday we had to fast. Daily we prayed and sang the psalms in Latin. Every day we began in silence and remained so, except for prayer, until 12.30. On Sunday we had to confess our sins before our classmates and our superiors. Often offenders were made to lie in the doorway where brother priests would walk over their prostrate forms.

Then I made a promise to remain in the order for three years. Immediately I began my philosophical studies. During three years I spent my time studying metaphysics, cosmology, psychology, methodology, the history of philosophy, Greek and Hebrew.

Afterwards I made my solemn vows, then I began my theological studies. In that year, 1961, I met the most progressive thinkers of the Roman Catholic Church. At the end of the year I received my first order, another step up the ecclesiastical ladder.

In the second year of theological studies, I received two more orders, or grades, of the Roman Catholic clergy. In the third year, I studied dogmatics, history and the Trinity, and I received the first of the major orders, that of subdeacon. The last year I studied moral law and pastoral duties and was ordained as a Roman Catholic priest.

The Living Word of God

But the Lord called me to a new way, and I would like to tell you something of what happened within me while I was preparing these many years. I read a speech by the Spanish writer Donoso Cortez in which he spoke of the greatness of the Bible and of its contribution to world literature. He concluded with a paragraph in which he spoke of the Bible as the Book of God for men. I understood then the importance of the Bible as a Book for salvation.

In our home we had a beautiful Bible in which we noted marriages, deaths and births, a Bible which was a silent witness to the activities of our home, and a witness which never spoke to us because we were never taught to read it. As I began to read some parts many doubts were created within me, and I wanted to resolve them. I believed that I should get closer to those who lived what the Bible taught. Thus I went to a Protestant Christian friend from whom I bought a Bible and with whom I had many discussions. I took their correspondence course but there were many questions still unresolved.

Once when attending a Protestant young people's meeting I was surprised at the knowledge these people had of the Bible. On my birthday my Protestant friend gave me a Scripture bookmark with John 3:16 on it, the text which became the key of my life: 'For God so loved the world, that he gave his only begotten Son, that whosoever believeth in him should not perish, but have everlasting life.'

I had gone to the seminary thinking that in this way I could give myself to the Lord. I had chosen one of the most noble of the orders of the Church because of its theologians, preachers and service in the defence of the Roman Catholic faith (the order of Thomas Aquinas and also of the Inquisition). But I found no peace in the seminary.

Always the Lord kept before me this text of John 3:16. I began to wonder why I was in the monastery if the Lord

could completely save me. All the practices of the
monastery and the Church were extra and not needed if
salvation was by faith. I tried to search for the practices
of the Church in the gospels, and one doubt grew into
another doubt.

The Way of Faith

From my second year of study I was accustomed to
reading the New Testament in Greek. Certain translations in Romans and Galatians seemed very strange to
me. The way of faith seemed to be presented as the
Christian's security. But when I asked my professor of
exegesis about my doubts he answered me in the
words of St John Chrysostom, 'The more I read of
Paul, the less do I understand.' My doubts became so
great that they created night about me. At this time I
did not believe in the resurrection of Jesus because I
had taken the liberal theology of Bultmann as my
guide.

Through further study of the Scriptures I was taken
out of these doubts. A verse in 1 Corinthians (15:14)
held the answer for me: 'And if Christ be not risen, then
is our preaching vain, and your faith is also vain.' The
resurrection of Christ became the greatest historical fact
of my life. I was already an evangelical at heart. I did not
believe in the ritual of the Church, although I was still in
it. Then I began to believe that all my life was a lie. I was
living a life in which I did not now believe.

So one afternoon I went to visit an evangelical pastor.
It was during my first vacation at home in seven years.
We studied the Word of God together, especially the
eleventh chapter of Hebrews, the faith chapter. I asked
him, 'If I believe this, then what do I have to do?' We
prayed together and I received Jesus Christ as my

personal and all-sufficient Saviour and Lord. Now I was a new man.

My Family's Reaction

After this many problems arose, especially concerning my family. For a Roman Catholic family to have a priest in the family is better than to give a golden altar to the Church. My father said, 'In two hundred years the Santamaria family has never had a murderer, a thief, a prostitute, or a Protestant – you are the first one.' I had to give up a precious family of six members for the gospel's sake, but I gained a family of thousands, true believers in Jesus.

The Roman Catholic authorities tried to put me in jail, but many born-again missionaries and believers stood with me and the Lord delivered me miraculously. I had to leave Colombia, but the Lord provided for my needs and opened the way for me to study his Word at a Bible seminary.

He has now burdened my heart for the Spanish people, and I am working as a missionary with The Conversion Center in the USA, seeking to bring the light of the gospel to darkened Spanish hearts. I need your prayers daily that many Spanish people might find peace in Jesus: 'Therefore being justified by faith, we have peace with God through our Lord Jesus Christ' (*Rom.* 5:1).

11

Miguel Carvajal

Why I Left the Monastery

It was four o'clock in the morning. I put as much clothing and other articles as possible into a suitcase. My decision to leave the monastery had been made. I carefully opened the door of my room without turning on a light, because it might be harmful to me personally if I were discovered slipping away from the monastery.

I went to a Roman Catholic church in a small town. Not knowing what course to take, I entered the church. The lamp was burning in front of the high altar. I tiptoed along the aisle, then decided to go through a side door which led into a silent courtyard. I had no place to go, and I thought perhaps the privacy afforded here would give me time to make the next move. I had removed the Franciscan habit and was now in civilian clothing.

The Cold Uncertainty of the Future

It was no easy matter to close the door behind me. Doubts would arise; the struggle was great, but I must not go back to the slavery of the Roman Catholic Church. When I left the courtyard and stepped out into the square of the little village the cold wind from the volcano Cayambe, six thousand metres high, nearly paralysed my body. The cold and fear of the future fell upon me.

Freedom I had found, but where I should go now was my problem. For the last time I looked towards the small window of my cell at the monastery, remembering the doubts, struggles, prayers and study to find peace for my soul. The walls of the monastery were a witness to my despair when I was confused and thought that perhaps God would not forgive my sins. I found that sacrifices and fasting were not enough; only an experience of the new birth would do. 'Jesus answered and said unto him, Verily, verily, I say unto thee except a man be born again he cannot see the kingdom of God' (*John* 3:3).

I walked across the square of the village, realizing that the bishop and his priests lived here and that I must not be seen. Now my thoughts were directed towards the future, and I travelled rapidly along the empty street. I was tired, and my breath was coming in short gulps, as I ascended and descended the hills with my suitcase on my shoulder. My steps were directed towards my mother's home in Quito. I could hear the church bells ringing in the village I had left. Wearily I sat down and wept. The temptation to return almost overwhelmed me. The sun was now rising in the Ecuadorian sky.

I had lived in the monastery for ten years. I thought of the students, priests and monks and how I had shared with them all the problems of life. I had known the bad and the good monks, their desires, conversations and

secrets, and the small amount of food that we shared
together. I longed for some of them to come with me
because the way seemed so lonely. They would, of
course, face the wrath of an angry Church if they did
leave. They would also have to face the struggles of life
and spiritual pressures.

Wounded Family

To leave the Roman Catholic Church one must
encounter the displeasure of family, relatives and
friends and all kinds of criticism and face an uncertain
life without employment. A mountain of trials and
frustrations presents itself before the new believer, but
we have a promise and the Bible for a guide. 'And ye
shall know the truth and the truth shall make you free'
(*John* 8:32). I preferred to leave the Church and be
independent. I was tired of hypocrisy and tired of a
religion without spirituality.

I finally came to a small town and found myself
without money and stranded at the railway station.
Because I had been a priest and was now travelling in
civilian clothes, I should not be seen by the public. It
would be very embarrassing for the people to see a priest
who, as they would think, had fallen so low. Therefore I
walked for about two hours to Quito, the capital of
Ecuador, and the home of my mother.

My Mother Cries

My mother cried because I had left the monastery. She
could not know how I had longed to find the Saviour.
Here was another temptation. I decided to remain a
Roman Catholic to please my mother, but not to return
to the monastery.

I had been at the monastery so long that it was hard to adjust to life on the outside. The customs of the people and those of the priests are so different. I was indeed miserable and depressed. I decided to seek pleasure in the youthful lusts of the world, such as drinking, smoking, dancing and visiting places of ill reputation. I did not think this was wrong, because these things were condoned in the monastery. I found work teaching in a Roman Catholic school, which lasted for two months. I desired to further my education, but God knew my heart and therefore my plans were thwarted.

I had a friend who worked at the HCJB broadcasting station. He wrote to me and testified of salvation in Christ. I scorned this and said that the priest knows best for the people. I had been taught that the Protestant Church was bad. A priest who was my history teacher in the monastery sent word that nothing would be said about my leaving if I returned.

A New Creature in Christ

One day I met some evangelical people. I talked with one of them for about two hours, discussing the Lord and the way of salvation. These verses were quoted:

'For God so loved the world that he gave his only begotten Son that whosoever believeth in him should not perish but have everlasting life. For God sent not his Son into the world to condemn the world but that the world through him might be saved. He that believeth on him is not condemned but he that believeth not is condemned already, because he hath not believed in the name of the only begotten Son of God' (*John* 3:16–18); and 'These are written that ye might believe that Jesus is the Christ, the Son of God; and that believing ye might have life through his name' (*John* 20:31).

It was at this moment that I received the Lord Jesus
Christ as my Saviour and became a new creature. My
life was changed, and for the first time I experienced
what salvation was. I was thirty-two years old. Since
my conversion I have resumed my real name, Miguel
Carvajal. In the monastery I was known as Friar
Fernando.

I was exceedingly happy. The neighbours began to
ridicule my mother and said that I had lost my mind.
They wanted to force me to return to the Roman
Catholic Church. They did not know that for me all
things had become new.

Temptations to Return

I experienced temptations to return. During the Roman
Catholic celebration of Holy Week in April 1960 the old
life began to bother me. I became confused. I decided to
go to Guayaquil although I had very little money and did
not know anyone there. In Guayaquil I became ill with
malaria. The thought came to my mind to return as a
prodigal son to my mother's home and to the monastery,
but God sent one of his faithful servants who took me
into his home and cared for me.

I Long that Others Should Believe

When I was better, I worked and began to serve the
Lord. I also studied in a seminary. I am now happy to
preach the salvation of the Lord and serve in the Berean
Church in Ecuador. I desire to read with you the words
of the Lord in John 6:47: 'Verily, verily, I say unto you,
he that believeth on me hath everlasting life.' The
meaning is very clear. However, to believe on Christ
alone is very difficult because to do this we must first

renounce all false human and religious traditions and place our faith exclusively in Jesus. On the basis of his finished sacrifice, we have eternal life. It is very important that a Roman Catholic deals with the gospel as it is declared in 1 Corinthians 15:3–4: 'For I delivered unto you first of all that which I also received, how that Christ died for our sins according to the scriptures; And that he was buried, and that he rose again the third day according to the scriptures.' If you truly believe that Jesus Christ completely paid the price of salvation and in faith you trust him with all your heart, you are then free from sin and have everlasting life.

12

Anibal Pereira Dos Reis

If I Had Stayed in Roman Catholicism, I Would Not Have Found Jesus

I was born in São Joaquim da Barra, São Paulo State, Brazil, on 9 March 1924, into a family deeply rooted in Roman Catholicism. My father was Portuguese, and in order not to be an exception to the common rule aligned himself with the admirers of the Lady of Fatima, fate and good wine. My mother was of Italian origin and boasted about the Pope's golden throne in the Italian peninsula.

My mother's father, who was very devoted to religious practices, used to take me to the solemn Roman Catholic rites in the Mother Church when I was very young. Even before I was seven years of age, I regularly attended parish instruction on the catechism. On one occasion a priest spoke to us, full of energy and vivacity, about hell. He introduced us to the danger, but he did not give us even a single clue as to how to be saved from this danger.

First Communion Day

My first communion was on 1 May 1932. I was moved with the purest feelings. One incident, though, obscured the solemn atmosphere of the hour. One of our companions, as soon as the priest placed the wafer on his tongue, began to shout, 'The wafer is stuck, Father.' The priest advised the nervous boy to keep quiet and not to take the wafer out of the 'heaven of the mouth' with his fingers. Touching the wafer with his fingers was sacrilege. After leaving the church, the boys and girls turned to the boy with loud recriminations, saying he had shown a lack of due respect to the sacred Lord.

In 1936 my family went to live in nearby Orlandia so that my brothers and I could take the secondary school course. My father wanted to give his sons the opportunity to study, something that he had never had.

A serious problem remained with me from childhood; it was the eternal salvation of my soul. I used to think constantly about it. Shivering with fear, I remembered the priest's words when we prepared for my first communion. He informed us of all the pious acts recommended by a very strict Spanish priest. A great desire awoke in me, even as a child, to serve God. Not knowing any other way I became a priest.

The Seminary and Ordination

I managed to enter a seminary at age seventeen. It was not a good environment. Never have I come across a

place with so much slander. I gave myself intensely to
studying all my subjects. My dissatisfaction, however,
continued.

I was ordained a priest on 8 December 1949 in the city
of Montes Claros, in the north of Minas Gerais. The
diocesan bishop gave me the responsibility of setting up
and leading the workers' circle. This duty met my
aspirations. I found the practice of social assistance a
relief for my spiritual anxieties. I was intensely active,
gaining sympathy from working people from every
region and a lot of praise from ecclesiastical authority.

A Priest in Social Work

At the beginning of 1952 the bishop of Montes Claros
was transferred by the Pope to Recife as an archbishop. I
was included in this change and was to live in Recife.

In this city, I was given the task of restoring a charity
company, a network of orphanages and Roman Catholic
education centres that had suffered a financial crisis. I
worked hard, aiming to rebuild the public reputation of
the institution. In fact I was weighed down by the heavy
responsibility. After little more than two years of work,
the institution's financial problems were remedied. The
orphanages and homes received a greater number of
children and old people. The schools made a fresh start.
I was referred to several times in the press.

No Peace with God

But in spite of these human victories and the applause of
admirers, I never felt any peace in my soul. Neither
complete dedication to my duties in the charity company
nor the applause of the ecclesiastical authorities provided an answer to my spiritual torments. I strongly

desired to be sure of my eternal salvation, and nobody could give me that assurance.

In 1960 I was transferred to Guaratinguetá in the interior of the State of São Paulo, a neighbouring locality of Aparecida do Norte. I rejoiced in this change, mainly because I would be with the 'patron saint of Brazil'. Also it was the first time that I would be involved in a task relevant to social management. I was very preoccupied with social work. I was supposed to find in my duties as a priest an answer for my spiritual anxiety. But I did not.

Parish Work

I developed a new parish in the district of Pedregulho in Guaratinguetá. I worked very hard. The construction of a parish home, a parish hall and three churches within only three years was proof of my dedication. Even up to this point in my life, with a long list of services rendered to Roman Catholicism, I was still not certain of my salvation.

In October 1956 my father died of lung cancer. I spent a whole year praying daily Masses for his soul. My family also prayed Masses for him. But not even the Mass, with all its claim to infinite value, gave us assurance of my father's salvation.

I used to cry out for this assurance for myself as well. Not the developing social work, nor the construction of churches, nor the ceremonies which I conducted, nor blind subjection to the ecclesiastical authorities, nor Roman Catholicism, were giving me any answer.

My Hatred of Evangelicals

With my spirit in rigorous subjection to Roman Catholic doctrines, I was feeling real hatred for the evangelicals,

whom I referred to in my preaching as 'goats', as
opposed to the Roman Catholics whom I called the
'lambs of Christ'.

One event demonstrates my anti-Protestantism. On the
occasion of All Souls' Day, in the cemetery of the district
of Pedregulho, the Bible believers carried out evangelistic
work by distributing tracts and Bible portions. In order to
give 'Glory to God' (the Jesuit motto) and to defend 'Holy
Mother Church', I resolved to damage their work. I got
the children from my church and divided them into groups
to pray hour after hour inside the cemetery. The idea was
to receive the literature and destroy it on candles burning
behind the mortuary.

However, one evening when I had finished this
merciless destruction of evangelical material, I went into
my library to find a book which would amuse me. By
God's marvellous grace I came across the Bible in the
translation by Matos Soares.

I opened this inspired volume and read chapter 11 of
John's Gospel. I felt relief come to my grief. I felt energy
transforming my spiritual depression. I continued to
read with more and more interest. I was constantly
thinking about this chapter.

A Beginning in Bible Study

Gradually I began to sense new horizons in my soul. I
decided to study the Bible free of my preconceptions.
Without anybody's interference and only through divine
grace I discovered through this study the real plan of
God for our salvation. Amazed, I discovered that we can
even have absolute and constant certainty of going to
heaven if we accept his plan. I resisted, however,
because my soul had conformed to standard Roman
Catholic practice.

A Talk with My Bishop

I went to see my bishop. I wanted to be completely sincere with him. He became confused with my questions, and finally told me that I was in Aparecida to take care of the construction of the new basilica. My preoccupations became the purchase of concrete, bricks and tools. I prayed to Our Lady of Aparecida.

God's Turning Point in My Life

The evangelical believers were at this time distributing leaflets in Guaratinguetá. One of them was about Roman Catholic idolatry and the worship of images. To answer its many claims, I decided to go into the pulpit to give an explanation about those doctrines, to tell them that the worship of images was not forbidden by God. I took my Bible. I began to explain by reading chapter 20 of Exodus. I skipped over verses 4 and 5 in order not to give any 'ammunition to my enemies'. When I came down from the pulpit I was totally ashamed of myself. I decided to make a sincere comparison of Roman Catholic doctrines and the Bible. Then I checked the infinite abyss that separated the two.

I Begin Using Bible Standards

In January 1963 I received an invitation to be a priest in the city of Orlandia where I had spent my adolescence. I was so pleased to go back where I had so many friends. This pleasure, however, was still not sufficient to drown my spiritual anxiety. I devoted myself entirely to work in the Roman Catholic parish, full of all the deficiencies of an old parish with rusty traditions. In spite of the opposition of a group of discontented but pious women,

I managed to develop a splendid work where everything fitted in, if possible, with the standards of the Bible. I cleaned up the church, withdrawing all the idols. My preaching was biblical. My daily programmes on the radio consisted simply of a commentary on the Word of God. Many religious hymns sung in the services were Christian songs.

My Hatred of Evangelicals Turns to Fear

An interesting thing happened to me. My former hatred of evangelicals had turned to fear. I wanted to talk with a pastor but did not have the courage. When I was in Guaratinguetá, I decided to go to São Paulo with the single intention of resolving this situation. On descending from the bus I went to the post office to send a telegram. On Post Office Square at that moment an evangelical was preaching. On seeing my cassock, he challenged me with a pointed finger, exposing me with harsh words. He did not know what was going through my soul and could not imagine the purpose of my visit. After this I immediately went back home.

A Servant of God Assists Me

In 1964 I came close to the end. I could not continue in this situation any more. In November I went to Santos. I had already worked out my plan. Wearing civilian clothes, I attended the Sunday service at the First Baptist Church and, incredibly, the Bible text used as the basis for the sermon was none other than chapter 11 from John's Gospel.

On the following day I managed to catch sight of Pastor Eliseu Ximenes. This servant of God responded to me in a manner which was so gentle that I was soon captivated and was free of all my earlier impressions. We began to plan my departure from Roman Catholicism. It was hardly a formal departure, because it was made over a long period of time.

Faith in the All-Sufficient Saviour

On 12 May 1965, with God's special protection, I managed to disentangle myself totally from the Roman Church. On 13 June, in the First Baptist Church of Santos, testifying publicly of my faith in my only and all-sufficient Saviour, Jesus Christ, I was baptized.

Besides having brought me into his kingdom, God placed in my heart the task of preaching his holy Word, and I entirely dedicated my life to this ministry. He has recently helped the work of this humble servant through giving me the joy of seeing hundreds of souls come to Jesus Christ.

In my sermons I stress God's plan of salvation through Jesus Christ alone. Every time I preach I can sense a more intimate communion with him.

I have never felt such spiritual happiness as I do now. I have total peace in my heart, because I am certain of my eternal salvation. My soul has been purified by the redeeming blood of Jesus Christ, to whom be all the glory for all eternity.

13

Arnaldo Uchoa Cavalcante

Grace and Truth Came to Me by Jesus Christ

I will try to summarize the forty years which led up to my conversion. I entered the seminary of my own free will, desiring to serve God as a priest. My family did not possess the financial resources to bear the cost of my studies, but fortunately a good friend kindly paid my expenses.

My twelve years of study included philosophy, theology and languages. I applied myself in a special way to a knowledge of philosophy and the Bible.

Finally on 15 August 1945, in the metropolitan cathedral of Maceió, Brazil, I received ordination to the priesthood by the hands of the archbishop. However, I did not receive what I really needed, the grace that comes from above, the divine power to preach the Word of God with authority! I was still like Thomas who, not believing in the resurrection power of the Lord Jesus, needed to touch the body of his Master to believe. In the same way I could not believe in the Word that I had read and studied. I needed a special revelation of the Lord Jesus.

A Priest, but with No Assurance of Salvation

For nine years, from 1945 to 1954, I exercised the ministry of a priest in the cities of Maceió and Recife, administering the 'sacraments' and preaching, still without peace, without conviction, and without feeling salvation in things in which I could not believe. My heart was aspiring for something greater and better. During this time I held several high academic and ecclesiastical positions. Meanwhile, at altars, in the pulpit and in the cathedral, I could not find what I was looking for. I resolved to leave the cassock in 1954 and set out in search of spiritual peace, the certainty of salvation for my soul, faith in the sacrifice of Christ and in the teaching of the Bible. Divine Providence is marvellous and prepared me for coming down to the valley of blessings, peace and salvation. My God proved that I was, to him, of more value than the birds and the lilies of the countryside.

How I Left My Parish

On the day of my liberation from black vestments, I was performing the rôle of factory chaplain in the city of Maceió. After having planned everything that my conscience advised me, I left for Recife by plane. I had bought some clothes that I needed in place of my cassock. I wanted to change my clothes in a hurry before looking for a hotel. I took a taxi and told the driver that I wanted to go to a particular district of the city. I warned him that during the journey I would change my clothes. When I got out of the car I was different and free. I found a hotel and spent the night there. On the following morning, I passed the superior from the Carmelite monastery on the street. I managed to escape him.

I left immediately for the city of Natal and from there for other cities. I would soon have to find the better way that I yearned for, but unfortunately I lived dominated by an unrestrained feeling of intolerance for the evangelicals that I called Protestants. I was like Saul of Tarsus, religious but a persecutor of evangelical Christians. I was certainly not converted to Christ inside, and, in contrast to Paul, it was only after some delay that I arrived at my conversion. Three years later I was married, on 10 May 1958, and in the following year our first son was born.

In the years that passed up to 1960, my search took me to Brazilian spiritists and other groups, always avoiding evangelical churches. However, I continued to feel the same emptiness in my soul and a burning thirst for salvation and peace.

God's Providence and Grace

In 1960 I went to Belo Horizonte and on to Aguai. In September I headed for Campinas to look for a better job and, walking in the streets of the centre, I came across a building labelled 'The Church of the Nazarene'. I looked for the entrance, and peeped inside. At that moment I was surprised by the pastor of the church. It was precisely 12 o'clock. The pastor received me as if he had expected me. And now I understand: he was led by divine Providence. That meeting resulted in precious blessings for my soul and was decisive, in that I took a new and surprising path. Days after my family was brought to Campinas, I got to know how true the evangelical faith was. I heard the sermons of Pastor Mosteller. On 18 September 1960 I fully accepted the genuine gospel of Christ publicly. On this date I really passed from death unto life – the real Christian life, having the divine Spirit and the peace of Christ in my soul.

Today I praise God, I bless Jesus, I preach the message of the gospel and, although working hard, I have joy, peace and happiness serving my Saviour, 'being born again, not of corruptible seed, but of incorruptible, by the word of God, which liveth and abideth for ever' (*1 Pet.* 1:23).

14

Thoufic Khouri

The Gospel of Grace in Jesus Christ

I was born in Lebanon of Roman Catholic parents and was enrolled in the register of their Church. In January 1923 I was baptized by a threefold immersion ceremony. This is the custom of the Syrian Catholic Church. Through this act I became a 'Christian' and a member of that Church. When I was three years old my mother died and I was put in a boarding school at Jerusalem where I stayed until I was thirteen. At a young age I loved the altar, the priests and everything connected with the priestly service.

The school was controlled by the Sisters of Mercy. One nun, Sister Germaine, noticing my piety and my interest in the liturgy, insisted that I become a priest. (Later on, I wrote twice to this nun and explained to her the way of salvation. After the second letter she did not reply.)

My Doubts in the Seminary

When I was thirteen years old, I had to choose either to study at college or to enrol in a seminary as a priest. I chose a seminary of the Syrian rite. Seminarians are carefully sifted and many are sent away, leaving only a few. These are of course not perfect. I did not feel worthy of the priesthood and asked my prior many times if I could leave. The answer was always the same: 'You are called by God; and if that is not so, then, when it is clear to us, you may go.' This continued for a long time. The last time that I went to the prior with this problem was just before my ordination as sub-deacon. I felt the difficulties that the priesthood would bring, particularly celibacy. When I had undergone this ordination I would then automatically face the obligation of lifelong celibacy.

I still felt unworthy to serve at the altar. My superiors ignored my pleas and eventually forced me to be ordained as a priest. I took the name Vincent after my patron, St Vincent de Paul.

A Little Piece of Paper by My Heart

After my ordination to the priesthood, the doubts remained. My superiors called these doubts 'an angelic virtue'. There were also difficulties on an intellectual level. I had these earlier as well when I was studying philosophy and especially theology. I could not accept certain things without great difficulty. I wanted to understand all the dogmas but wondered how they originated and how important they were. I could not remain in uncertainty about this. My superior once told me, 'If you have difficulties of belief don't be desperate; imitate your patron, St Vincent de Paul.' He had written the Creed on a piece of paper which he rolled up. When he was attacked by doubts he kissed the paper and pressed it to his heart saying, 'Lord, I do not understand, but I still believe.' I followed his advice and experienced a short period of peace. It was not, however, strong enough to settle me fully in my beliefs.

Diplomacy against a Dictatorship

To be brief, there were disciplinary, intellectual and ethical difficulties. First I had an aversion to submitting my will completely to my superiors. The bishop could really do as he wished with us. The effect was that many got their own way by using other means. This was especially so in the case of appointments. If one had a little cunning and a feeling for diplomacy, then one could prevent an unwelcome appointment or even alter it to something a little better. For example, I was appointed chaplain in a small village away in the wilderness. I manipulated things so that this appointment was cancelled and I was appointed instead as a lecturer in a seminary.

The Advice of a Franciscan of Gethsemane

This appointment brought its own difficulties. I now had to try with the utmost effort to be a good example to my students. I still had to read the Mass in the morning, alternating with another priest. We were the only two lecturer-priests at the seminary who belonged to the Syrian rite. The others were Benedictines. My longing after perfection of life greatly increased and I sought to obtain the power for this through the sacraments. The sacraments did not give me the power for which I sought. This disappointment caused a crisis. I began to doubt the value and the truth of the sacraments. From that moment on I began to consider resignation from the priesthood, not that I wanted to leave the Roman Catholic Church, but I wanted to be relieved of the burden of my priestly functions. I felt totally unworthy of this holy way of life. I spoke with my confessor, an old Franciscan who lived in the cloister of Gethsemane. He simply said: 'Oh, dear boy, even the greatest saints have had trouble with temptations against their beliefs. There is no valid reason for resigning. Just carry on peacefully. It is Satan who does not want you to do things well.'

Pastor in Beirut

After five years I was nominated as priest of a Syrian-rite parish in Beirut. I came more in contact with people and their misery. I got to know the suffering of the poor and came to love them, but I could never find peace for my soul nor peace and harmony with my colleague, another priest.

This priest, a rascally old fellow, loved money very much. He had the management of a school of which he retained the gifts as much as possible. He was able to do this because the Lebanese schools are not under the control of the government but privately run. Although I did not have anything to do with him he did not leave me in peace but continually complained to the bishop about me. The bishop loved me and I him, for he had ordained me as a priest. In the end I had a great aversion for my fellow priest and for others like him. Still, I did not yet have a reason to say good-bye to the Church. I dared not.

The Soul Cannot Be Contented with Money

In the meantime my ethical difficulties continued and still I performed the sacraments. This again caused several tensions. In order to perform the Mass one's conscience has to have a certain purity and this purity is obtained by means of confession. Many times I had the opportunity to confess before the Mass, but I did not always do so. I then had to satisfy myself with an exercise of penitence involving a very firm intention to confess my sin at the next opportunity. It was still very difficult to adjust myself to this psychological act of penitence, because I had to do it in love to a perfect God.

Many times I had to satisfy myself with the saying of this act of penitence and then went on to read the Mass. I often had the feeling that although I had to do it, I celebrated a sacrilegious Mass. The necessity to serve in this condition was a growing burden to me. At last I went to the papal nuncio with a request to be relieved of my priestly functions.

Again I was discouraged. The nuncio thought it was only depression, a passing psychological state. He gave me some money, about $35, to cheer me up. This was not the way to help me. My purse was fuller, but my soul emptier.

Love for Such a Hard Church

I was tired of all the priestly functions and wanted to leave officially, without any grudges, trouble, discussion or difficulties with my Church. I did not want to cause great trouble in leaving, but the Church did not allow me to leave quietly. I began to feel that I was a slave to that terrible system. How the Roman Catholic Church sought to tyrannize my whole life! I wanted to be a simple layman in the Church. However, I began to realize that this could never be. I could not escape from the pressures of the hierarchy. How could I ever have loved such a Church that was so hard on me? I began to think of saying farewell to my priesthood at all costs, but I dared not. I was afraid because I had my religious beliefs. I believed, for instance, that Rome alone was the custodian of salvation and outside her there was no salvation. Certainly, I was afraid that I would be lost if I died at that moment, but nevertheless I continued to believe that inside the Church my salvation was secure.

A Priest Who Poisoned Himself

About this time, a priest took his own life by poisoning. He had been a bad priest who had occupied himself with all kinds of obscene business. He had been addicted to gambling. Sometimes he won and sometimes he lost. In the end he committed suicide. I began to consider following his example. Before I took my life, I would surrender myself to the mercy of God and ask him to awaken in me a perfect act of contrition. I was afraid of that thought. I felt so helpless and depressed.

The Frightening Image of an Apostate Priest

In spite of the terrible state I was in, I dared not break with the Roman Catholic Church, as I would then become an apostate priest. Many times the terrible image of the renegade priest had been portrayed to us, but we had been told only about those priests who had been unfrocked and who had left the Church. I did not know that there were many other priests who had left the Church because the love of Jesus Christ had claimed them. To leave the Roman Catholic Church meant for me to go the same way as Renan, or as ex-priests De Lammenais and Loisy. Such priests were portrayed as monstrous examples of pride or as slaves to animal instincts. No, I would never want to become one of them.

I Wanted to Commit Suicide

Still, I was in an acute state and needed urgent help. One day I went to the church of my parish and beat on the altar and begged, 'Lord, if you are really here now, help me, please.' But I did not get any help, just the opposite. I suddenly realized that I had committed a new sin against my faith because I had said, '*If* you are really here now . . .'. I had expressed doubts concerning the dogma of the Real Presence and of the transubstantiation of Christ in the host. When one wilfully doubts a Roman Catholic dogma, it is a mortal sin. I returned to my room very, very depressed and again contemplated taking my life and plunging into eternity, but I dared not.

Suddenly I *Had* to Pray

Suddenly I had a strong desire to pray, but not the prayers from my Syrian breviary. I wanted to turn to God in personal prayer from the depths of my heart. I knelt down and said, 'Lord, I do not want to be an apostate and yet I am still afraid that I will lose all my faith. Therefore, I pray now let me die while I still have faith in you, in your Son Jesus Christ and in your Holy Ghost, in your Holy Church and in everything that she teaches me.'

From Scripture Jesus Speaks to Me

Very soon after this, I had the impulse to open my New Testament. I had several kinds of Bibles in Arabic, Aramaic, Latin and French, but I had never really read it thoughtfully, that is to say, grasping it with a hungry heart. I did not have reverence for the Word of God or respect for this Book of the Lord. I had never had time or inclination for it because I never had any expectations for my soul. On that day I opened my Bible and my eyes fell on Matthew 11:28: 'Come unto me, all ye that labour and are heavy laden, and I will give you rest.' It was, viewed from a human standpoint, accidental, but God who has everything in his hands and who guides everything had prepared this text for me. I did not read those words for the first time. Many times I had read them from my breviary and in the Mass, but they did not mean anything to me. On that day those words were a personal message from Jesus to me. Then I prayed a second time and said: 'Lord, I take you at your Word. It is you who are calling me. Here I am. You promised to take my burdens away. Well, here are my burdens. Remove them from me and give me rest from them.' I got some rest, but I did not then know Jesus as my personal Saviour.

A Foolish Plan

I had to return to my routine work as a priest. The people of the parish demanded my attention, and my sad and weary life continued One day I reminded myself that the first time I had received any enlightenment had been through the Bible. Why should I not go to the Bible House in Beirut to inquire about a book on comparative religions? When I think about this I have to smile that I was so naïve. I was looking for a book about several religions so that I could then choose a suitable one.

I tell you this as an illustration of how far a Roman Catholic priest can wander from the truth. I had never known a living, personal religion. I was looking for something difficult. I wanted to choose between Islam, Buddhism, Confucianism, Hinduism, the Greek Orthodox Church and Protestantism. For me they all had the same value. I wanted to choose from these, but it was clear that I wanted to make only an intellectual choice.

When I went to the Beirut Bible House in my priestly garb, I was very conscious that I was visiting 'heretics'. I rang the bell and asked for a book on religions. I received a friendly welcome. They spoke with me, helped me and above all they prayed for me. That was the first time I prayed with Protestants. They did not speak about other religions or about a church but about Jesus Christ alone. I thank the Lord that he inspired them to speak about his Son. I was happy to listen. They gave me a booklet called *Towards Assurance*. It was printed in Switzerland and contained some Bible texts with illustrations and references.

Salvation in Christ Alone

I took this simple booklet to my room and read a little from it every day. So I began to understand the message of the gospel. I came to a decision which had been prepared a long time before by the guidance of God. So my life had now ripened by reading and meditation from this booklet and from the Word of God. I knelt down to trust Jesus only. By God's grace everything in me was open to receive him. I closed my eyes and opened only the eyes of my heart in faith and love, and I said to the

Lord: 'Jesus, you alone are the Saviour; your name means Saviour. I receive you as my Saviour, and from this moment I will not build on anything except you. Henceforth I will look for my salvation only in you.'

So the miracle happened, that which I needed so much: a spiritual birth. I became a new creature, a child of God. Outwardly I was still a Roman Catholic. I still wore my priestly garb. The books in my room were still all Roman Catholic. Inwardly, however, I was a Roman Catholic no longer. Inwardly, I had become a Christian. Also, in my thinking I was still a Roman Catholic, because so many years of pseudo-biblical, scholastic teaching is difficult to discard. Within my spirit, the Spirit of God witnessed to me that I had become a child of God. 'For ye have not received the spirit of bondage again to fear; but ye have received the Spirit of adoption, whereby we cry, Abba, Father. The Spirit itself beareth witness with our spirit, that we are the children of God' (*Rom.* 8:15–16).

My Departure

When I told my bishop of my desire to leave the Roman Catholic Church, he told me that my 'strange ideas' were 'Protestant fallacies'. He wanted me to have a talk with a Jesuit priest, who asked me if I prayed to St Vincent de Paul and the Holy Virgin. When I told him I only prayed to God in the name of Jesus Christ he said to me, 'It is very clear to me you are too much of a Protestant. I cannot speak any longer with you, I am sorry.' When the bishop heard of this he said, 'I will give you two weeks to think things over.' I declared that I would never celebrate another Mass, hear another confession or pray to any of the saints. He said, 'Then do what is necessary so that we are not

forced to take the most extreme measure.' I knew what
that meant. I packed my luggage and departed because I
wanted to avoid being removed from the presbytery by
the police.

Accursed be Pastor Khouri!

I left my Church, but I left it with complete peace of
heart. I could not leave the Roman Church so long as I
was a Roman Catholic. There was a need to meet Jesus,
for a meeting person to person, to complete this step. I
was too afraid to break with my Church and become an
apostate, an excommunicated person, a heretic. In my
spirit I could already see my name added to the list of
excommunicated persons at the back of the churches in
Beirut and of the whole Syrian Catholic world, because
that is the way things are done in our part of the world.
Everyone who is under the ban of the Church is
mentioned on a list which is nailed for at least a year to
this shameful board. I could already hear the people
saying, 'Pastor Vincent Khouri is excommunicated. He
became a heretic. He is accursed. Let him be Anathema,
he is damned!'

I always had this frightful image before me and this
was the reason I had never dared leave the Church. But
those fears totally disappeared when I came to know
Christ as my personal Saviour. In earlier times I had
prayed to Jesus but never to *my* Jesus, *my* Saviour.
Many times the people prayed to God in the name of
Jesus but without knowing Jesus as their own Saviour.
'If ye then be risen with Christ, seek those things which
are above, where Christ sitteth on the right hand of God.
Set your affection on things above, not on things on the
earth. For ye are dead, and your life is hid with Christ in
God' (*Col.* 3:1–3).

A Call to Witness

I cannot end without emphasizing this: I am very sure that God has given each one a call to become a witness for Jesus Christ. The preparation may have been lengthy, but God has freed you to help free others. Be always aware of this call. But again, a call to tell others of the joy available, can only be obeyed if we ourselves possess this joy. Joy is only found in Jesus Christ. Any human being can experience this joy if he is guided by the Spirit of God and believes in the written Word and in the Word become flesh.

I pray that this joy in Jesus Christ will become your full possession. All over the world my brothers and sisters and redeemed children of God are praying for you priests. I tell you this to encourage you during the time when the dark hours and depressing thoughts come. What a wonderful thing to know that we are allowed to be real priests, kingly priests to God. Not Levitical priests, sighing under a special Church system, we are now priests by the Holy Spirit's anointing of our souls: 'But ye are a chosen generation, a royal priesthood, an holy nation, a peculiar people; that ye should shew forth the praises of him who hath called you out of darkness into his marvellous light' (*1 Pet.* 2:9).

15

Victor J. Affonso

Following Jesus Without Compromise

At the age of twenty-three I was a successful commercial artist on the verge of going abroad where
a job was awaiting me. I was happy at the prospect of
leaving India and thereby also escaping the terrible
anguish caused by seeing the misery of the poor in the
streets of Bombay.

Political saviours like Gandhi and Nehru had failed to
give true freedom and justice to India's poor majority.
Murder and divisions assailed independent India. All the
work for social improvement was but a few drops of water
in a desert. Yet there was still one solution left. The words
of Jesus kept coming to me during prayer: 'With God all
things are possible' (*Mark* 10:27). They seemed to say to

me, 'Don't run away!' On another day I heard the words, 'Follow my Son – Jesus!' These words finally led me to leave the world and join the Society of Jesus, a missionary order that promised by its very title, its spiritual exercises and its constitutions to serve Jesus at any cost and to lead men to know him, his peace and his justice.

To Give India the Gospel

My desire when I joined was to know Jesus intimately, to study and obey his Word, to be completely free of outside encumbrances, even a girl I loved, in order to follow him uncompromisingly. Like Paul, I wanted to preach the gospel and bring India to Christ. The misery of India hurt me, and I hoped that with other fully committed Christians I could help lead the people of India to Christ that they might be saved spiritually and socially and live truly as God's children. When I studied communications media and taught at St Xavier's College, it was for the same purpose: to give India the gospel.

The Mission Factor

During the fourteen years of my studies my Jesuit superiors and companions also seemed to have dedicated their lives to the same goal, to know and to serve Jesus and to proclaim him to the whole world that men might become his disciples. I was also one of the rare privileged Jesuits who was able to travel and to live abroad for studies and was given freedom to act responsibly. As a man I felt fulfilled. Yet, something very important was missing! I could not satisfy the hunger in my heart to experience Jesus, the risen Lord, as he was experienced by simple 'unschooled' men in the apostolic church, as described in the Scriptures.

In the 1960s and early 1970s I studied in the Philippines, in many countries of Europe and later in the USA. I witnessed the exodus from Roman Catholic churches in Europe in the 1960s while I studied in Spain. Only six per cent attended Sunday Mass! Later in Los Angeles, USA, I saw the double standards of the lives of the Sunday Catholics, including myself and the other priests and nuns. I questioned my Christianity, imported from the West, and wondered if Jesus Christ and the Bible were not mere fables for which I was giving up my life in vain.

The Church Opens to Accept Hindus

I had experienced no church other than the Roman Catholic Church. I was brainwashed to believe that it was the one and only true Church, outside which there was no salvation. Vatican Council II had changed the emphasis a bit but not too much. The Protestants, though now called 'brethren' and their churches called 'ecclesial communities', were still treated as 'heretics' and their churches were imperfect, 'truncated'. I faithfully remained anti-Protestant and avoided any contact with their heretical teachings and television programmes. On the other hand, I was encouraged by the Jesuits in India to be more open with non-Christians, Hindus and Muslims, even to the extent of calling them 'God's children', and to study their religions for 'dialogue', which meant engaging only in mutual appreciation of religions but avoiding any intention of converting them to Christ.

Professional but Lost

In 1971, while studying in California, I was enveloped in an atmosphere of hippies, gurus, drugs, divorce, sexual hedonism and perversion of every kind. All my psychological counselling and prayers were not helping the 'sinners' at all. I felt helpless. At that time thousands of priests and nuns were leaving the Church in western countries. Others, like myself, were becoming professional in the media, in psychological counselling, or in social programmes to justify our priestly vocation and to save the world by every method except 'the gospel . . . the power of God unto salvation' (*Rom.* 1:16).

In my late thirties I had already been a Jesuit for seventeen years. I was equipped with several university degrees and a 'green card' for permanent residency in the USA. I considered leaving the powerless and unexciting priesthood along with the rest. But just in case there was a heaven and judgment, I would remain a Sunday Catholic and pay my heavenly insurance. Outwardly I appeared to be an efficient and 'happy' popular priest studying film and television at the University of California at Los Angeles and living the 'yuppie life' at St Martin of Tours Church in Brentwood, near Beverley Hills and Hollywood. I mingled with my favourite stars at their cocktail parties and never felt discriminated against by this 'white' parish. On the contrary, I felt loved and materially speaking was very happy. With a good but deceived conscience I also believed in horoscopes, taught yoga exercises on the campus to young Americans, and never knew that the Bible strictly forbids the occult activities into which I had delved. I needed help!

Unknown to me, some Christians, whom I had accused and preached against as being Protestant 'fundamentalists' were praying for me to be delivered from my deception. They prayed, and I received the grace to come to a point of confusion and desperation regarding my faith and vocation and to cry out to the Lord, 'O God, show me if you are true, if Jesus is your Son, and if the Bible is your true Word.'

Turning Point

On Pentecost Sunday 1972 the Lord dramatically saved me. I had prepared to preach a sermon on the Holy Spirit, to be repeated at five consecutive Masses in Brentwood. I had no faith in what I preached.

My back gave out early that morning, for the first time in my life, and I did not preach. An ambulance hurried me to St John's Hospital. A leading orthopaedic surgeon diagnosed my serious condition as congenital scoliosis of the spine in need of major surgery. I lay on my back in traction, in pain and in confusion. The Lord arranged for Christians to come to my room and to pray for me. Against my will, they placed their hands on me and while I patiently suffered their 'foolishness', I tried to forgive these 'heretics' who had begun praying. I sighed, 'Father, forgive them, for they know not what they do.' But in his own way, the Lord had heard my cry and was answering it through his servants, the very ones I was rejecting. The Lord opened my heart from that day on to know Jesus as my personal Lord and Saviour and assured me of salvation there and then in a way I had never experienced before. I then knew the big difference between experiencing Jesus as my personal Saviour after being born again and leaving all things to work for Jesus as a Roman Catholic, religious but still not sure of my salvation and destination after death. Words cannot describe this wonderful experience of Jesus my Saviour.

The Lord Opens My Eyes and Heals Me

During that month in the hospital the scales slowly fell from my eyes. The risen Lord sovereignly removed from my heart all doubt and confusion about his reality and about eternal life. The Bible, which I had once laboured to study as professional knowledge, now became an exciting real-life spiritual revelation to me. I could easily understand the Word, enjoy it and remember it. I was also given grace to believe I would be healed. With faith in Jesus I walked out of the hospital refusing surgery, unafraid of the risk. I was healed of the scoliosis without surgery, to the amazement of the surgeon. This greatly strengthened my faith and proclamation of the gospel.

The Lord also convicted me that I had fought against many people. I had always prided myself on being a friendly and forgiving priest who loved everybody, including the Hindus, Muslims, my enemies and sinners, giving my life to convert them to the Roman Catholic Church for salvation. But now I heard a clear inner voice of the Holy Spirit convicting me of unloving ways, wrongly judging many Christians as 'heretics'. Years of prejudice dissolved and I suddenly hungered to meet my long-lost Christian brothers and sisters. It was as if a dark screen had been drawn from my heart, and my mind and eye could see the truth plainly. I was so joyful. Love for Jesus burned within me, with a new zeal to return to India and a boldness to proclaim the gospel to the whole world.

My Subsequent Life and Marriage

I launched out into all churches, beginning with some Protestant ones, and found great love among my Christian brothers as I witnessed to the risen Lord, 'Jesus Christ the same yesterday, and today, and for ever' (*Heb.* 13:8).

The Roman Catholic hierarchy requested me to stop teaching because I had publicly stated that some of their main dogmas and practices were contrary to God's Word, the Bible. To the best of my ability I had always

respected and obeyed the Roman Catholic Church
leaders as unto the Lord. But now my conscience
convinced me that in remaining under their authority I
would be forced to submit to teachings that were false
and lies coming from the anti-Christ spirit. The false
dogmas have not been changed at all by Vatican II. This
Council fully supported Trent in totality. In 1988, in
Bombay, India, I resigned from the Roman Catholic
Church and the Jesuit Order. It broke my heart to leave
the Roman Catholic people, with all my friends and
relatives, and not be able to teach them the Bible good
news. May the Lord sovereignly bless them with his
truth and set the prisoners free to follow Jesus without
compromise. In 1993 I married Julie Laschiazza Baden
of Brentwood, Los Angeles, who had ministered with
me in Roman Catholic churches all over India and the
USA. Together we founded Cornerstone International
ministries in India and the USA for discipling believers
to pray and labour by the power of the Holy Spirit and
also to use the mass media for India to come to Jesus
Christ.

16

Simon Kottoor

There is Power in Christ's Atoning Blood

The love of Christ compels me to give testimony to my conversion from the Roman Catholic priesthood to the born-again life in Jesus Christ. For twenty-five years I was a Roman Catholic priest strictly following the rituals of a system which enveloped me as a huge and indomitable fortress of darkness and ignorance of the written Word of God.

The Lord Teaches Me

I baptized many infants, pouring water on their heads. I officiated at public processions in honour and veneration of dead 'saints', holding their wooden images, even though the second commandment of God strictly forbids even the making of graven images. I offered the daily Mass, which I falsely believed was the repetition of the sacrifice of Jesus Christ on Calvary, and I believed that the bread and wine literally became Jesus' flesh and blood. Only later, when I had studied and prayed over the words of Jesus as recorded in the Bible, were my eyes opened. The Lord taught me that there could neither be a repetition of the consummated sacrifice on the cross nor did Jesus literally change bread and wine into his body and blood when he instituted the Last Supper.

Very seriously, steadfastly and sincerely I sought the intercession of dead 'saints' and prayed for the dead in purgatory, not knowing the biblical teaching that there is only 'one God and one Mediator between God and men, the man Christ Jesus' (*1 Tim.* 2:5). He alone died in place of the believer and paid the full ransom for sin. This being true, we understand why there is no mention in the Bible of a place of expiation called purgatory, where souls are released through suffering and the prayers of those living on earth. As a sincere Roman Catholic I had great faith in the veneration of relics and the sacraments to which divine power is attributed when they are used for spiritual needs.

Only God Can Forgive Sin

While a priest I heard many confessions and 'absolved' others from their sins, being ignorant of the biblical teaching that only God can forgive sin. The Bible says, 'If we confess our sins, he is faithful and just to forgive us our sins, and to cleanse us from all unrighteousness' (*1 John* 1:9).

I adhered to these and other beliefs and disciplines not only because I was born and brought up in that traditional system, but mainly because I was obliged to obey, for I believed the lie that 'outside the Roman Catholic Church there is no salvation'. The teaching of the Church, called the *magisterium*, based on tradition, was accepted as the final authority, not the written Word of God, the Bible (which was an unopened book, even for those studying for the priesthood).

No Peace Apart from God

My education for the Roman Catholic priesthood took place in Rome. I took my doctorate in theology in 1954 and afterwards did post-graduate studies in economics in Canada. For eight years I was professor of economics at BCM College, Kottayam, India. I was also principal of St Stephen's College, Uzhavoor, for nine years. These were high positions which gave me regard in society and material prosperity. During twenty-five years as a priest, I did not have spiritual joy or peace of soul even when performing the various rituals. There was an increasing sense of darkness and emptiness growing in my soul until I felt that there was no meaning in infant baptism, confession of sins, the 'real presence of Christ' in the Mass, or in any of the other rituals. I did not know what to do. I turned to smoking, drinking, gluttony, theatre attendance and other secular activities in an effort to gain happiness and peace. But none of this could give me what my spirit needed. Those were years of agony and spiritual unrest. What I needed was eternal salvation.

Thy Word Is a Light unto My Path

Somehow I began to turn my attention to the Bible. Certain verses caught my attention. 'Heaven and earth shall pass away: but my words shall not pass away' (*Mark* 13:31). I realized that this was because 'All scripture is given by inspiration of God, and is profitable for doctrine, for reproof, for correction, for instruction in righteousness: that the man of God may be perfect, thoroughly furnished unto all good works' (*2 Tim.* 3:16–17).

I thank God for bringing into my life some born-again men who helped me in my study. The Word of God became the 'lamp unto my feet' and the 'light unto my path'. I became convinced of the reason for my spiritual aridity and emptiness of soul. 'Whosoever transgresseth, and abideth not in the doctrine of Christ, hath not God. He that abideth in the doctrine of Christ, he hath both the Father and the Son' (*2 John* 9). Even though I had been very religious, I was not abiding in the doctrine of Christ. My eyes were opened to the doctrine of Christ as found in the Bible, the only 'power of God unto salvation'. Matthew 16:26 rang in my ears: 'For what is a man profited, if he shall gain the whole world, and lose his own soul? or what shall a man give in exchange for his soul?'

Through the Word of God I became convinced that it takes more than baptism to make a person a Christian. Infant baptism certainly cannot do it. An infant cannot believe, experience conviction, confess sin; cannot trust and accept Jesus Christ as personal Saviour. Soon I realized my spiritual need and was convicted of my sin and of Christ's righteousness.

A New Creature

I praise the Lord for granting me the courage and strength to leave everything behind and trust Jesus Christ as my personal Saviour and Lord. The day was 5 April 1980. After I was born again by his Spirit and baptized in water, the Lord filled me with a divine peace, a joy of heart, and new meaning in my life. The emptiness of soul that had plagued me for so long vanished and I now know what it means to become a new creature. Old things are passed away; behold, all things are become new.

Satan, however, has not left me alone. He has been roaming about like a roaring lion. He began to make use of his agents to persecute me through physical assaults, isolation and ostracism, and by false litigation against me. I have suffered the kinds of persecution described in Psalm 69:4, 8 and 12. Through all this the Lord remained my comfort and strength. He has never failed nor forsaken me. His words in Psalm 27:10 and Luke 6:22–23 have given me added confidence, inspiration and even joy.

The Lord has blessed me with a Christian wife, formerly a nun for twelve years, and we have been living by faith and serving the Lord ever since. I have travelled to many places in India and abroad to preach the truth about the saving power of Jesus Christ and give the testimony of my conversion. I have visited many families and individuals in an effort to bring them to the Lord. It seems miraculous to realize how the Lord took me and my family from place to place in India in spite of persecution. Finally, in 1987, he opened a way for me to take my family to America. Through Dr Bart Brewer of Mission to Catholics International we were introduced to Pastor Ted Duncan of Liberty Baptist Church in San Jose, California. I will always be grateful to these men for their benevolence and spiritual help. They were indeed good Samaritans. My wife and I have been blessed with a son and daughter. We live in San Jose and worship at Liberty Baptist Church.

Reader, look to Jesus Christ. There is power in his atoning blood to wash away your sins as he did mine. No one can limit the efficacy of the precious blood of Christ. Trust on him alone and be 'justified freely by [God's] grace through the redemption that is in Christ Jesus' (*Rom.* 3:24).

17

José Borras

From the Monastery to the Ministry

'Father, you must start a campaign against the Protestants. They are growing more and more,' said Sister Dolores, a nun in a cloister where I went on Sundays to say Mass and preach.

I was a young priest and teacher in a school in Spain when the nun asked me Sunday after Sunday to do something against the Protestants.

'They are deceiving the simple people, and with material gifts they are winning many good persons for their heretical group,' the nun said.

Willing to defend the gospel of Christ, I decided to fight against the Protestants. The only thing I knew about them was that they were bad and their doctrine was full of errors and heresies.

A few days later a pupil came to my class with a thick book in his hands. 'Father,' he said to me, 'This is a Protestant Bible. A woman gave it to my mother, but she is afraid of keeping it because she thinks it would be a sin to do so. Would you like to burn it?'

'Oh, yes. I will destroy it,' was my answer. 'We must finish with all the Protestant propaganda.'

After I had torn out some of the first pages I changed my mind, thinking that since I needed to preach against the Protestants and did not know their errors, I could read their Bible to find out their main heresies.

I read some portions of the New Testament and compared the text with my Roman Catholic Bible. When I discovered that both Bibles were almost the same, I became very confused and wondered how there could be such great differences between Roman Catholics and Protestants when they both apparently had the same Bible. My conclusion was that the Protestants did not read their Bible or, if they did, surely they did not practise its teachings.

A Family and a Pastor

Thinking that the best way of knowing who the Protestants were would be to observe their lives and customs, I went to visit a Protestant family. I told them that I was a teacher and would like to know their doctrine to teach my pupils better what Protestantism was.

I was surprised that they were polite with me. I was astonished to see that they knew the Bible better than I. I was ashamed when I heard them speaking to me about Christ with a conviction that I, priest that I was, never felt.

They answered some of my questions and invited me to speak with their Baptist pastor. I met him the next day, but my first words were: 'Do not try to convince me, because you will waste your time. I believe that the Roman Catholic Church is the only true one. I would only like to know why you are not a Roman Catholic.'

He invited me to meet every week and to study the New Testament, discussing in a friendly way our different points of view. We did so.

The pastor answered all my questions with texts from the New Testament. My arguments were always the sayings of the popes and the definitions of the councils. Although I did not accept his arguments externally, in my own mind I realized that the words of the Gospels had more value than the decisions of the councils, and that what Peter and Paul said was of more authority than the teaching of the popes.

As a result of our conversations I began reading the New Testament assiduously in order to find some arguments against the Protestant doctrine. I wanted not only to show that the pastor was mistaken, but even to win him for the Roman Catholic Church. But after each one of our interviews, I came back to my school feeling that he had defeated me in argument.

For a long time I was very concerned, reading the New Testament and praying that God would increase my faith and dispel my doubts so that I should not make a mistake. But the more I read and prayed the more confused I became. Could it be possible that the Roman Catholic Church might not be the Church of Christ? Could I be wrong in my faith? If so, what had I to do?

I heard that other priests and monks became Protestants by studying the Bible, but I could not imagine myself doing the same. Be a Protestant? Be a heretic? Be an apostate from my faith? Never! What would my parents, my pupils and my friends say? My eleven years of study would be declared invalid. What would I do for a living?

These thoughts disturbed me greatly. I preferred not to change my faith. I wished I had never spoken with that pastor. I tried to convince myself that he was mistaken. I read the New Testament more and more, seeking for an answer to confirm my position as a Roman Catholic priest. As I read more I saw more clearly my wrong situation, but I was so afraid of leaving the Roman Catholic Church that I decided to continue as a priest even though I could no longer believe in Roman Catholic doctrine.

Light in the Darkness

One Sunday, Sister Dolores said to me, 'Father, you didn't preach against the Protestants as you promised me to do. They continue growing every day and are winning many people for their Church.'

'Sister,' I said to her, 'I have been studying the Protestant doctrine during all this time, but I have discovered that they are not as bad as we think. They base their doctrine on the Bible and we cannot preach against the Word of God.'

'You are quite mistaken, Father,' answered the nun. 'They are very bad. They are wolves in sheep's clothing. They are enemies of our country. They hate Mary. They are undermining our faith in the Pope. We must start a campaign against them.'

I told her how some priests who wanted to preach against the Protestants had been converted and had become Protestants when they studied their doctrine without prejudice and in the light of the Scriptures.

The nun interrupted me. 'Don't tell me this, Father; they were not converted, but perverted. They went over to Protestantism either because they were demented or because they wanted to get married. You can study this doctrine without fear,' she continued, 'and I am sure you will never go to Protestantism, because you are not demented; neither would you sell Christ for a woman.'

'I am thinking the same, Sister,' I replied. 'I promise you that I will study this question seriously. If I come to the conviction that the Protestants are wrong, I will start a campaign against them. If I discover that they are right, I shall become one of them.'

'Don't worry, Father,' said the nun, smiling, quite satisfied with my decision. 'You will never be a Protestant.'

I read my New Testament again and again, and I prayed to God with all my heart, asking for wisdom and guidance to arrive at a clear and right decision. I knew I would never be happy otherwise.

God's Grace

Three months later I left the Roman Catholic Church because I could not go on doing things and pretending to believe doctrines that deep in my heart I knew were wrong. I thought of all the possible difficulties, but I decided to follow Jesus Christ in spite of them.

The most important thing that could have happened to me was my personal encounter with Jesus Christ, when I came to know him as a personal Saviour.

It is not enough to be a good Roman Catholic: the important and necessary thing is to be born again in Christ. This has been my experience. When I entered into Christ, I experienced that he not only liberated me from my sins, but also from the heavy load I had to carry being in a monastic order. 'Blessed be the God and Father of our Lord Jesus Christ, who hath blessed us with all spiritual blessings in heavenly places in Christ. In whom we have redemption through his blood, the

forgiveness of sins, according to the riches of his grace'
(*Eph.* 1:3, 7).

Thank God for the many who have sought and found
that grace. The same God who transformed the life of
Saul the persecutor on the way to Damascus, and
transformed the life of Father Borras in the cell of a
monastery, is able to transform your life wherever you
are.

'I will greatly rejoice in the Lord, my soul shall be
joyful in my God; for he hath clothed me with the
garments of salvation, he hath covered me with the robe
of righteousness' (*Isa.* 61:10).

18

Enrique Fernandez

I Discovered the Word of God

Born in Madrid to devout parents in 1929, I studied in the Metropolitan Seminary of Oviedo for twelve years. I was ordained on 30 May 1954. I then became a Roman Catholic chaplain in a convent of nuns in Navelgas, a tranquil village in Asturias, Spain. In the evenings I usually visited the village priest, an older man who was companionable and friendly. One night in 1960 he showed me a pamphlet entitled 'The Gift' (an excerpt from the autobiographical writings of the former Canadian priest, Charles Chiniquy). I asked permission to borrow it and read it.

The pamphlet created an intense desire to read the Bible. I wanted to know if there was a real difference between the Roman Catholic and Protestant Bibles.

Withholding my identity, I wrote to the address on the pamphlet, requesting a Bible or a New Testament.

I began to study the New Testament, especially Acts and Hebrews. As I did, a conviction grew that the Roman Catholic Church had deviated from the Bible and that its priesthood had usurped Christ's place.

The discovery of the Word of God became a thrilling adventure for me. As I continued reading, I felt the cutting reality of Hebrews 4:12: 'The word of God is quick, and powerful, and sharper than any two-edged sword, piercing even to the dividing asunder of soul and spirit, and of the joints and marrow, and is a discerner of the thoughts and intents of the heart.'

Theology Not the Bible

During my four years of theological studies, I had never seriously read the Bible. For me, the Holy Scriptures were only consulted as a reference book in the study of Roman Catholic dogma. I knew only those parts of the Bible which were included in the Mass and in the texts of the Roman breviary.

Salvation, the Roman Catholic Church said, depended on absolution from sins by a priest, and whoever refused to confess his mortal sins to a priest was eternally condemned. But I could not find in Acts or in any other New Testament book any statement that this was so. All the sacred writers insisted that man must go directly to God for forgiveness.

On the other hand, in Hebrews I read very clearly that Christ had been offered once for all for the sinner. 'Then,' I said, 'how dared the Council of Trent declare in 1562 that in the Mass Christ offers himself by the hands of the priest as a true and real sacrifice to God?'

Faith Alone

I also found that justification was only by faith, and I asked myself whether, if I had not found peace of soul in the Roman Catholic Church, it could perhaps be because I had expected to gain it as a reward for my own efforts? 'But to him that worketh not, but believeth on him that justifieth the ungodly, his faith is counted for righteousness' (*Rom.* 4:5).

In such a manner, I suddenly understood that Jesus Christ asked nothing of me, and I relinquished all my own effort to gain salvation. So Jesus Christ became my only Lord and Saviour.

Later Developments

Through the Spanish Evangelical Mission in the Netherlands, I was put in touch with a former Spanish priest of the Roman Catholic Church who directed me to the Dutch foundation *'In de Rechte Straat'* (In Straight Street). This Christian organization had for several years been helping priests who left the Roman Catholic Church to understand the principles of the sixteenth-century Reformation and return to the doctrines of the Bible.

On 2 May 1961, I arrived in Brussels. Later I went to Hilversum, Holland. Then I sent a letter to my archbishop, telling him, 'I have discovered the Word of God, and Jesus Christ has presented himself to me as my only Lord and Saviour. Rome claims that Catholicism is centred in Christ, but in reality it has turned its back on him.'

Afterwards I went to San José, Costa Rica, where I received on 25 November 1963, a Bachelor of Theology degree in the Latin American Theological Seminary.

Finally, I spent several months in Guatemala in consultation with the Lutheran Church Missouri Synod before coming to the United States, where I have been preaching the gospel since 1 June 1964 to the Spanish-speaking people.

My fervent desire is to serve the Lord Jesus Christ, to carry the gospel of grace to the people and to tell them what great things the Lord has done for me. What he has done for me, he can do for them, and for you.

19

Francisco Lacueva

My 'Damascus Road'

I was born of Roman Catholic parents on 28 September 1911 in San Celoni, Barcelona, Spain. My father died in 1918 at an early age during the influenza epidemic which visited so many homes in my country. I was only six and my mother had to work hard from then on, as we were left very poor.

Two years later a friend obtained a post for my mother as a servant in a convent of Conceptionist-Franciscan nuns in Tarazona of Aragon, a small city in the province of Zaragoza. The nuns accepted her on condition that I study to be a priest, as they did not want boys in the porter's lodge of the convent, unless they were destined for later entry into the seminary.

Thus, at the age of eight years, I found myself already

committed to a future about which I knew less than nothing. The overbearing influence of the nuns was such that during my career in the seminary, though I told my mother several times that I did not feel the vocation for a life of celibacy, she threatened to send me to the Civil Guard orphanage, which she proceeded to describe in very dark colours.

As a Young Priest

When I was ten I entered the seminary of Tarazona to study for the priesthood. I did not study very hard until the senior courses, but even so I was able to pass all the exams with the highest marks. This I felt was some slight compensation to my pride to counter-balance the attractions of an ordinary job in which I could have realized my desires of making a home.

I was ordained a priest on 10 June 1934 in Tarazona by Dr Goma, archbishop of Toledo. Then passed the fifteen years of my ministry to the Church, classes in the seminary and in private, as well as burials, baptisms, marriages and other religious ceremonies.

Doubts Suppressed

In September 1948 I was promoted by my bishop to the chair of special dogmatic theology in the diocesan seminary of Tarazona of Aragon. One year later I was also appointed as Magister Canon, that is, the official preacher in the cathedral. Up to that time, I had managed to suppress all doubts and difficulties which I had experienced with regard to many of the doctrines of the Roman Catholic Church which the faithful are taught and obliged to believe. This had been achieved partly because of the immediate and unconditional submission which, under pain of excommunication, all true Romanists render to the Pope.

Then one day I read in a Roman Catholic magazine, *Cultura Biblica,* the name of a Spanish evangelical pastor, Don Samuel Vila. He was attacked for some remarks he made in his book *The Fountain of Christianity,* with reference to the brothers of Jesus. I wrote him a letter describing with utter sincerity my spiritual problems.

A True Conversion to God

Pastor Vila replied with a letter full of understanding and unction of the Holy Spirit, in which he explained many of the fundamental truths of the Word of God. These amazed me, as they were against everything which I had believed. Mr Vila did not ask me to become a Protestant but told me quite candidly that the solution to my spiritual problem did not lie in changing from one religious confession to another but in a true conversion to God. This was my first surprise and it was not to be my last. He added that my salvation depended on my simple reception by faith of Jesus as my personal Saviour and (another great surprise) that I should consider Christian living as a loving spiritual relationship with God. This was extraordinary to me. So these were the maligned Protestants.

I continued my correspondence with him and he sent me some evangelical literature. I shall always remember the impression I received from reading his book *The Fountain of Christianity.* There I found a reasoned exposition of the solutions to my personal research, undertaken against the dogmas of Romanism. Why had I not seen these things? Simply because I did not possess the extensive knowledge of the Bible and history which

Don Vila proved to have. It was thus that I devoted myself to the detailed study of and meditation on the Word of God, accompanied by much prayer in which I sought abundant grace of the Holy Spirit to discover the real sense of the Word, to treasure it in my memory and heart, to live it out in my life, and to communicate it to others. In a little over a year I had read the whole Bible through twice and the New Testament many times. I also studied the best Romanist and Protestant commentaries.

The Word of Truth

I was soon enjoying the fruits of this very pleasant task. My students were often amazed at the pertinent and varied biblical references with which I supported my theological explanations. But above all I saw with clarity, and for the first time the falsity of many of the doctrines of the Roman Catholic Church which are the articles of faith.

Though the light had begun to filter into my soul in January 1961, I was still not saved, even though I was convinced of the falseness of Romanism. I was most encouraged at this stage in my conversion by the first personal visit I made to Samuel Vila in Tarrasa (Barcelona) in May of that year. The fervour and devotion with which he spoke to me and particularly when he prayed to the Lord with me impressed and moved me greatly.

The Power of the Grace of God

Following the advice of brother Vila, I put God to the test in moments of great difficulty for me, and with wonderful results. At last on 16 October 1961, and in the

midst of a trial which hemmed me in like a veritable bull
of Bashan, I raised my eyes and heart to heaven, not
resting on my own strength, but sure of the power of the
grace of God, which harvests its greatest triumphs in the
face of human weakness and impotence. 'And he said
unto me, My grace is sufficient for thee: for my strength
is made perfect in weakness. Most gladly therefore will I
rather glory in my infirmities, that the power of Christ
may rest upon me' (*2 Cor.* 12:9). 'Blessed are they
whose iniquities are forgiven, and whose sins are
covered. Blessed is the man to whom the Lord will not
impute sin' (*Rom.* 4:7–8).

Since that time I have seen quite clearly that I have
been born into a new life, abandoning my life of sin, and
surrendering unconditionally to Christ, ready to take up
his cross and follow faithfully in his footsteps. Every day
I have prayed that the Holy Spirit might keep me ever on
the alert to obey his slightest wish, and that I might be an
instrument under his almighty guidance. From October
1961 to June 1962, my friends, my pupils, and my closest
companions were able to see the change which had been
wrought in me. My sermons had a fire of conviction
which they never had before. My heart was filled with an
enthusiasm, an inner joy, a wonderful happiness, and
my greatest delight was in prayer and in the continuous
reading and study of the Holy Scriptures. I began to read
methodically; and many were the Bibles and New
Testaments which I gave to my friends on their birthdays
and holidays.

Romanism: Another Gospel

I realized after some time, that it was impossible to
continue in the Roman Catholic Church. On 16 June
1962 I wrote letters to my bishop and to the President of

the Canonical Council of the Cathedral of Tarazona to which I was attached for thirteen years as Canon Magister renouncing all my honours and position. I told them I was leaving the Roman Catholic Church because I did not wish to fall under the anathema of Galatians 1:8–9, 'But though we, or an angel from heaven, preach any other gospel unto you than that which we have preached unto you, let him be accursed. As we said before, so say I now again, If any man preach any other gospel unto you than that ye have received, let him be accursed.'

The same day that I wrote my letter of resignation I left Spain for England. My friend Mr Luis de Wirtz received me with open arms at Newhaven.

I would not end without offering a vibrant testimony of my conversion to Jesus Christ. With great joy I have renounced the high positions which were mine in the Roman Catholic Church and the handsome living which accompanied them. I follow confidently under the providential guidance of my heavenly Father to the sure goal of my salvation. Since leaving the Roman Catholic Church I have seen quite clearly that in order to possess all things it is necessary first to give up all things.

By Grace

To my former companions in the priesthood, I say with all my heart, I am very happy in the new life which I have embraced in Christ and in his gospel; I would that all of you were touched by this same grace. I shall not forget you in my prayers, and I trust I have a place in the prayers of all who seek the truth sincerely and with an upright heart. Be assured that salvation is a personal matter between God and each one of you. Salvation does not lie in membership in a church, nor in pious practices, services, rosaries or messages of Fatima. It is obviously wrong to believe that one can be saved by observing the 'First Fridays' or the 'First Sabbaths'. Only our personal acceptance by faith of the redemption of Jesus Christ can save our souls. 'For all have sinned, and come short of the glory of God; being justified freely by his grace through the redemption that is in Christ Jesus: whom God hath set forth to be a propitiation through faith in his blood, to declare his righteousness for the remission of sins that are past, through the forbearance of God' (*Rom.* 3:23–25).

This is biblical doctrine; it is the doctrine of Paul in Romans. Study the Scriptures and they will guide you to the truth. Beware of following a mistaken road. Think on this today. Tomorrow may be too late.

20

Juan T. Sanz

'Thou Knowest That I Love Thee'

I was born on 28 April 1930, in Somosiera, Madrid (Spain), the eighth child in a Roman Catholic family.

I felt the call to the priesthood when I was thirteen, while listening to a sermon during the Mass (19 March 1943). For economic reasons I did not enter the minor seminary of the diocese of Madrid until the academic year of 1945–6.

During the first five years of my course I studied Latin and humanities. The following three years I studied philosophy, theology and ethics. In September 1953 I began studying theology and ethics as basic subjects.

No seminarian could possess or read a Bible during his first eight years. On my twenty-first birthday a woman,

who would later be godmother to my first Mass gave me a
Bible which, to her surprise, she had to take back home
until I was twenty-four years old and started my theological studies. So my interest in knowing more about the
Bible would be more of a curiosity than a necessity.

My First Mass

I was ordained a priest on 14 July 1957, and on the 18th
of the same month I celebrated my first Mass in my home
town.

My first parish church was La Horiuela, Madrid. I
took possession on 23 August 1957, and continued there
until 1959, when, due to my parents' health, I resigned
and was assigned coadjutor to the parish church in the
neighbourhood of Canillejas, Madrid.

I took my parents and my sister with me to this new
post, where both the parish priest and the parishioners
received us with open arms. But after a while my
fellowship with the parish priest gradually began to
deteriorate due to his fundamentalist and conservative
attitude concerning the content of the preaching, the
administration of the sacraments, the liturgy of the
Mass, and devotion to the Virgin Mary and the saints.

Why did I have to preach what the parish priest wanted?
Why did I have to hear the confession of the penitents
before celebrating Mass, as if this were the expiation of
their sins? Why was the specific devotion to Mary and the
saints allowed during the celebration of the Mass? Why
use Latin in the Mass and administration of the sacraments
if the parishioners could not understand it? In my first
parish I had used Spanish in various parts of the Mass, in
funerals and baptisms. This so pleased the vast majority of
parishioners that their attendance and participation in
worship gradually increased.

Reform in the Parish

After two years in my new parish I told my parish priest about my use of Spanish and the Bible in my previous work. Later he informed me that, with the bishop's permission, we would be using Spanish during much of the liturgy and sacraments. But the Sunday and quarterly preaching would have to remain unchanged, even though I thought that they moralized too much and consequently were not very biblical. The themes were chosen by a group of conservative priests with the aim that all clerical diocesans would preach on the same theme at a particular Sunday Mass. Even so, I managed to 'restyle' the proposed themes, giving them a new direction towards Christ. My parish priest came to hear about this and, to my great surprise, told me that he would substitute for me in the pulpit whenever he could, leaving me to officiate at the Mass.

In those difficult days I used the Bible as my bedside book and searched more and more for its truthful, profound and eternal message of salvation, for me and the rest of the world.

The Lord Answers

One day the Lord answered all my questions when he led me to read and understand chapter 3 of the Gospel of John. God's love and promises were now and would henceforth be for me the only rule, power, authority and mirror. But had they not always been so for me? They had: but now they were so in another way, since God had regenerated me by his Word and Spirit: 'For God so loved the world, that he gave his only begotten Son, that whosoever believeth in him should not perish, but have everlasting life' (*John* 3:16). Therefore God was my

Father and his Son Jesus Christ was my only and perfect personal Saviour. This was something completely new for me. A big change had taken place in my heart.

In the summer of 1964 I asked the Lord to tell me what to do with my life. I could no longer continue in the Roman Catholic Church because its hierarchy forced me to preach 'another gospel', different from the message of salvation by grace and through faith, only to be found in Christ.

But when and how could I leave my priestly ministry? Who would support my parents and my sister financially? Would I find understanding and support in the bishop if I gave up my post for the sake of faith and conscience? How would the Protestants, to whom I was thinking of going for advice, receive me?

In the spring of 1965, I heard about the 'desertion' of a priest, also from Madrid and a superior of the seminary, who, with the help of the pastor of an evangelical church, had left the Roman Catholic Church and had gone abroad to study Protestantism in a European Protestant university. So my colleague's attitude and determination were the answer as to how I could leave the priesthood to know in a deeper way the gospel of liberty of God's children.

With this aim I contacted the German Church, La Iglesia de los Alemanes, in Madrid, and they gave me Pastor Luis Ruiz Poveda's telephone number. As soon as I told him that I was a priest with problems of conscience and faith, he advised me to stop the conversation and to arrange to meet on a certain day and place, as his telephone was frequently tapped by the police. And that is what we did.

Mortal Sin or New Life?

Meanwhile I felt as if my spiritual and psychological life were collapsing. Under the terms of Roman Catholic doctrine, I lived constantly in a state of 'mortal sin' because I formally doubted my faith; because I did not search for the pardon of this and other sins in the sacrament of penitence; because I searched for biblical truth in Protestantism and not in my bishop and theology professors; because I rejected the Roman Catholic ecclesiastical hierarchy and authority; because I rejected the doctrinal authority of my Church concerning the Bible; because it seemed to me that the aural confession of sins robbed God of the right and power which only he has in his own person and through the work of his Son Jesus Christ; because the celebration of the Mass seemed to me to supplant the merits of Christ on the cross.

Did all these reasons mean a full stop to my pastoral ministry? The Lord told me by his Word that they did not. But this brought about a conflict against the Lord's will, against my Roman Catholic mentality, and against my stubborn pride. This inner battle affected my health and sleep and produced many fears. In the end it required me to renounce everything for love of Christ and for my own eternal salvation.

I Respond to the Lord's Grace

At the end of the tunnel of anguish and fears, the Lord Jesus invited me to respond to him as the Apostle Peter had done for the third time near the lake. It was these words I had already chosen as my motto for life before being ordained as a priest: 'Lord, thou knowest all things; thou knowest that I love thee' (*John* 21:17). Thus the Lord led me out of the shadows of Roman Catholicism into the light of the gospel of grace: 'For by grace are ye saved through faith; and that not of yourselves: it is the gift of God: not of works, lest any man should boast' (*Eph.* 2:8–9).

21

Celso Muñiz

The Professor's Methods Did Not Work

From childhood on I looked restlessly for reality and certainty. In my youthful opinion it was through the priesthood that I could best experience truth and salvation for the soul. A schoolteacher once said to me, 'It is more difficult for a priest to be lost than for a stone to float in water.'

I entered seminary for a twelve-year period of study. There I gave myself completely to a life in accordance with the regulations of the Roman Catholic Church. I did all the ascetic exercises and I also taught asceticism when I was professor of ascetic and mystic theology and principal of the Metropolitan Seminary at Oviedo in Spain. (Asceticism is the art of mastering 'self' and bringing under control all passions, desires and lusts by severe self-discipline, abstinence, or inflicting punishments on the body.)

Yet I could never find for myself the self-control, peace and certainty which I taught other people to acquire. My inner restlessness, added to the many disappointments I experienced from the Roman Catholic Church when comparing her teaching with the Bible, brought about an increasing struggle within me. While in this spiritual turmoil my attention was caught by Protestant radio broadcasts from abroad. These made me hunger for the true message of God, and so the Bible became light and food for my soul.

The Bible, the Source of Truth

My desire to understand precisely what Jesus had taught led me to seek contact with a church I had heard of, one where the Bible was the only source of guidance for their faith. As I studied the Bible and spoke with these Christians, I saw Jesus Christ in a completely new way – as a perfect Saviour who must be approached directly and personally by faith alone.

As I continued to search the Bible, I recognized more and more clearly the errors of Roman Catholicism and I wanted to experience the kind of conversion of which the Bible spoke. On the other hand, because I was very tied to my Church, I wanted to have this experience without leaving Roman Catholicism.

However, I gradually became convinced that the Roman Catholic Church had pushed Christ aside with her wrong teaching and her highly complex organization. For me this was a most painful conclusion to reach.

Jesus Is the Truth and the Way

I can never forget the actual night of my conversion. Another day of severe inward conflict had ended with my seeking refuge in the Lord and in his Word, the Bible. I could not sleep.

It was not so much that I tried to pray, but prayer suddenly welled up in my heart and I could not hold it back. More than ever before I felt the burden and weight of the sins of my past life. I thought, I am completely sinful. I cannot deliver myself; I am useless and good for nothing in the sight of God. Never before had I felt so incapable of doing any good. I thought of how many times the Lord Jesus Christ in the Bible had invited those who felt utterly lost to come to him. I felt strongly drawn towards him, for he offered free and undeserved forgiveness. Indeed, Christ had been ready to come to suffer the punishment of men's sins in their place.

At last, without any further desire to do anything myself, I threw myself into the arms of God my Father, who had given Jesus Christ for my salvation. I prayed, 'Come to me, Lord Jesus, I give myself to you as my only, personal and all-sufficient Saviour.' The hours flew by as minutes. I felt as never before completely at one with the Lord my God. Deep down within myself I thought, Thou art mine, O Lord, and I am thine, thy possession for all eternity. I do not know how it happened, but it is a fact that all my wavering, doubting and vacillation disappeared, and my happiness became complete.

My decision was now made, and standing before the choice of Jesus Christ or the Roman Catholic Church, I chose to follow the Lord Jesus Christ whatever the consequences might be.

I discovered that Christ took over my life and made

me one with himself simply because I trusted my soul to him. The Lord is not merely a good man who shows us the way, but he *is* the way. The Lord is not just a teacher of truths, but he *is* himself the truth. The Lord is not a hero who gave his life for a human cause, but he is the only Saviour who is life for all who turn to him.

We can never find salvation while part of us trusts in what Christ has done to take away the punishment of sin, and another part of us still trusts in sacraments, indulgences, and our own attempted good works. Real salvation comes only when we fully trust Jesus Christ.

22

Manuel Garrido Aldama

From Roman Priest to Radio Evangelist

I was born of long Basque ancestry in a typical Roman Catholic family in the north of Spain. The Basques have the reputation of being the strictest and most devout of all the Spanish people. We were a family of six boys and one girl who was the youngest of all. My father, a lawyer, intended that we should have the best education. My mother, a fervent Roman Catholic, took care of our strict religious life.

For My Mother's Sake

During his regular pastoral visits to my mother's home the priest would remind her that her six boys had been given to her by God and it was for her to show her gratitude by giving at least one of them to serve at the altar. 'If you love your children, give them the greatest honour a mother can give her boys. The greatest honour is the priesthood,' he used to say to my mother. It is no wonder that she, being of such religious tendencies and so devout, thought that it was really her duty to dedicate some of her boys to God in the priesthood. My father, although not anti-religious, paid little heed to the priest's advice for he was not of the same opinion. He wanted to have his boys follow some secular profession. I would not have been allowed to study for the priest-hood had not my father died when I was ten years of age. It did not take my mother long to make the necessary arrangements to have me accepted in the seminary, and some months afterwards, when I was scarcely eleven years of age, I was taken to the minor seminary in Madrid. I promised my mother that I would do my best, for I would not have displeased her willingly for anything on earth. But how could a boy of eleven years of age understand the meaning of the priesthood? Rome maintains that 'once a priest always a priest', and such a lot was cast on me at the impressionable age of eleven years and under the pressure of a loving mother.

Things went quite easily for the first six or seven years of my training, but they began to change when we came to the study of the dogmas of the Church. The classes of theology were conducted in Latin, and at the end of every class the professor, who had received his Doctorate of Divinity in Rome, gave the students an opportunity of presenting questions or putting objections or asking for a better explanation of some of the points which he had treated in his lecture.

Is God Not Just?

When we came to the dogma of the 'infallibility' of the
Pope, I decided to put a question to him, not with the
object of denying anything, but so he might help me to
reconcile the justice of God towards man with the
declaration of this dogma in the Church some years
previously. My argument was that God was making
salvation more and more difficult for man as the years
went by, and this did not seem to me to be very just on the
part of God. Why was it that men could be saved and go to
heaven before the year 1870 without believing this dogma,
while we that were living after that could not be saved if we
did not believe in it? Does it not imply injustice on the part
of God to place additional obstacles before men every few
years in order that they might obtain salvation? God is not
just if to enter heaven I have to overcome greater doctrinal
difficulties than my ancestors.

I could see that the professor did not like my raising
such questions. When on another occasion I sought
further enlightenment, he answered in an irate manner,
'If you do not refrain from your dangerous ways of
thinking, some day you will be a heretic.'

We often saw one of the professors in the seminary
walking up and down the corridors with his New
Testament, studying and meditating on it. When he
preached he always preached Christ; he never mentioned the saints, and in one of his classes he said more
than once, 'I am afraid we are in the wrong somewhere.
The Christ we know is not the Christ represented to us in
the New Testament, and that may be the reason our
preaching appeals so much to the feminine sentiment,
while the men keep away from us.' He, no doubt, knew
something of the truth as it is in Christ Jesus, but was
afraid to be outspoken.

The time had arrived for me to be ordained a priest, and I was not very happy about it, in spite of all the importance attached to ordination and all the honours I was supposed to receive. My faith in the Church and even in God had been on the decline for a long while.

Ordination and My Mother's Joy

The ceremony of ordination took place in Madrid. My mother and other members of the family had come for the unique occasion. My fellow students and I were ordained with the elaborate ritualism and sumptuous pomp that Rome's experts have arranged for such occasions. Some days after the ordination I said my first Mass and administered the communion to my own mother and sister. I could see the tears running down my mother's cheeks, and I myself could not help feeling the extraordinary emotion that such a ceremony was intended to produce.

Men as Mice

Some months after ordination I secured a post teaching Spanish literature in one of the colleges in the north of Spain, in the province of Santander. I was obliged to say Mass every day and occasionally was invited to hear confessions. Since, according to the dogma of transubstantiation, I had God in my hands every day and since I saw men and women coming to me for confession, I began to drift further and further away from God. There were men as strong as an oak kneeling before me at the confessional box shaking with fear as if they were little mice. They did not feel like confessing their sins and they did not know how to do it, but they feared the eternal punishment with which they were threatened if

they did not come to confession at least once a year.
Labouring men like these did not know how to begin so
they would say, 'Father, help me by asking me some
questions', and I had to review the sinful acts that I felt
men of their position might commit. Although I did not
believe in the power of men to forgive sins, I never
refused to pronounce the formula of absolution to any
one who came to me in good faith.

Trapped by Our Position

There were other priests connected with the school in
which I was teaching with whom I naturally came into
close friendship. More than once I asked them, 'Do you
really believe that because we say of a piece of bread,
"This is my body", or because we say to a sinner, "I
absolve thee", the bread is turned into the body of Christ
and the sinner has his sins forgiven?' I remember one of
them answering, 'Why do you bother about those
things? We are in this position and cannot help it now.
We can do nothing about it.' By then I had resolved to
leave the priesthood. I did not have the courage to face
the opposition and consequent ostracism which would
have been my lot had I given up the priesthood in Spain.
I knew that in many places my very life would have been
endangered, so I decided to leave Spain in order to carry
out my convictions. For a time I had another teaching
job in North America. Then on my return to Spain I
found the religious surroundings unbearably narrow and
oppressive.

   In London I found circumstances the most favourable
for leaving the Roman Church. I was fairly popular with
the pupils and in no need of the support of the Church.
Therefore I decided to separate there and then. So I
dispatched a notice to the Roman Catholic authorities in

London, advising them of my resolution and asking them to appoint someone in my place. In this apparently easy way I realized a desire that had been in my heart for several years. I thought I had rid myself at last of all religion. It was not so, however. God had his plan to draw me unto himself.

Faith in Christ Alone

A minister of the Church of England, a real man of God, hearing of my spiritual predicament became interested in me and invited me to converse with him on religious matters. He endeavoured to show me the truth, not just because I had given up the Church of Rome, but because I thought that by doing so I had done away with all religion in my life, and with God in particular. In our conversations he would always conclude, 'In spite of all your studies, there is one thing you do not know and one thing you lack; you do not know Christ as your Saviour, and you do not have him in your heart.' I could not help admiring the sincerity of the man as well as his earnestness, and I had to admit that I had never before heard God's plan of salvation as he was now telling me: that Jesus Christ had paid the price of sin in full and that I needed to know him in a real way and have heartfelt faith in him.

'Now to him that worketh is the reward not reckoned of grace, but of debt. But to him that worketh not, but believeth on him that justifieth the ungodly, his faith is counted for righteousness. Even as David also describeth the blessedness of the man, unto whom God imputeth righteousness without works. Saying, Blessed are they whose iniquities are forgiven and whose sins are covered' (*Rom.* 4:4–7).

The minister repeated God's plan of salvation to me many times, until God in his grace gave spiritual light to my spirit. I began to have a new hunger for the things of God, a hunger given to me by God himself.

Effectual Prayer

One Saturday afternoon the minister invited me to his home, and after speaking to me on the same subject, took me into an adjoining room where some members of his church were meeting for prayer. I was greatly surprised when I heard them praying for me. Their interest in my spiritual welfare was quite evident. The pastor had told them about me, and they had met there solely for my sake. I felt that Christ was very real to them. They spoke to him as if he were really present among them. This was a totally new experience for me. I never thought that men and women could call on God so fervently and spontaneously as those people did. For Roman Catholics, even for the priests, prayer consists almost exclusively in the mechanical recitation of certain formulas written by the Church or by some person who has tried to put his own feelings towards God or the saints into writing for the help of those who might want to use them.

God Gives Me Faith

Deep spiritual conviction came upon me and God gave me faith in Christ and a heart to repent. I could not help praying earnestly to God, 'God, it is true that Jesus Christ saves and brings peace to the soul; I want him to draw near and give it to me.' I did not know exactly what was happening within me, but the doubts and spiritual darkness which had troubled me for so long vanished and I experienced a peace and tranquillity such as I had never known before. The Lord had accomplished his purpose. I had 'passed from death unto life'.

'Therefore being justified by faith, we have peace with God through our Lord Jesus Christ' (*Rom.* 5:1). 'In whom we have redemption through his blood, the forgiveness of sins, according to the riches of his grace' (*Eph.* 1:7).

It Is Not Good that a Man Should Be Alone

Not long after my conversion I met a lady who later became my wife. She had been a pupil in one of my Spanish groups. Later on when I proposed marriage to her, she refused at first on the ground of the Roman Catholic saying, 'Once a priest, always a priest.' She was a Roman Catholic, though no longer in communion with the Church. Finally she accepted, on condition that I would never ask her to accept the Protestant faith. 'I will never go over to the enemy's camp,' she used to tell me. I knew, however, that if Christ's grace had been powerful enough to bring me to him, he would also save her, and he did. Leading her from the errors of Romanism was not difficult and the Lord drew her to himself also.

The Need for the Gospel

I began to have a burden from the Lord for Spain and the Spanish-speaking world. In time the Lord led me as an evangelist to a radio ministry in South America called 'The Voice of the Andes' (HCJB). Quite a number of Roman Catholics came to Christ through this.

I believe we need to preach the gospel, 'for it is the power of God unto salvation to every one that believeth' (*Rom.* 1:16), and to utilize every means of doing so, to meet the spiritual needs of this dying world. 'So then faith cometh by hearing, and hearing by the word of God' (*Rom.* 10:17).

23

José Manuel de León

Jesus Saved Even Me

I was born in Vizcaya, Spain, on 9 April 1925. At age eleven I lost my father, a victim of the Spanish Civil War. Some uncles, sincere yet deceived, set me on the road to studying for the priesthood. I was ordained a priest on 24 September 1949. Although for eight years I had been working in Spain instructing youth, I myself needed peace. In spite of all the vows of poverty, chastity and obedience, and interminable prayers and confessions, I did not manage to resolve the anguish of my soul.

I observed with qualms of conscience countless rules and laws; I received sacraments and practised cere- monies, all without knowing Christ as my Saviour or even wishing to read the Word of God. Besides, I could not teach what I was ignoring. Of course, it had never occurred to me to think that I was practising a ministry contrary to the Holy Scriptures.

God in His Mercy Guides Me

Meanwhile I was designated for the parish of 'Our Lady of the Remedies' in Rocha, Uruguay, in the capacity of Father Curate. I faithfully carried out my mission, yet did not find the remedy for my troubles.

I had never spoken with evangelical Christians (or Protestants as they are usually called) nor desired to become one. However, God in his mercy was guiding me. In September 1958 I met two evangelical ladies from Buenos Aires whose conversation left a pleasant impression in my soul. They prayed to God with confidence and had thorough knowledge of his Word. They asked me if I was saved. I replied that I was expecting to be saved by the merits of Christ and my good works. They replied that we can only have peace with God through being justified by faith in Jesus Christ and that 'the blood of Jesus Christ his Son cleanseth us from all sin' (*1 John* 1:7). I responded, 'This is understood by the Church of the Mass in which daily sacrifices are offered for our sins and for the dead.' The ladies replied, 'The Roman Church and you priests would say many such things; however, the Bible assures us: "Now where remission of these is, there is no more offering for sin" (*Heb.* 10:18).'

Reading and Preaching the Word of God

Immediately I wrote to friends from Spain and asked them to send me two translations of the Bible, the Roman Catholic one of Nacar-Colunga and the evangelical

one of Reina-Valera. As soon as they arrived, I began to
read them avidly at the rate of seven or eight hours a
day. I ascertained that the books were the same, only
differing in some words used by the translators. The
Word of God was revolutionizing my spirit. After three
months in the true 'school of God' I travelled to Buenos
Aires desiring to know the evangelicals personally.
Three days, in which I attended services and conversed
with them, were enough to convince me that people who
enjoyed so much peace and happiness, who prayed to
God asking always in the name of the Lord Jesus, could
not be wrong. It was impossible.

On returning to Rocha I could not stop preaching the
Bible to the faithful of my parish. Included in the Mass
of those days were references to the parable of the
sower, the healing of the blind man of Jericho, the
temptation of the Lord in the desert, and so on. The
occasion was favourable to exhorting the parish to
read the Holy Scriptures. I did not attack any Roman
Catholic dogma and in my spirit I held firm the
resolution of not attacking the Roman Catholic Church.
At that time I believed that I was far from being saved.
Besides, I was bound by personal interests.

Therefore my surprise was great when on the anniversary of my arrival at Rocha (21 February 1959), the
senior bishop told me that in view of accusations that I
had preached 'as a Protestant' I was expelled from the
diocese and had to go back to Spain.

If I had preached against Christian doctrine I would
have willingly recanted publicly. But according to the
Church's own legislation, notification must be sent to
the accused party before ecclesiastic censure can be
imposed. I was restricted in my duties. Although my
conscience did not accuse me before God, I headed for
Nuncio, asking for a new interview with the bishop. He

was a little more amiable, but I decided that I must leave Rocha; and after eight days of spiritual retreat I took the office of priest in Rio Branco.

No Other Foundation than Christ

Those days of retreat helped me to get to know the Bible better. The more I read, the more convinced I was that the Roman Church was completely removed from the spirit of the gospel. In my book *Why I Embraced the Priesthood and Why I Left It* I explain the reasons that induced me to leave the Roman Church. There everything is put in its place: Christ, the fundamental rock of his Church, not Peter; the Scriptures, not the traditions; the Virgin Mary as mother of the Saviour, not as mother of God; the holy men of God, privileged but not intercessors. I noted that in the Roman Catholic Bible already cited, in the second commandment that Rome cut out of the catechism, it was prohibited by God not only to worship but to make images. 'Thou shalt not make unto thee any graven image, nor any likeness of any thing . . . thou shalt not bow down thyself to them' (*Exod.* 20:4–5).

The Roman Catholic Church teaches that (1) the priest, called Father, is placed by God to instruct; (2) that one must confess sins to him for them to be absolved; and (3) that only through him and through the Church can one obtain salvation.

God teaches in his Word that: (1) we must call no one father on earth because he is our Father, that Christ is our Master, and that the Holy Spirit teaches us and guides us into all truth (*Matt.* 23:9–10; *John* 14:26 and 16:13); (2) that sins must be confessed to the Lord, and that this is what cleanses us from all unrighteousness (*1 John* 1:8–10); and (3) that outside Christ who died on

the cross for sinners there is no other name given to men
by which we can be saved (*Acts* 4:12 and 5:31, *Heb.*
7:25).

Consequently, not being able to continue struggling
against God, against his Word and against my own
conscience, I decided to yield myself into his hands and
release myself from the Church of Rome. The Word of
Christ was fulfilled more than once 'And ye shall know
the truth, and the truth shall make you free' (*John* 8:32).
I did nothing more than obey one of the solemn
exhortations which conclude the Bible: 'Come out of
her, my people, that ye be not partakers of her sins and
that ye receive not of her plagues' (*Rev.* 18:4).

Now, like the apostle Paul, I preach the gospel.
'Having therefore obtained help of God, I continue unto
this day, witnessing both to small and great' that it is
Christ that must 'show light unto the people, and to the
Gentiles' (*Acts* 26:22–23).

24

José A. Fernandez

I Was Blind, Now I See

I was born blind, not physically but spiritually, in 1899 in one of the most mountainous and inaccessible regions of Asturias, rightly called the 'Spanish Switzerland'.

My parents were devout Roman Catholics who believed implicitly everything that the Roman Catholic Church taught. They had, indeed, a blind faith, which they transmitted to their seventeen children. Roman Catholicism permeated the heart, the mind and even the body of the individual; the baby was nursed and nourished with love and devotion to Mary and the saints; the child was later on impressed with the value of medals, scapulars, beads and holy pictures; the priest's word was law and had to be obeyed.

As early as I can remember, I had a strong inclination towards everything connected with the Church and the priest, whom we regarded as a super-human being devoid of ordinary human needs and weaknesses. My greatest delight was to serve as an altar boy, considering it a great privilege and honour to rise early in the morning and walk two miles in the snow through mountainous terrain to assist the priest at the Mass. At the age of seven I was able to recite the prayers of the Mass in Latin.

Blind Faith in the Church

The family devotions, consisting of the recitation of the rosary and a long litany of prayers to all the patron saints, were held every night without exception. The whole family, including the small children, gathered in the kitchen, which also served as the living room. We formed quite a congregation! When my father took the beads from his pocket, it was the signal for all of us to go down on our knees on the bare stone floor, ready for the coming ordeal which usually lasted forty minutes.

The recitation of the beads, consisting of the Apostles' Creed, fifty-three 'Hail Marys', six repetitions of 'Glory Be', five of 'Our Father,' the 'Hail, Holy Queen' and the Litany of the Blessed Virgin, was trying enough. Far more so was what followed, a seemingly endless series of prayers to the different virgins, angels and saints noted for their special advocacy and protection in all the circumstances of life.

The Worship of Images

My early religious life was centred on one main event during the year: the Festival of the Virgin of Dawn, commemorating the assumption of Mary into heaven on 15 August.

The Virgin of Dawn was the patroness of the region. According to a legend, the virgin appeared to a certain shepherd on a nearby mountain called 'Alba' or 'Dawn'. A sanctuary was erected on that spot to honour the apparition. Every year a religious pageant is enacted, and the shrine is visited by thousands of pilgrims from far and near. The statue of the virgin, attired in splendid regalia, is carried in procession through the mountainside, to the acclaim and veneration of the devotees who come either to pray for a miracle or to thank her for the miracles already performed. Each region in Spain claims at least one such miraculous virgin. Fatima is reproduced hundreds of times!

Although Roman Catholic theology distinguishes between the statue and the person it represents, that distinction is theoretical only. There was no doubt in my mind that both I and those simple mountain people really worshipped the image. To us, a supernatural power was attached to the physical part of the figure, for it was not even a statue in the proper sense of the word. It consisted of a few sticks arranged so as to provide the skeleton on which a face was placed. The figure was then dressed in silk and gold. I was shocked beyond words when one day I saw the altar ladies undress the statue and noticed that the virgin of my dreams was only a dummy. That mental picture has remained with me ever since.

Having observed my religious inclinations, the parish priest approached me with the idea of studying for the priesthood. Guided by the exalted opinion I had of that profession, I yielded readily to his persuasion, much to the joy and satisfaction of my deeply religious father and the consternation of my equally religious mother, who opposed the idea on the grounds of her maternal instinct and love.

A Friar and Priest

At the age of twelve I left home, father, mother, brothers and sisters, never to see them again. The glory of the priestly life, the enchantments of the monastery, and the salvation of my soul envisaged on the horizon of my mind overcame the natural sadness that came over me as I took leave of my family and the scenes of my childhood.

I was sent to a high school in the province of Valladolid. The high school was conducted by priests of the Dominican Order for the purpose of training young boys already set aside by their parents for the priesthood.

During the four years of my stay there, I not only studied the high school subjects but became proficient in the Roman Catholic catechism. It was there that Romanism took hold of me body and soul; the seed of intolerance was sown in my soul, since the catechism insisted that there was only one true Church of Jesus Christ outside of which there was no salvation. That Church was the 'Holy Roman Catholic Apostolic Church'. God was presented to my young mind as a stern judge ready to render to us according to our sins, an angry God who had to be appeased by good works, penances and mortifications.

During the first two years of my training, my life was exemplary in the observance of every rule and in the assiduity to my studies. I was honoured on several occasions with special awards.

From this school I was sent to the Dominican Novitiate in Avila, and in the famous monastery of Santo

Tomas I was invested with the black and white habit of the Dominican Order at the age of sixteen.

A Time of Torture

One full year was devoted to the intensive study of the rule and constitution of the order, the rigid observance of the same, the chanting of the office of the virgin, and constant vigilance on the part of the novice master. It was a year of trial and probation which only the strongest characters could survive. Fasting was prescribed from 14 September to Easter. The incoming and outgoing mail was carefully censored by the master. All contact with the outside world was prohibited. No conversation or communication could be held between the priest and the professed members of the monastery. Auricular confession was obligatory every week, and this was generally held on Saturday and had to be made to the same novice master who was at the same time our superior and constant supervisor.

It is not difficult to imagine the anxiety and mental torture that such unmerciful practice, since changed by the canon law of the Church, inflicted on the young novices, who literally dreaded the approach of Saturday. But the dream and anticipation of one day becoming a full-fledged friar provided me with the courage needed to complete that year of probation and absolute self-renunciation successfully.

The day of partial liberation came on 8 September 1917, the Feast of the Nativity of the Virgin Mary, when I made my profession as a member of the Dominican Order. The next four years were spent in Santo Tomas College, adjoining the novitiate.

From the time I left home at twelve until I finished college at twenty-one I had not spoken to a woman.

Womanhood was presented to our young minds as
something evil, and on numerous occasions the religious
instructors related to us stories of saints who never
looked at their mothers' faces, citing this as an example
of chastity to be imitated by us.

Studies in America and Ordination

After four years of college I went to the United States to
study theology and learn English. I spent three years in
the Dominican Theological Seminary in Louisiana and
some time in Notre Dame University.

Soon after my ordination to the priesthood in 1924 I
was sent as assistant pastor to one of the largest
Roman Catholic churches in New Orleans, Louisiana.
I served in that capacity nine years and in 1932 I was
appointed pastor of the same church, at the age of
thirty-two.

For six years I laboured untiringly, zealously and with
great success. The church grew in membership, attendance at religious services, reception of the sacraments,
and even in material goods. When I became pastor, the
parochial school had an enrolment of about 450 pupils;
two years later the enrolment went over the one
thousand mark. I made it possible for hundreds of poor
children to receive free religious education.

The Dominican Order had honoured me with the
office of superior of the Dominican House connected
with the church. My community was composed of five
priests and two lay brothers. I was also the Father
Confessor of several convents of nuns, facts which prove
the high esteem in which I was held by the archbishop,
the congregation, and my religious superiors. I was in
fact a 'Pharisee of the Pharisees', who needed a personal
encounter with the living Christ.

A Penitent Soul

During the last years of my pastorate I began to doubt the validity of some of the doctrines of the Roman Catholic Church. The first thing that I doubted and rejected was the power of the priest to forgive sins in confession. Neither could I make myself believe in the doctrine of transubstantiation, or the real physical bodily presence of Christ in the host (wafer) and in the chalice (cup).

My faith in the Roman Catholic Church weakened. I felt that I could no longer remain a hypocrite. I was entertaining the idea of leaving the priesthood. God intervened and provided the occasion by the instrument of human agents. This time it was the Master General of the Dominican Order who issued orders from Rome to the effect that Spanish Dominican priests of Louisiana should leave their churches and turn them over to the American Dominicans. Some were ordered to Spain, others to the Philippines.

I resigned myself to abandon the parish without any protest, feeling that the hand of God was present in this new turn of events. But I refused to leave the country of my adoption which I had learned to love. I left the priesthood and took the road that leads to the gutter of sin, but somewhere along that road God took pity on me and saved me from a disastrous end. For a year and a half a terrific struggle went on within my soul. I felt tempted to turn away from God and everything sacred. But then I would remember the words of Peter: 'Lord, to whom shall we go? Thou hast the words of eternal life.'

The world with all its pleasures and allurements could not fill the vacuum in my soul. After vainly trying to find happiness in the things of the world, and wishing to save my soul, I went to a monastery in Florida. It was my

purpose to consecrate my life to God in the solitude of
the monastic life, to bury myself in that sacred precinct,
to work for and earn my own salvation. In the seclusion
of a monastery I thought God would surely give me that
assurance of salvation and the happiness of soul that I
was seeking.

That was my purpose but God had other designs for
me. From now on God's hand leading me was manifest.
It was in the monastery that I became acquainted with
evangelical Christianity.

The Inspired Word of God

For a while I worked in the library of the monastery.
There was in that library a particular cabinet with the
inscription 'Forbidden Books'. Curiosity got the better
of me. One day I unlocked the cabinet and saw six or
seven books. I read them all one by one. They were
religious books dealing with the evidences against
Roman Catholicism as the true Church of Jesus Christ.

I also began to read the Bible. Until then the Bible did
not mean much to me personally. It was indeed the
inspired Word of God, but I was told that the ordinary
human mind is not able to understand its true meaning.
A superior mind, an infallible authority was necessary, I
believed, to impart the meaning of what was in the mind
of the Holy Spirit when he inspired the sacred writers. I
preferred to read the Word of God as understood by this
infallible authority and as found in the Roman Catholic
missals and prayer books.

Gradually the reading of the Bible became a source of
comfort and inspiration in the solitude of the monastery,
and I began to understand the real meaning of certain
passages of the Bible to which I had not paid particular
attention in the past.

I was particularly impressed with the following verses as I read them in the Bible: 'For there is one God, and one mediator between God and men, the man Christ Jesus; who gave himself a ransom for all, to be testified in due time' (*1 Tim.* 2:5–6). 'Grace be with all them that love our Lord Jesus Christ in sincerity. Amen' (*Eph.* 6:24). 'Believe on the Lord Jesus Christ, and thou shalt be saved, and thy house' (*Acts* 16:31). 'Now the Spirit speaketh expressly, that in the latter times some shall depart from the faith, giving heed to seducing spirits, and doctrines of devils; speaking lies in hypocrisy; having their conscience seared with a hot iron; forbidding to marry, and commanding to abstain from meats, which God hath created to be received with thanksgiving of them which believe and know the truth. For every creature of God is good, and nothing to be refused, if it be received with thanksgiving' (*1 Tim.* 4:1–3).

The seed of the Word of God was then planted in the garden of my soul. It is true that I tried to smother it, but that little seed was to grow and bear fruit in due time.

Teaching church history to the young monks, I became acquainted with the corruption of the Roman Catholic Church, both in doctrine and in practice; and in my heart, I felt a deep admiration for the courageous leaders of the Reformation.

After two years in the monastery, I had not found the peace of mind nor the happiness of soul that I was seeking. What should I do next?

An American Soldier

Not wishing to go on living in those surroundings, anxious to be useful in some way to humanity, and knowing that my adopted country was at war, I did the most honourable thing: enlisted in the US Army as a private. After my basic training I was sent to the Military

Intelligence Training Center at Camp Ritchie, Maryland. The men selected to attend this Intelligence School were highly educated. We had to take orders from corporals and sergeants who, for the most part, in their civilian life did nothing, perhaps, but sweep streets or wash dishes, but who could use strong language, and the stronger the language the more the stripes. But I thank God for these men, for they fitted me for my future Christian ministry as they taught me humility, obedience, discipline and spiritual democracy.

Furthermore, I was assigned for a while to the chaplain's office. The chaplain, Major Herman J. Kregel, was a minister of the Dutch Reformed Church, a man with a brilliant mind and a heart of gold. I loved to listen to his sermons on Sunday morning, for he was a fluent and interesting speaker. While my mind was reacting favourably to his full and lucid explanations in doctrinal matters, my heart became captivated by the example of his conduct, his charity, unselfishness, broad-mindedness and naturalness. For the first time I realized that a Protestant minister could be happy and sincere in his faith and work.

In the American army, unlike other places, proselytizing of members of another faith by a chaplain is not done. The relations between the Protestant chaplain and myself were cordial in the usual chaplain–soldier relationship, but no more. He had no objections to my attending the Protestant services. After all, the right to worship when and where one pleases is one of the things that we were fighting for.

Salvation through Faith Alone

One Sunday Major Kregel preached on Paul's doctrine of salvation through faith alone. Until then I had clung tenaciously to my belief in salvation by works. After the service I went to his office to let him know how I felt about his 'heretical' statements. Armed with the text from James 2:24: 'Ye see then how that by works a man is justified, and not by faith only.' I said to him, 'If what you said is right, then James is wrong; if James is right, you and Paul are wrong. Otherwise you must admit there is a contradiction in the Bible.' He replied, 'José, there can be no contradictions in the Bible, for the Holy Spirit is its only author, and the Spirit cannot contradict himself.' With that, of course, I fully agreed.

'Now,' he continued, 'when Paul says that salvation is by faith alone, he speaks from the point of view of God, who reads our minds and sees our hearts. So far as God is concerned, we are saved the moment that we believe. But this belief is a faith of trust and not just a mental assent to a few doctrinal statements. On the other hand,' the chaplain went on, 'when James states that salvation is by works also, he speaks from the point of view of men who, being unable to read our minds or see our hearts, must have something visible and tangible by which to judge whether or not we are saved. As far as men are concerned, we are saved when we produce good works, but good works are not the root; they are the result of salvation.'

I fully agreed with this explanation. The last mental barrier had been removed. I became an intellectual believer and promised the Lord to give my life to the Protestant ministry. But I was not fit for that ministry yet. My mind had been converted, but my heart remained untouched.

A Sinner Saved by Grace

I prayed for light, studied for information, and on my days off visited the different churches in Maryland and

Pennsylvania to find out which one appealed to me the most on biblical grounds.

During one of my visits to Baltimore, I met the one who was going to be my life partner, a deeply religious lady of the Baptist communion. She possessed a winning personality, a delightful sense of humour, and a fine Christian heart. Our short courtship ended in a most happy union brought about by a Baptist minister in a Baptist church. The good lady could not give me salvation, but the merciful Lord was going to grant it to me six months after our marriage.

In the fall of 1944, I was assigned as interpreter for South American officers studying the military science of mechanized cavalry at Fort Riley, Kansas. While doing army reconnaissance, I also engaged in spiritual reconnaissance, searching for the truth.

One Saturday night I attended the Salvation Army open air service on a street corner of Junction City, Kansas. At first my attitude towards the meeting was one of indifference and even scorn. But as the meeting went on, I was being driven by a supernatural force to give earnest attention. A young Salvation Army lady gave a stirring message which ended by appealing to those standing by to believe on the all-sufficient sacrifice of Christ. Then she quoted the words of Jesus as recorded in John 5:24: 'Verily, verily, I say unto you, He that heareth my word, and believeth on him that sent me, hath everlasting life, and shall not come into condemnation; but is passed from death unto life.'

At that moment I felt myself passing from death to life under the influence of a supernatural force. I went down on my knees, confessed Christ as the Lord of my life, and received him as my Saviour. What happened, how it happened, I cannot tell; all I can do is to repeat with the blind man of the Gospel, 'Whereas I was blind, now I see' (*John* 9:25).

In the face of the transformed life, there can be no denial of the power of the Holy Spirit. Something happened in my life; I am not the same man. I love the things that I used to hate and hate the things that I used to love. For the unregenerate man and woman, this may seem foolishness because 'the natural man receiveth not the things of the Spirit of God: for they are foolishness unto him: neither can he know them, because they are spiritually discerned' (*1 Cor.* 2:14). My life since then has been a public testimony to the transforming power of the Holy Spirit. I am a sinner saved by grace.

Gospel Minister

Soon after our marriage, my wife and I went to live in Blue Ridge Summit, on the mountain range dividing Maryland from Pennsylvania. The pastor of the Presbyterian church was the Rev. C. P. Muyskens, a college classmate of chaplain Kregel and, like him, a former minister of the Dutch Reformed denomination. Worshipping regularly in his church, we became acquainted with his sterling qualities as preacher and pastor. Visiting him at his home, we were impressed with his Christian family life. He did not leave his religion in the pulpit but took it with him to the home. In him I found the inspiration, guidance and encouragement that I needed during the transition period from soldier to gospel minister.

On 24 April 1945, while still in the Army, I was ordained a Presbyterian minister at the Hawley Memorial Presbyterian Church of Blue Ridge Summit. Two months later I was given the piece of paper I was avidly waiting for, an honourable discharge from the US Army!

That fall I entered Princeton Theological Seminary, where I worked for and obtained the degree of Master of Theology. My year there was without doubt the happiest of my life. There I found spiritual uplift, Christian fellowship, intellectual growth and deep religious experience. It was indeed, as in the case of the apostle Paul, an 'Arabia' for me. When I compared conditions there with those of my early seminary days the difference was striking. Fear, regimentation, and constant supervision had given way to love, joy and the freedom of the children of God.

25

José Rico

Life Begins for a Jesuit Priest

After nineteen years of continual threatened ship-wreck in the Roman Catholic priesthood, on 15 April 1956 I arrived on the tranquil shores of peace with God through Jesus Christ.

Among the reasons for leaving my native Spain was the call of South American bishops in the face of the avalanche of Protestantism in Latin America. There is something in the soul of a Spaniard that makes him instinctively react against Protestantism. From the reign of Charles V and Philip II onward, the history of Spain is full of religious episodes, battles, decrees of faith and the Inquisition. Thus when the pope told the Spanish clergy that Latin America is the mission field for Spanish priests, it was a clarion call to me. Coupled with this was

my desire to labour in that part of the world which I
loved, though I had not been there, because it had been
the most precious possession of our empire.

I soon learned that Latin America is a new and
different world in every sense of the word. In São Paulo,
Brazil, later in Argentina, and finally in Chile I saw
the Protestant chapel alongside the Roman Catholic
church, claiming right of social recognition. From my
prejudiced viewpoint, this was an intolerable abuse.
Nevertheless, the divine providence was soon to bring
light to my mind on all this.

'He Which Hath Begun a Good Work . . .'

I arrived in Antofagasta, Chile, where as a priest of the
cathedral I found excellent opportunities to promote my
anti-Protestant ideas. When evangelical literature
began to reach me I was ready to commence my fight. I
read it with disgust. Later I read some Protestant books
that I had dared to place in my private library. Little by
little a current of sympathy began to replace the mortal
hatred that I had up to that time against Protestantism. I
saw clearly that Protestantism is not what it is said to be,
nor what it is taught to be in Roman Catholic halls of
theological learning. The evangelical books were full of
profound teaching drawn from the holy books of the
Bible. Between them and Roman Catholic books there
existed no difference that I could see, other than that
they lacked the *imprimi potest* of the Roman-approved
books. But when it came to the lives of the evangelical
believers, there was a notable difference between them
and the average Roman Catholic. I would have desired
that my faithful adherents live as morally and correctly
as those hated Protestants.

Unforeseen circumstances took me from Chile to

Bolivia. A few months later I was appointed to the honourable position of National Counsellor to the Roman Catholic student organization called the JEC. The nomination was made and signed by the archbishop of La Paz. My heavy responsibilities retarded for a time the evolution that had commenced in my soul towards Protestantism. Yet God continued the work that he had started and I not only had the opportunity to get acquainted with evangelical books and tracts, but also to meet some strong evangelicals.

Christ by Himself Purged Our Sins

My Roman Catholic faith and priesthood were close to irreparable shipwreck. I wanted to make some supreme effort to save them. Could it not be that all this was a diabolical temptation like similar cases I had heard of? I wrote a book called *The Priest and the Host* which, though not published, had the official approbation of the diocese. I went to the Epistle to the Hebrews for inspiration in writing the book, but I failed to find there the Roman Catholic priesthood that I was looking for. The only priest spoken of was Jesus Christ, who 'once in the end of the world . . . appeared to put away sin by the sacrifice of himself' (*Heb.* 9:26). Then I read in Hebrews 10:17–18 of the impossibility of another offering for sin. How is it that from the Roman Catholic pulpits it is preached that the Mass is the bloodless renewal of the very sacrifice of the cross if this epistle teaches that there is no possibility of repeating that which Christ did once and for all? And of what value is a bloodless sacrifice if the same writer teaches that 'without shedding of blood is no remission' (*Heb.* 9:22)? For this reason he says that, having accomplished eternal redemption, the eternal High Priest of the new covenant ascended on high where now he intercedes for us in the presence of God (*Heb*. 1:3; 7:25).

When I finished studying the Epistle to the Hebrews I felt that an invisible and omnipotent hand had stripped me of my vestments and my priestly character. The only priesthood found was that recorded by St Peter: 'Ye also, as lively stones, are built up a spiritual house, an holy priesthood, to offer up spiritual sacrifices, acceptable to God by Jesus Christ' (*1 Pet*. 2:5). It is the same that is referred to in Hebrews: 'By him therefore let us offer the sacrifice of praise to God continually, that is, the fruit of our lips giving thanks to his name' (*Heb*. 13:15).

I then saw the uselessness and falsity of purgatory, since the same writer says that Jesus Christ accomplished our purgation by offering his life on the cross, when he 'by himself purged our sins' (*Heb*. 1:3). If Christ purges our sins, how is it that souls that are saved now have to go to purgatory to be purified? What kind of purgatory do the Roman Catholics have that is not once mentioned in the Bible?

Jesus Is the Only Way

After this there only lacked the opportunity to reach the goal that with such clarity appeared in the distance. God intervened by putting me in touch with a young pastor whose natural intelligence was combined with a profound love for God and an extraordinary knowledge of the Scriptures. He was the director of the Indian Bible Institute in La Paz, Samuel Joshua Smith. This was my first real personal contact with a 'heretic'. His conversation illuminated my mind, dispelled my doubts, and comforted my heart to the point of making it valiant.

The next day I repeated the visit and at its close

Samuel Joshua said, 'What keeps you from receiving Christ as your only and sufficient Saviour?' I felt my heart melt with a happiness which choked me with emotion, while tears ran down my cheeks. Nothing more was needed: I received him with full conviction.

Christ became my 'only' Saviour, for none other had died on the cross for me. He also became my 'sufficient' Saviour because his blood is all-powerful to wash my sins from my soul. How miserably the rites and ceremonies and human traditions of Romanism had failed to cleanse my soul for God. It was only then that I understood what Jesus meant when he said, 'I am the way, the truth, and the life: no man cometh unto the Father, but by me' (*John* 14:6). I asked forgiveness for having wandered for so many years in wrong paths and I was determined to walk by that way which is Christ Jesus.

From that moment I knew myself a new creature in Christ Jesus (*2 Cor.* 5:17). I realized at the same time that God had justified me and lifted the enormous burden from my heart that until that moment had mercilessly weighed me down. Yes, I had 'passed from death unto life' (*1 John* 3:14).

I still had to continue my normal activities in Romanism for two months. It was necessary to evaluate all the details before taking a definite step. Those months were the darkest days of my life, but God finally broke the cords that had held me prisoner for so long. One bright afternoon I arrived at the evangelical church in Miraflores, La Paz. I quickly took off my gown. Dressed in civilian clothes, I sat down to a cup of tea and entered into the simple, spiritual, intimate conversation with the brethren, feeling as though I had always known them.

In this manner the curtain fell that put an end to the tragedy that had existed throughout my nineteen long years in the priesthood.

26

Mark Peña

The Lord Became My Righteousness

I was born in a little town north of Burgos called Villamediana de Lomas, Spain. Because I wanted to be a missionary I decided to enter the novitiate to became a Roman Catholic priest.

I began the novitiate 24 July 1949. After a year and a day we had to swear to God before the holy community to observe for one year the vows of poverty, chastity and obedience. With this ceremony we began as members of the congregation of the Oblate Missionaries of Mary the Immaculate. After this we moved to Madrid to the larger seminary that the Oblates have in Pozuelo de Alarcon, where we studied two years of philosophy and four of theology to be priests.

After three years it was necessary to profess for our entire lives the vows of poverty, chastity and obedience. Before arriving at ordination, the seminary student has to climb several steps on his ascent towards the top. They are called orders, minor orders and major orders. It begins with the tonsure during the first year of theology. Then follow the other orders.

On 17 March 1956, in the church of the seminary of Madrid at the hands of the bishop of Madrid-Alcala, Dr Eyjo Garay, I, together with four classmates, received ordination to the priesthood.

My First Mass and Fireworks

My first Mass took place in the church of the Religiosas de San Jose de Cluny in Pozuelo de Alarcon the following day, Sunday 18 March 1956. I sensed great internal emotion and sublime sentiment for this first Mass and remember my nervousness that I should not wrongly perform any of the rites and ceremonies.

The first Mass with the family in our home town was something humanly great for a little town such as mine. Everyone lived two days of intense emotion and fiesta during 8 and 9 July 1956. It was all fireworks, music, floral displays, games and joy. I was the first priest from that town and because of that it was a matter of great pride for all the families.

I taught Spanish literature and music, Latin and French, but what I liked best was preparing the Sunday sermon for the 11 o'clock Mass in our church.

Co-Pastor

As the Provincial Patriarch knew of my missionary desires, he assigned me, together with another Oblate

Father, as co-pastor of a poor and miserable parish in the city of Badajoz. On 14 November 1958 I arrived at the parish of Our Lady of the Assumption at Badajoz, composed of a populace of great spiritual and material misery. It was made up of nine thousand souls. For three years I worked in this parish to the joy and satisfaction of the people. Truthfully they felt proud of me, and I loved them and sought to win them by every means.

Increasingly I felt burdened by my sins and realized that there was no assurance of forgiveness through confessions and other Roman Catholic practices. I felt that I was lost forever. The Mass became meaningless. Like John Knox, the former Roman Catholic priest turned Reformer, I could say, 'The Mass is blasphemy'. I determined that I must leave the priesthood, go into the world, obtain secular employment and 'enjoy life'.

Evangelicals – Rare Insects?

My dissatisfaction with the Mass and the spiritual emptiness of the Roman Catholic Church increased. I contacted a Protestant pastor in Madrid, Alberto Arajo Fernandez. I did not know him but had been told that he was a prudent man and an earnest Christian. The first contact with him was very simple and cordial. And to think that the great majority of Roman Catholics, at least in Spain, think that evangelical Protestants are something like rare insects! He let me explain my problem, and with a wisdom and a love before unknown to me he counselled me and encouraged me to spend much time reading the New Testament. We corresponded regularly.

In February 1962 I resolved to take the great step, to leave the Roman Catholic priesthood. I could not continue where there was only ritualistic coldness; as it is written, 'Having a form of godliness, but denying the power thereof' (*2 Tim.* 3:5). I wrote to Arajo asking him to look for a place where I could hide, and also to another pastor in Bilbao, Juan Eizaguirre, asking him the same thing, because at the first opportunity I was determined to leave the priesthood.

'The Lord Our Righteousness'

My superior had arranged for me to preach at the celebration of the appearances of the Virgin in Fatima. I chose this as my time to leave the priesthood and my religious state. I arrived in Madrid on 8 May 1962. Then I flew immediately to Holland, to get out of Spain before my superior could learn of my defection and have the police close the Spanish frontiers to me.

At this time I knew nothing of true biblical salvation, but in Holland I lived with an evangelical Protestant family. They read the Bible together and prayed in family devotions and at meals. They recommended me to Dr Hegger, a converted priest and director of a work in Holland which helps priests who want to leave the Roman system. It is called *'In de Rechte Straat'* (In Straight Street), from the reference in Acts 9:11. Dr Hegger counselled with me and answered many of my doctrinal questions from the Word of God.

Shortly afterwards I returned to Spain via Portugal (for safety) to visit my mother, who was sick and worrying about me. The Lord enabled me to live in safety with my family for a month and my mother improved greatly. On my return by train I was reading the Bible and praising the Lord. In this attitude of praise, passages of Scripture came to me, emphasizing that Jesus Christ is a perfect Saviour, the only Saviour, the all-sufficient Saviour; that he made one perfect,

never-to-be-repeated sacrifice on the cross of Calvary
for my sins; that he was my substitute, my sin-bearer;
and that he would impute his righteousness to me and
forgive all my sins if I would but trust him with all my
heart. In one moment, I did so. I gave him my life, my
soul, and received him, trusting him as my Lord and
Saviour forever. The words of God were fulfilled in my
heart and life: 'To him give all the prophets witness, that
through his name whosoever believeth in him shall
receive remission of sins' (*Acts* 10:43). My sins were
forgiven; my soul was saved; heaven became my home;
Christ was mine, and I was his forever.

My Prayer for Roman Catholics

I returned to Holland. From there I contacted The
Conversion Center in Havertown, Pennsylvania, about
coming to America and studying the Word of God. The
Lord enabled me, after some difficulty, to reach the
USA in September 1963, where I commenced studies at
Faith Theological Seminary. I then took some special
courses at Temple University leading to a Master's
degree in Spanish Literature.

As Paul's heart went out for the salvation of Israel, so
I pray for my beloved Roman Catholics: 'Brethren, my
heart's desire and prayer to God for Israel is that they
might be saved. For I bear them record that they have a
zeal of God, but not according to knowledge. For they
being ignorant of God's righteousness, and going about
to establish their own righteousness, have not submitted
themselves unto the righteousness of God. For Christ is
the end of the law for righteousness to every one that
believeth' (*Rom.* 10:1–4).

27

Luis Padrosa

Twenty-Three Years in the Jesuit Order

'**I** have found that there is no foundation in the gospel for the dogmas of the Roman Catholic Church.' Such a statement from me, dressed in my priest's robes, must have left evangelical pastor Samuel Vila, whose advice I sought, almost speechless with astonishment.

I came to talk with Samuel Vila already persuaded by the force of the truth and constrained by the Spirit of God, eager to explain what I had discovered in the pages of the Sacred Scriptures, the Bible.

I had now decided to take the painful and dangerous step (dangerous especially in Spain) of renouncing my office and position as lecturer and director of the Loyola

Institutes of Barcelona and Tarrasa, to be faithful to the
light I had received.

Rome Is Not the True Church

The reasons behind my decision were not one, but
many. After living forty-three years a sincere Roman
Catholic, fifteen of intense ecclesiastical training, ten as
a priest and a popular preacher to great multitudes, and
twenty-three of religious life in the Jesuit Order, I
arrived at the conviction that the Roman Catholic
Church was not the true Church of Jesus Christ.
Thirteen years of intense study of apologetics brought
me to an unbreakable conviction. I know the arguments
on both sides. I have analysed them.

I took the Holy Scriptures and began to search, but
where was the infallibility of the Pope? I could not find it
anywhere. Where was eucharistic fasting, and the Mass?
Where was it all? I could not find it. The more I studied,
the more I came to see that Christianity is one thing and
Roman Catholicism another, completely distinct; the
more I searched the Scriptures, the more convinced I
became of this truth. In Roman Catholicism, Jesus
Christ is presented as a fossil, a corpse, a man nailed to a
cross, but dead, no longer alive. Thus the Church cannot
get a Roman Catholic to love Jesus Christ, and if there is
no love, there is no possibility of salvation, however
many Masses, scapulars, medallions, novenas and
images you have. It is useless unless there is sincere love
and faith, and there cannot be such love unless a man is
convinced that Christ is alive, his sacrifice finished. In
Roman Catholicism your salvation depends on yourself,
on your saying many prayers, on your using many
scapulars, on your devotion to the Virgin, on your
taking communion. From this and from many other

things I came to see that Roman Catholic doctrine cannot be the truth. If you only knew what I was going through! It was a very serious matter to me.

Torture of Soul

In this position you find yourself up against your lifelong tradition, your native atmosphere, your family, your relations, and all your friends. They are all going to say one of two things (or both at once) because they have no other argument for one who leaves the Roman Catholic Church for Christianity: you have gone mad or you have fallen in love.

Few know the torture of soul that Roman Catholics suffer. People who go to Mass every day and are constantly in attendance at the Roman Catholic churches live in torment of soul, saying to themselves, 'Shall I be saved or lost? Did I make a good confession or not?' They have no peace. Is this the true religion? What is all this? Where in the Gospels do we find this method of tormenting the sinner? When did Jesus Christ or his apostles torment sinners with their questions?

How wonderful to know in our hearts that Jesus Christ our Lord has redeemed us, that by grace we are saved! Does not Paul say, 'I do not frustrate the grace of God: for if righteousness come by the law, then Christ is dead in vain' (*Gal.* 2:21)? The salvation of men depends only on Jesus Christ, our divine Redeemer.

Jesus Is the True Way

He is the way. He never said that the way was the church. 'I am the way, the truth, and the life' (*John* 14:6). On the other hand, the Roman Catholic Church wants to be the way herself and to be absolute mistress of the truth, so as to modify it at her will. To accomplish this she has put the clergy in place of Jesus Christ and the Church in place of the Bible.

I can offer a single word of advice to the one who wants to possess the truth: read as frequently as you can the holy Gospels and the epistles contained in the New Testament. There you will see what it is that one who desires to be a Christian ought to believe and practice.

Never shall I be able to thank the Lord enough for bringing me to himself and into the truth. My father and other relatives feel very sad, thinking that I have apostatized from the faith. But to follow Jesus and to read the Word of God in all its purity, free from the additions and distortions which, in the passing of the centuries, have been accumulated by Roman Catholicism, is not to apostatize from the Christian religion.

28

Joseph Zacchello

I Could Not Serve Two Masters

I was born in Venice, north Italy, on 22 March 1917. At the age of ten, I was sent to a Roman Catholic Seminary in Piacenza, and ordained a priest, after twelve years of study, on 22 October 1939.

Two months later Cardinal R. Rossi, my superior, sent me to America as assistant pastor of the new Italian church of 'Blessed Mother Cabrini' in Chicago. For four years I preached in Chicago, and later in New York. I never questioned if my sermons or instructions were against the Bible. My only worry and ambition was to please the Pope.

Believe on the Lord

One Sunday in February 1944 I turned on the radio and
accidentally tuned in on a Protestant church programme. The pastor was giving his message. I was going
to change the programme because I was not allowed to
listen to Protestant sermons, but I was interested and
kept on listening.

My old theology was shaken by one text from the
Bible I heard over the radio: 'Believe on the Lord Jesus
Christ, and thou shalt be saved.' Therefore, it was not a
sin against the Holy Spirit to believe that one was saved.

The Lord Rebukes Me

I was not yet converted, but my mind was full of doubts
about the Roman religion. I was beginning to worry
about the teachings of the Bible more than about
dogmas and decrees of the Pope. Every day poor people
were giving me from five to thirty dollars for twenty
minutes of ceremony called Mass, because I promised
them to free the souls of their relatives from the fires of
purgatory. But every time I looked at the big crucifix
upon the altar, it seemed to me that Christ was rebuking
me, saying, 'You are stealing money from poor, hard-
working people by false promises. You teach doctrines
against my teaching. Souls of believers do not go to a
place of torment, because I have said, "Blessed are the
dead which die in the Lord from henceforth: Yea, saith
the Spirit, that they may rest from their labours; and
their works do follow them" (*Rev.* 14:13). I do not need
a repetition of the sacrifice of the cross, because my
sacrifice was complete. My work of salvation was
perfect, and God has sanctioned it by raising me from
the dead. "For by one offering he hath perfected for ever

them that are sanctified" (*Heb.* 10:14). If you priests and the Pope have the power of liberating souls from purgatory with Masses and indulgences, why do you wait for an offering? If you see a dog burning in the fire, you do not wait for the owner to give you five dollars to take the dog away from it.'

I could no longer face the Christ on the altar. When I was preaching that the Pope is the vicar of Christ, the successor of Peter, the infallible rock upon which Christ's church was built, a voice seemed to rebuke me again: 'You saw the Pope in Rome: his large, rich palace, his guards, men kissing his foot. Do you really believe that he represents me? I came to serve the people; I washed men's feet: I had nowhere to lay my head. Look at me on the cross. Do you really believe that God has built his Church upon a man? The Bible clearly says that Christ's vicar on earth is the Holy Ghost, and not a man (*John* 14:26). If the Roman Catholic Church is built upon a man, then it is not my Church.'

God's Word Is Sufficient

I was still preaching that the Bible is not a sufficient rule of faith but that we need the tradition and dogmas of the Church to understand the Scriptures. But again a voice within me was saying, 'You preach against the Bible teaching; you preach nonsense. If Christians need the Pope to understand the Scriptures, what do they need to understand the Pope? I have condemned tradition because everyone can understand what is necessary to know for personal salvation. "But these are written, that ye might believe that Jesus is the Christ, the Son of God; and that believing ye might have life through his name" (*John* 20:31).'

Whose Blood Was Shed?

I was teaching my people to go to Mary, to the saints, instead of going directly to Christ. But a voice within me was asking, 'Who has saved you upon the cross? Who paid your debts by shedding his blood? Was it Mary, the saints, or I, Jesus? You and many other priests do not believe in scapulars, novenas, rosaries, statues, candles, but you continue to keep them in your churches because you say simple people need simple things to remind them of God. You keep them in your churches because they are a good source of income. But I do not want any merchandizing in my church. My believers should adore me in spirit and in truth. Destroy these idols; teach your people to pray, to come to me only.'

Who Forgives Sin?

Where my doubts were really tormenting me was inside the confessional box. People were coming to me, kneeling before me, confessing their sins to me. And I, with a sign of the cross, was promising that I had the power to forgive their sins. I, a sinner, a man, was taking God's place, God's right, and that terrible voice was penetrating me, saying, 'You are depriving God of his glory. If sinners want to obtain forgiveness of their sins they must go to God and not to you. It is God's law they have broken. To God, therefore, they must make confession; to God alone they must pray for forgiveness. No man can forgive sins, but Jesus can and does forgive sins.'

These Scripture verses were constantly in my mind:

'And she shall bring forth a son, and thou shalt call his name JESUS: for he shall save his people from their sins' (*Matt.* 1:21).

'Neither is there salvation in any other: for there is none other name under heaven given among men, whereby we must be saved' (*Acts* 4:12).

'If we confess our sins, he is faithful and just to forgive us our sins, and to cleanse us from all unrighteousness' (*1 John* 1:9).

'My little children, these things write I unto you, that ye sin not. And if any man sin, we have an advocate with the Father, Jesus Christ the righteous' (*1 John* 2:1).

One Master: The Lord

I could not stay any longer in the Roman Catholic Church, because I could not continue to serve two masters, the Pope and Christ. I could not believe two contradictory teachings, tradition and the Bible. I had to choose between Christ and the Pope, between tradition and the Bible; and by God's grace I have chosen Christ and the Bible. I left the Roman priesthood and the Roman religion in 1944, and since I have been led by the Holy Spirit to evangelize Roman Catholics and urge Christians to witness to them without fear.

29

Joseph Lulich

The Word of God Came to My Rescue

I am really glad to be able to tell you what the grace of God has done in my life. I speak to you as one who has lived most of his life as an ex-Roman Catholic priest, one who once served faithfully and sincerely the Roman Church for fourteen years, and who then served as a missionary used by God to spread his glorious gospel in one part of our needy world.

I was born on the eastern border of northern Italy, where I lived during my childhood. I grew up knowing the horrors of the first World War, and fear of the future gripped me. At the age of twelve I was taken by my father to a monastery for my education. I well remember my farewell to my family. I was so young, but in my heart

I had a strong desire to find peace in my soul, to become a priest and so be able to help others in their physical and spiritual needs. Fifteen years passed by.

A Priest but Disappointed

I had spent all my time in study, prayer and good works, to become a priest. But when the time came for me to say my first Mass in my native town, I felt bitterly disappointed. The peace I had dreamed of was not yet in my soul. I was technically well-prepared: philosophy, theology, medical training, languages, ability to endure physical and spiritual hardships, these were my equipment.

I was ordained a priest, and I was ready to serve the Roman Catholic Church for the rest of my life. I had experienced the agony which Martin Luther went through. I had gone through many months of long fasting, prayers, etc., but all this did not give me any assurance of my sins being forgiven. I was afraid of hell and of purgatory, but the theological teaching of my church did not allow me any doubts. I had to accept her infallibility and authority and trust her as the only way of salvation.

Being in touch with other needy souls who came to me for a word of comfort, I felt inadequate to speak in the name of Christ.

World War II

I served my country as a chaplain in the Second World War. Many times on the battlefield or after a bombardment, I forgot to raise my hand and pronounce the words, 'I absolve you' to the dying soldiers or civilians to whom I was ministering. I used to remind them of the crucified Christ their Redeemer. Looking back, I see that maybe I was like the prophet Balaam who spoke guided by the Spirit, not knowing what he said. In fact, all this behaviour of mine was in conflict with my conscience, and I felt guilty of betraying the teaching I had received. I remember sharing this with another priest, and he was disappointed because I was not exercising the authority of mediator which the Church had given me.

After the War

After the war, I had experience of life in communist Yugoslavia. I need not tell you the physical suffering I endured, but the terror of death was with me night after night. Every night some of my companions were taken to unknown destinations. I felt that if I were to be killed by the Communists I would be a martyr of the Roman Catholic Church, but this did not offer me any light or help in my uncertainty of having my sins forgiven. I used to pray, 'Blessed holy Mary, Mother of God, pray for me now in the hour of my death', but the fear of the judgment of God, hell and purgatory was constantly with me.

Some months later I fled to northern Italy where I spent three years working with poor people. I organized a group of one thousand homeless and jobless people. I had two hundred children under my care, most of them illegitimate, for whom I provided food, clothing and schooling. People were bitter against the Pope, bishops and Church, but they loved me – not as a priest, but as a good, honest man. They trusted me and listened to me, whereas they had stoned the bishop of a nearby town when he tried to visit them. I remember once I was speaking in an open air Mass, and among those present were more than twenty women of the red light district, a

number of Communists, and many others living in sin. I
read the account of the adulterous woman to whom
Jesus said, 'Go and sin no more.' They were touched,
and so was I. I realized that only Christ could forgive
their sins, not I as a priest. I invited them to receive his
forgiveness. I knew that I was guilty against the teaching
of my Church. I could not sleep. But the lives of my
people were changing. Newspapers carried daily reports
of crimes committed by the people I cared for, but then
they stopped. I remember at night the young people
were singing, 'Let Christ Reign'.

Contact with Protestants

In 1950 I was appointed chaplain on an ocean liner which
took Italians all over the world. I travelled across to
Asia, Africa, Indonesia, Australia. I was still struggling
in my soul, but I thought this struggle the work of the
devil. It was then that I came into contact with Protestants for the first time. I had been taught that branches
cut off from Christ did not bear fruit and that Protestants
were those branches. But I could see many good fruits
among Protestants. I will never forget one Christmas in
the middle of the Indian Ocean. I could not organize a
choir, so five Protestant girls asked me if they could sing
some carols. All the Roman Catholics were so very
much moved, and I more than they. The struggle in my
spirit was stronger and stronger. My faith and trust in the
Roman Catholic Church was undermined. I had to
review my studies.

Truth and Life in Christ Alone

To understand my fears and doubts, you must remember that as a Roman Catholic priest I had to have

nothing to do with Protestants, and I was afraid I could be accused and sent into some desert monastery to rot. The tremendous storms I had experienced on the high seas of the Atlantic were nothing in comparison with the storms that had broken out in my soul. I did not believe any longer in the authority of the Church, but where could I find any security? The Word of God came to my rescue, offering me that spiritual source of power and courage to face the world, when, through some simple words of Jesus, the Holy Spirit enlightened my soul and gave me that peace of sins forgiven and that joy which only God can give in believing that 'I am the way, the truth, and the life: no man cometh unto the Father, but by me' (*John* 14:6). My trust in Jesus for salvation gave me direction in my life. Only Christ could offer me truth, and only in him could I have life, joy, peace and purpose. I had to leave the officers and crew who loved me, but they were also disappointed at my decision. I had to flee from my superiors, relatives and friends. Having been excommunicated by the Roman Church, I had no dignity and work, and every door was closed to me. But I praise God that the peace I had in my soul was so great that I overcame that stage in my life without fear.

I went to Canada, where I worked for nine months as a general labourer in a hospital. It was hard work compared to the easy life on the ship, where I used to travel first class and had enjoyed every comfort. I had to come back to Italy since my visa was not extended. I lived for a time with my sister, who was a refugee, and I remember how my family often told me to go back into the Roman Church or I could not survive. It was then that I came into contact with two converted priests (and now evangelical pastors). They could well understand my position, and they helped me very much. I was given a job as a teacher in an orphanage, and then I was put in touch with Western Bible College in the United States where I spent time in Bible studies. That was a time of growth in my spiritual life, as well as my academic life. The college put me in touch with some local churches, since I felt I had to come back to Italy for missionary service. The Lord has been very good in providing for me for the last twenty-five years, during which time I have come back to the States only once.

New Life, New Partner, New Mission

Back in Italy, the Lord provided a faithful partner and fellow worker in the gospel through all these years, my wife Agnes. For family reasons we were brought back into the place where I had served as a Roman Catholic priest for some time, and the work was very difficult. The police were checking our moves. The bishop spoke against us and tried to have us removed. People hated us. I remember having to wipe spit from the front door of our little meeting place and paint over the nasty writings on the walls.

With time we were able to win the people's confidence and trust. Four hundred years earlier the last evangelical family had been forced to flee from Rovigo because of persecution. Now the Lord gave us the joy of seeing a church started to his glory in that town. I felt that I was the least able to be used by God in such an adverse city because of my past, but God in his mercy has found in me an instrument for his use.

Our church has many young families, and we continue to grow in the Lord. When he put into our hearts the idea of extension, we had to overcome the indifference of the people. The Lord opened the way for us to start a local radio station, which has gone forward in spite of many difficulties. Our equipment was stolen, but the Lord has been good to us and through it all he has led us into victory. Many letters show that the radio is listened to and enjoyed, and we are continuing all the time to try to improve our quality of service to our fellow men, those who dwell in the darkness in which we were at one time. As the name of the radio station suggests, we want to be a 'Voice in the Desert', like John the Baptist, and to point men and women to the Lamb of God who alone can take away the sin of the world.

30

Mariano Rughi

Living Water – Peace with God

My conversion from Romanism to Christ did not come about in a moment but was the result of a long and painful process which took several years. It began during my college days in Assisi, Italy. One day my professor was dealing in a lecture on church history with Pope Honorius I (626–38), one of the many popes who, according to the Church, taught error. Pope Honorius I became involved in the controversy regarding the Monothelite heresy, with which he agreed. This doctrine taught that Christ had one will, his own personal will. This was in contrast with the biblical teaching that he has two natures and therefore two wills, both the human and the divine. The Third Council of Constantinople (680–1) condemned those who

supported the Monothelite heresy and this included
Pope Honorius I.

I was forcibly struck by the fact that even the Church
of Rome recognized that Pope Honorius I accepted
heretical teaching whereas in 1870 the Vatican Council
defined the dogma of papal infallibility which declared
that the Pope of Rome was absolutely inerrant in his
solemn *ex cathedra* definitions and decrees in matters of
faith and morals. I had also learned how the Fathers of
the 1870 Council explicitly stated that, although the
dogma had only just been defined, its truth had always
existed, thus implying that all the popes from Peter to
Pope Pius IX, who was still alive at the time, were all
infallible. It was claimed that they were all inspired by
God and that their succession was from the same divine
source. I felt impelled to ask my professor how the belief
of Pope Honorius could be contrary to the official
teaching of the Church. My professor replied that Pope
Honorius did teach error but that when he did so he was
not speaking *ex cathedra* as the Pope but as a private
theologian.

Rome's Lack of Assurance

In the seminary where I was living we did not follow a
strict monastic life, although we had to perform certain
penances and acts of self-denial which included fasting
and abstinence. We also had to go to the confessional
and practise meditation as well as take part in spiritual
retreats. We were taught that in spite of all this we could
not be certain of our salvation since one of the dogmas of
the Church is that anyone who claims to be sure of his
salvation is certainly lost.

Doubting Castle

I realized once more that the Church was contradicting itself but I did not dare say this to anybody for a time, and so I kept on fighting my doubts single-handedly. Then one day, being deeply concerned, I felt I must speak to my Father Confessor. His reply was quick and blunt, 'My boy, these thoughts are just temptations of the devil.'

It was clear to me that he was trying to pervert the truth in saying that my convictions which I believed were from the Holy Spirit were the work of the devil. I quoted John 3:16 to prove that my concern had a solid foundation, but my boldness merely earned me a terrific lesson on humility and on blind obedience to the Church. As you will notice, it was blind obedience to the Church that I was told to have and not to the Lord Jesus Christ.

The Confession Box

By this time I had ceased to go to the confessional regularly. I had never been enthusiastic about the spoken confessional and when I went I did so more because of outward compulsion than by inner conviction. At times I found the confessional to be a real burden and a cruel torturing of the conscience.

I stress this point because one of the arguments brought by Roman Catholics is that the practice brings a sense of comfort to the penitent as he pours out his sins into the ear of the priest, whose absolution removes the burden of sin and guilt. It is true that a kind of comfort may be experienced in this way, but it has no lasting effect and is nothing more than a passing emotion.

Later on I served five years as a priest in the Roman

Church. This may seem a short period, but it was long enough for me to learn a great deal about confession and the confessional. I heard the confessions of many people, some of whom I knew personally. In some of them there was deep sincerity and a longing to get deliverance from some besetting sin or vice and yet these people, much to their own distress, had to come week after week, confessing the same sins which quite often were shameful and hated sins. 'Why don't I get deliverance?' was their anxious question. My duty as their Father Confessor was supposed to bring them peace, but I could never give them a convincing assurance and neither could anyone else in my position.

Living Water

Think of that lovely incident when Jesus met the woman of Samaria at Jacob's well. There we have the true answer needed by thirsty souls. However, people who are deceived by being continually compelled to go to the priest for the quenching of their spiritual thirst never find the true answer. 'Jesus answered and said unto her, Whosoever drinketh of this water shall thirst again.' The Roman confessional is just like the water of Jacob's well. It is water that may satisfy but only for a time. Jesus went on to say, 'But whosoever drinketh of the water that I shall give him shall never thirst; but the water that I shall give him shall be in him a well of water springing up into everlasting life' (*John* 4:13–14).

We see here that the true source of lasting satisfaction is the Lord Jesus Christ, who knows the secret need of every sinner and who has the water for each one. Jesus also said, 'Come unto me, all ye that labour and are heavy laden, and I will give you rest' (*Matt.* 11:28). This offer comes from the heart of God, but no priest, bishop, or pope in the Church of Rome can ever give this peace of heart which they lack themselves. People remain thirsty, heavy-laden, and helpless until God himself satisfies them. Then, just as a stream fills a well, so the gift of God gives blessing after blessing with the promise of eternal life.

Ordained but Perplexed

In my own search I suddenly came up against a personal problem. The idea of giving up the vocation to the priesthood occurred to me, but I at once rejected it as a heinous temptation. I was doing my last year of theological studies and was almost ready to receive ordination. I also thought about the honour of my family, since in a Roman Catholic country it is considered a great privilege and honour to have a priest in the family. I knew that my parents and friends were all looking forward to seeing me celebrate the Mass as a priest. I now realize that these were insignificant considerations, but as I did not then know the Lord Jesus Christ as my Saviour and Lord, I felt powerless to follow my convictions. So I went through with my ordination and became a priest, after which I was sent to a parish as curate-in-charge. I began my ministry with enthusiasm and even had some success, which removed some of my old doubts. In my parish work I was in a new atmosphere and in different surroundings and I felt I had a certain freedom which I did not have in my college life. I began to take the liberty of reading the Bible and other books which were forbidden by the Church. Later on, as a parish priest, I entered into religious discussions with many people.

My Doubts Intensify

One day, during an intimate conversation with a Franciscan monk, I had a revelation that shocked me. I
discovered that he was going through the same painful
experiences regarding the assurance of salvation as
those through which I had gone. I began to ask myself,
'If the Church of Rome is the true Church of Christ, how
is it that one of its best followers, a man of integrity and a
disciplined life, is uncertain of his salvation and is
suffering intense spiritual perplexity?' My doubts revived and I found myself in another spiritual crisis, but
one which this time eventually led to my release. The
immediate consequence of this crisis was that the Mass,
the confessional and other priestly duties became a great
burden.

God's Light

Then for a time I sought release in amusements. I found
I was beginning to lose my sense of duty and, much to my
shame, I found myself falling to worldly standards of
life. My real need was not amusements but cleansing,
not pleasures but spiritual renewal. What I needed was
Jesus Christ. Was the Church able to lead me to the one
who could release me from this terrible situation? No,
Rome could only apply its canonical punishment and so
I was sent for a week to a monastery. The treatment was
not adequate to the disease. I was still fighting alone a
seemingly lost battle. Then one day a flash of divine light
revealed the darkness of my heart. What was I to do? I
decided to leave my parish and my parents and go to
Rome. I had no definite plan in mind and had no friend
in Rome to whom I could turn for help. On my first day's
search in Rome, however, I discovered an Episcopalian

Methodist church. I was able to contact its minister, to whom I opened my heart and told him about my desperate situation. I soon learned, however, that leaving the Church of Rome was not as easy as I had thought.

Rome's Stated Curse on Converted Priests

The Lateran Treaty of 1929 was a great obstacle. Its fifth article, paragraph 2 reads: 'Under no circumstances may apostate priests or those subjected to censure be appointed as teachers or allowed to continue as such nor may they hold office or be employed as clerks where they are in immediate contact with the public.' This meant that I had to choose between retiring from any kind of public life or leave my country, parents and everything that was dear to me. The latter was a terrific sacrifice, but I was given strength to do it and God opened the door for me in a remarkable way. The Methodist minister whom I had met introduced me to Professor E. Buonaiuti, an ex-Roman Catholic priest who, as a result of the Lateran Treaty, had to give up his position as a teacher of comparative religions and who was himself subject to canonical censure. This man made contact with Protestant societies in Switzerland, France and Germany for me to find a place to which I could go for refuge from Rome.

In His Light We See

Weeks and months went by with no prospect in sight, when God brought into the picture another ex-priest, the Rev. M. Casella, who was working in a parish in Northern Ireland. This was indeed a providential happening. Dr Casella happened to be writing to Prof.

Buonaiuti in Rome about a book. In his letter, Dr
Casella mentioned how he had been enabled to leave the
Church of Rome through an evangelical society in
Dublin called the Priests' Protection Society. In his
reply, Prof. Buonaiuti referred to my case, and through
this contact the final stage of my journey began.

The Priests' Protection Society came to my aid and
enabled me to get a thorough training in evangelical
Reformed doctrine at Trinity College, Dublin, spon-
sored by the Irish Church Missions. I would like to
express at this time my deep gratitude to the Priests'
Protection Society for enabling me to come out of the
darkness of Rome into the light of the gospel.

Of course it has cost me much to leave my parents, my
friends, and everything that was dear to me in Italy, but
when I decided to obey the voice of God rather than the
voice of the flesh and of the world, all my hardships were
transformed into sweetness, especially since I have
completed my spiritual journey from a sinful life to a
personal knowledge of the living Christ.

I would like to add a word of gratitude to the Irish
Church Missions in whose buildings in Dublin I was
taught to read the Word of God and where my eyes were
opened to the light of the gospel. The prophet Isaiah
taught about true, right standing before God: 'Surely,
shall one say, in the LORD have I righteousness and
strength' (*Isa.* 45:24). The apostle Paul teaches that
God's righteousness is given to the believer through
faith: 'But now the righteousness of God without the law
is manifested, being witnessed by the law and the
prophets; even the righteousness of God which is by
faith of Jesus Christ unto all and upon all them that
believe: for there is no difference' (*Rom.* 3:21–22). The
sinful condition of all men is also clearly detailed by the
apostle Paul, together with the teaching of God's grace

given freely without any human merit: 'For all have sinned, and come short of the glory of God; being justified freely by his grace through the redemption that is in Christ Jesus' (*Rom.* 3:23–24). By grace through faith a real transaction took place between God and myself. Like the apostle Paul, I can confidently say, 'I count all things but loss for the excellency of the knowledge of Christ Jesus my Lord: for whom I have suffered the loss of all things, and do count them but dung, that I may win Christ, and be found in him, not having mine own righteousness, which is of the law, but that which is through the faith of Christ, the righteousness which is of God by faith' (*Phil.* 3:8–9).

31

John Zanon

I Found Christ the Only Mediator

I was born in 1910 to poor but devout Roman Catholic parents in northern Italy. Following my ordination by Cardinal Rossi, 29 June 1935, I was sent to the United States.

A few years later I was given a table radio as a birthday gift. To my surprise and joy I was able to receive some Protestant programmes. I loved their messages and songs from the very beginning. The thing that impressed me most was that they put a great emphasis on the Bible. It seemed to me these preachers were really fulfilling Christ's mandate to 'preach the gospel to every creature' (*Mark* 16:15). In an attempt to prove how right I was in being with the Roman Catholic Church and how wrong those were who were outside of it, I began to read the Bible earnestly and prayerfully. The more I read and the harder I prayed to God, the more clearly I understood how wrong the Church of Rome was.

In the Gospel of John I read, 'But as many as received him, to them gave he power to become the sons of God' (*John* 1:12); 'For God so loved the world, that he gave his only begotten Son, that whosoever believeth in him should not perish, but have everlasting life' (*John* 3:16). The Bible could not be more clear in this all-important matter of our salvation.

Teachings Not in the Bible

Even being a Roman Catholic priest did not assure the salvation of my soul. I came to realize that my zeal and good works as a priest could not save me, because I read in the Bible: 'For by grace are ye saved through faith; and that not of yourselves: it is the gift of God: not of works, lest any man should boast' (*Eph.* 2:8–9)

This shook my faith in Roman Catholic teachings. Until now I had blindly accepted all of Rome's teachings. A Roman Catholic has no choice: either he accepts Rome's doctrines without question, or he is excommunicated. Because I was beginning to doubt everything, I started searching the Scriptures more diligently than ever. I discovered that the sacrifice of Jesus Christ on the cross was all-sufficient, 'By the which will we are sanctified through the offering of the body of Jesus Christ once for all' (*Heb.* 10:10). 'For by one offering he hath perfected for ever them that are sanctified' (*Heb.* 10:14). 'Who needeth not daily, as those high priests, to offer up sacrifice, first for his own sins, and then for the people's: for this he did once, when he offered up himself' (*Heb.* 7:27). There is no need then of Mass, confession, or purgatory.

Go to Jesus, Not to Rome

I began to realize that all these doctrines of the so-called only true Church were nothing but Roman inventions. Pursuing my studies further, I learned that devotions to Mary the mother of our Saviour and the saints were not even mentioned in the Bible. Mary herself directed the attendants at the marriage feast of Cana to go to Jesus: 'Whatsoever he saith unto you, do it' (*John* 2:5). Christ invites us to come directly to him and not through the saints as the Roman Church teaches: 'Come unto me, all ye that labour and are heavy laden, and I will give you rest' (*Matt.* 11:28). 'Jesus saith unto him, I am the way, the truth, and the life: no man cometh unto the Father, but by me' (*John* 14:6). 'If ye shall ask any thing in my name, I will do it' (*John* 14:14). And Paul, divinely inspired, wrote: 'For there is one God, and one mediator between God and men, the man Christ Jesus' (*1 Tim.* 2:5).

Once again I had to conclude from my Bible study that the thousand and one devotions to the saints were all inventions of Rome. For the first time in my life it became crystal clear that the teachings of the Roman Catholic Church were wrong. I thanked the Lord for enlightening my mind. I had no choice but to leave the Roman Catholic Church. I began formulating my plans, but the decision frightened me. I knew my parents and brothers would be hurt and the Roman Catholics would feel I had disgraced them. It would also cost me many life-long friends, security, prestige and a comfortable life. I delayed and prayed. The voice of the Lord came clear and firm, 'He that loveth father or mother more than me is not worthy of me: and he that loveth son or daughter more than me is not worthy of me' (*Matt.* 10:37).

To still this divine warning I put aside my Bible and began to work harder than ever. I recalled the vows made in seminary and particularly on the day of my ordination: to be one of the best priests. This gave me a relative peace of mind for quite a few years.

The Sword of the Word of God

In January 1955, I had a pleasant surprise. Rev. Joseph Zacchello, the editor of *The Convert* magazine, came to visit me while he was in Kansas City, Missouri. I was startled when he asked me if I was saved. This question haunted me and I prayed to God again to show me the way of salvation. The voice of the Lord came clearly and reproachfully to me: 'Think not that I am come to send peace on earth: I came not to send peace, but a sword' (*Matt.* 10:34). That sword I used to cut myself off from everybody near and dear to me.

Today, having believed on the Lord as my personal Saviour, I am experiencing how right he was when he said, 'There is no man that hath left house, or parents, or brethren, or wife, or children, for the kingdom of God's sake, who shall not receive manifold more in this present time, and in the world to come life everlasting' (*Luke* 18:29–30).

32

John Preston

From Works to the Light of the Gospel

'The truth shall make you free' (*John* 8:32). The truth of Jesus' gospel has set millions of people free from their sins, burdens and worries. This is a clear proof that the unadulterated gospel of the Holy Scriptures is still 'the power of God unto salvation to everyone that believeth' (*Rom*. 1:16). The story of my liberation from the darkness of Romanism into 'the glorious liberty of the children of God' (*Rom*. 8:21) is only another evidence of the same power.

There was nothing striking in my conversion, no sudden change or miraculous event to compel me to abandon the Roman Catholic Church and to surrender to Christ. It was only the quiet and steady working of

God's grace and the daily realization of the wrongness of a system that is erroneously called Catholic and Christian.

Finding No Assurance of Forgiveness

Born in the north of Italy of Roman Catholic parents, I was baptized and confirmed in the same faith. At the age of twelve I felt called by God to the priesthood and entered a seminary, where I spent nine years of intense and severe training. During these years a deep and lengthy crisis brought home to me for the first time the uselessness of auricular confession. My soul was darkened by sin and my spirit tortured by doubt. I sought desperately for light and peace. I went to confession almost every day, thinking to find in it forgiveness and happiness, but no matter how hard I tried or how often I confessed my sins to my Father Confessor, no assurance of forgiveness was ever given to me, no strength ever flowed into my heart to keep it pure from more and worse sins.

What a joyous contrast between my past and my present life! Now I have put all my trust in Christ; now I know whom I have believed and know that he is able to keep me 'until that day'; now I confess my sins directly to God who has cleansed me and given me a new heart, and made me a new creature, through the purifying power of Jesus' blood.

Seeking Salvation in Works

It was to overcome this inward crisis that I decided to dedicate myself to a more sacrificial life to be spent among the African people. Thus, I joined a Missionary Order, which in Italy boasts the glorious name of 'The

Sons of the Sacred Heart of Jesus' and here in England is known as the 'Verona Fathers'.

Although I am deeply indebted to the Verona Fathers for the help they gave me during my last five years of training, I cannot overlook the way in which they prepare their candidates for the religious profession and for the priesthood. The whole preparation is centred in works, in doing things. Salvation depends entirely on what we do, not on what Jesus did. We merit our eternal life or our everlasting damnation. Jesus is no longer 'the author and finisher of our faith', 'Alpha and Omega, the first and the last'. Our actions, our merits, our prayers, our year's alms and our penances take us into heaven, not Jesus. That is why, during my two years of novitiate, I was invited to flog myself and to kiss the floor of the dining room or the feet of other novices.

Seeing the Light of the Gospel

At the end of my novitiate I attended a four-year course of theological training and was ordained in Milan in 1952. After one year of ministry and of missionary deputation in northern and central Italy, I was sent to Asmara, in Eritrea, as a missionary and teacher in a big Roman Catholic college. There I made my first personal contact with Protestant missionaries and was given some literature to read. There also I realized more than ever how tyrannical the Roman Catholic system can be.

Coming to London two years later to improve my English, I went on studying the biblical faith and praying to God for light. There I happened to listen now and then to evangelical speakers at 'Speakers' Corner' in Hyde Park, and their fearless and bold exposure of Roman heresies helped me to break away at last from the Roman Catholic Church. Mr P. Pengilly, senior outdoor speaker of the Protestant Alliance, was one that influenced me.

In conclusion, I would like to assure you that while writing this testimony I do not bear any grudge against anybody. On the contrary, it is 'my heart's desire and prayer to God' (*Rom.* 10:1) that many Roman Catholic people might see the light of the gospel as I have seen it and come to rejoice in the knowledge of Jesus as their own personal Saviour. It was the great joy of this spiritual discovery and the desire to communicate it to others that prompted me to write these lines, trusting that God will have all the glory.

33

Guido Scalzi

My Encounter with God

Our little house at Mesoraca, Italy, was situated in a hamlet called Filippa which was not very far from the monastery of the Franciscan Friars, located on top of a beautiful hill. It was there that I went as a child with my family to hear Mass.

The Attraction of the Monastery

I remember one particular morning I was moved as I heard the strains of the church organ. This, with Spring just awakening, produced in my mind a strange attraction. I felt it would be wonderful to live the rest of my days in a monastery in close communion with God and with nature. I met my mother when she came out of church and cried out, 'Mama, how wonderful it would be if I could become a priest.' To say my mother was happy with my sudden decision would be an understatement. She was happier still when as the days passed I told her that I was more and more confirmed in what I sincerely considered to be the call of God for my life.

One day I asked my mother to go to the monastery with me to speak to the Father Superior. After our interview he seemed satisfied with the seriousness of my intentions and told my mother I definitely would be a priest some day. Eventually I was accepted by the director of the Franciscan seminary called Seraphic College. On 28 September 1928 I took leave of my family and, accompanied by Father Carlo, made my way by train to the seminary in the province of Cosenza.

First Years in Seminary

During the trip, my thoughts drifted back to those I had left behind. Often, without letting my companions see me, I wiped away the tears which dropped silently down my cheeks. The first days of seminary were characterized by a great flurry of activity due to the arrival of new students, and some confusion, since many of the boys did not adapt quickly to their new regimented lifestyle, quite different from the freedom they had previously enjoyed. As the cold winter approached I suffered from frostbite, flu and other illnesses. There was no heat at the college. In the morning when we awoke at the sound of the alarm, we had to walk through an open terrace to wash our faces, since there was no running water. The water would freeze in the basins so that the ice had to be broken, and we used the ice as though it were soap. Sometimes two or three days would pass before most of us would dare wash our faces. It was a hard life. The cold had a debilitating effect on my morale, which sank lower and lower each day. Though I tried to overcome all these things, I withdrew into myself more and more. I was surprised to find myself weeping. During those times, no one could console me. I remember one time Father Carlo, annoyed because of the disturbance I was creating, began slapping, punching and even kicking me. I must say that those relentless blows achieved the desired effect. From that moment on I decided to live that seminary life, even if it was most disagreeable to me. One thing I learned quickly was that I could confide in no one and that it was impossible to have a friend. Spies seemed to be everywhere. Very few memories remain of these first four years of seminary.

Brother Felice

In September 1932 I left for the monastery, where I spent my year as a novice. According to the novitiate rules of the Order of the Minor Friars of St Francis, the day one is inducted one is given a new name. So from then on I was known as 'Brother Felice' (Brother Happy). I remember the awful boredom that plagues novices, boredom coming from a forced idleness and a false solitude. Even though the novices are supposedly growing in the ways of God, in reality they are suspicious of one another and jealous over trifles, which leads to envy, quarrelling and vulgarity.

Happiness and Disillusionment as a Priest

My year as a novice ended with the ceremony of the 'simple profession' on 4 October 1933. On 7 July 1940 I was ordained to the priesthood. I received congratulations from the bishop, my superiors, and the priests who were present. I was very happy. At last I was a priest. However, my first Mass was a sad disappointment. It seemed to me to be merely acting out the rôle that I had been ordained to perform. There was no joy, no spiritual satisfaction. Where was the presence of God that I had been promised I would savour in a very real way? There was nothing but mere empty formality.

After a few years at St Francis of Assisi Convent, where I taught Italian, history, geography and religion at the intermediate junior high levels, I went to the monastery at Bisignane (Cosenza) and then to a monastery in Reggio di Calabria. It was here that I had my first face-to-face encounter with evangelical Christians.

A Fountain of Water for the Thirsty

On 15 August 1945, while passing the Evangelical Baptist Church of Reggio di Calabria, I suddenly felt a strong desire to see the minister. Finally, I found the courage to write a letter asking to see him. 'Come, you are welcome to meet with me at your convenience', was Pastor Salvatore Tortorelli's response to my note. The pastor advised me to read the Bible. 'Read it with simplicity and without preconceived notions,' he said.

I returned to the monastery and began to read the Holy Bible in Italian. To my spirit and soul it was like a fountain of water for the thirsty and sight for the blind. Each page brought new surprises and new light, like opened windows in the walls of a prison. 'Is it possible?' I would repeat to myself. 'Is it possible that I have lived so many years without ever knowing all of these marvellous things?' One day I told Pastor Tortorelli how I felt. 'The Lord is calling you out of falsehood. Leave everything, and be converted to the gospel of Jesus Christ', was his response.

My Real Fears

There were two obstacles preventing me from leaving the monastery. First of all there was the shame of being despised as an infamous person, a defrocked priest. Secondly, there was the fear of venturing out into the unknown world without having security or employment of any kind. This last point was most crucial, since the fifth article of the Concordat between the Italian government and the Vatican forbade employment of all ex-priests. With such conditions, I could not muster enough courage to leave the monastery.

Jesus Wants to Save You

Not long after I was transferred to a monastery at Staletti. One day in the village a peasant farmer signalled me to stop. He had heard of me from the Baptist pastor at Reggio di Calabria and explained that his own pastor, Domenico Fulginiti, in Gasperini, about six kilometres away, would like to meet me.

Some nights later I went to the meeting place. The house was small and very simply furnished, as are most of the homes of the Calabrian peasant farmers. There was a table with some chairs, a fireplace, and near it a dough tray and two sifters for sifting flour for bread. Near the fireplace, on the wall, hung pots and pans. Through an open door one could see a bedroom. The pastor did not make a very good first impression on me. He wore a very modest suit, without a tie. One could see he was just a simple peasant. 'What kind of pastor is this?' I thought, as Pastor Domenico Fulginiti was introduced to me. I thought that at any moment he would pull out his Bible to witness to me, but instead, looking at me with great tenderness, he said, 'By now you know everything there is to know about the Word of God. What you need now is salvation. Jesus wants to save you. He died on the cross to save your soul.' He continued speaking to me about the 'new birth'. He told me the story of Nicodemus, who went to look for Jesus by night, and then repeated the words of the Master: 'Art thou a master of Israel, and knowest not these things?' 'Born again, if I could only be born again,' I thought to myself. To blot out all of my painful past, all of my errors, all of my delusions, all of my sins, all of the filth and mire my soul had accumulated, and begin a new life, a pure life before God and man: if I could only be born again!

A Real Prayer of Faith

'You must be born again,' the peasant kindly repeated to me. I did not know what to say, but I was content to agree with him, as he continued saying these things with great conviction. He spoke with simplicity. There was no trace of superiority in his words. He used no flowery professorial tones. After a little while he got up and said to me, 'If you don't mind, may we pray before we go our separate ways?' 'Of course we can pray,' I answered him. He knelt and raised his hands toward heaven as he closed his eyes in prayer. My eyes were wide open. He began by thanking God for the opportunity that he gave me to hear the words of salvation. He went on asking God to purify my heart from all sin and wash my soul in the precious blood of Jesus, his only begotten Son, who died on the cross to pay the price to redeem my soul. He continued that way for a while. I was kneeling also, of course, with some reluctance, and I followed his prayer with scepticism, smiling within myself when he alluded to my sins. What could he know? I kept looking at him;

he kept his eyes closed, while his hands reached towards heaven imploringly. The intensity of his prayer exuded from his entire being. It was truly a prayer of faith. I had never heard anyone pray like that in all my life. Nevertheless, that prayer seemed to be true prayer, fully corresponding to the teachings of Jesus, who warned against mechanical repetitions but rather encouraged prayers according to the need of the moment. What could have been more urgent than the salvation of my soul?

Eternal Life Is in His Son

Suddenly I closed my eyes and my past life flashed before me. All of my sins, all of my vices, all of my pride, my lustfulness, my hypocrisy, my lies and many other things. I saw myself covered with every type of sin, as a leper covered with his repulsive sickness. My condition frightened me. With anguish, I wondered how I could free myself from this oppressive situation. In that instant, I remembered certain words mentioned earlier in the prayer: 'The blood of Jesus purifies us from all sin.' It was then I understood what it meant to be truly free. It was then I abandoned myself into the hands of Jesus, my Saviour, desperately seeking his help. 'Lord, have mercy on me, a sinner. Save my soul,' I cried. I was going through a great crisis. On one hand I saw my present life, the pleasures and comfort it offered; I saw my relatives, friends and all those who respected me for what I was. On the other hand I saw the unknown, a life of work and sacrifice; but I also saw Jesus with open arms, ready to receive me unto himself, ready to give me a new heart, a new soul, a new life, full of his grace, his love, and peace. In the words of Scripture, I knew that 'this is the record, that God hath given to us eternal life, and this life is in his Son' (*1 John* 5:11).

Trusting Jesus Totally

I sensed peace come into my heart. For the first time in my life, I truly felt the presence of Jesus. He was there with us in that room. He accepted my repentance. He received me unto himself and he spoke to me. His voice was sweet to my ear. He calmed the anxiety of the heart. Darkness fled from my mind. His presence was so alive I had the impression that if I extended my hand, I could touch his garment. It was he, my Lord, my Master, Jesus.

Brother Fulginiti became aware that something very important had taken place within me and that the Lord had answered his prayer. He embraced me and said, 'The Lord touched your heart; believe on him only; do not postpone it. Who knows if you will be given another opportunity to hear Jesus' invitation? The enemy will always try to hinder you from entering into the way of salvation.' With my eyes full of tears, I replied, 'Brother, I have decided to serve the Lord for life or death.'

Since my conversion and departure from Roman Catholicism, I have had the privilege of working as a missionary pastor, evangelist and founder and director of 'La Voce Della Speranza' (The Voice of Hope) which is broadcast from several radio stations in the United States and Europe. May the Lord continue to fulfil through us the ministry foretold by Isaiah: 'To appoint unto them that mourn in Zion, to give unto them beauty for ashes, the oil of joy for mourning, the garment of praise for the spirit of heaviness; that they might be called trees of righteousness, the planting of the Lord, that he might be glorified' (*Isa.* 61:3).

34

Benigno Zuniga

Transformed by Christ

Until I was over fifty years of age I lived in complete
spiritual darkness. Despite having been a priest
for many years, my knowledge about Jesus Christ was
very limited and distorted. In fact, for me, the real
Christ of the Bible had been hidden under a blanket of
complex religious teaching.

I believed that outside the Roman Catholic Church
there was no possibility of salvation and that the Pope,
as Christ's representative on earth, was infallible. My
loyalty was so great that I would have been willing to
give my life in defence of the Pope.

The Teaching of the Church

I had been educated by Jesuit Fathers and decided to become a Jesuit monk at the age of sixteen. I studied in Peru, Ecuador, Spain and Belgium and was later ordained a priest. For many years I taught in Roman Catholic schools, held a position as a professor in a seminary, served as Vice-Chancellor of the Ecclesiastical Tribunal in my diocese, held the office of a chaplain in the army and served as a priest of two of the principal parishes of my country.

As a parish priest I set myself to opposing the Protestants in my area. I treated them as heretics, and I taught my people that they all held the lowest possible moral standards. As some of these Protestants continually appealed to the authority of the Bible, I decided to write a book exposing their error in the light of the Bible.

The Teaching of God

As I studied the Bible chapter by chapter over a period of three years, it came as a terrible shock to me to discover that I was the one in error. Far from being able to refute these heretics I found myself being refuted by my own Roman Catholic Bible. I began to see how far away from the Bible my Roman Catholic beliefs were. Often as I studied I found myself moved to tears to think that I had submissively followed human ideas rather than the teaching of God.

Another effect of reading the Bible chapter by chapter was that I found my conscience came to life within me. I saw that personally I was a long way from God. As a priest I projected an image of holiness, but in reality I gave way to all kinds of sin and lived a thoroughly worldly life. The black robes which I wore symbolized the darkness of my heart. No amount of sacraments, prayers to the saints, penitence, holy water or confession of sin to a human confessor could give me the peace which my soul began to long for.

Transformed by Christ

One day, although a priest over fifty years of age, I at last surrendered my heart to God. I knelt before Christ, who, though invisible, became real and living to me. Feeling like a nobody and with sorrow in my heart, I repented of having offended him by my awful life of sin. In my imagination I saw the cross, where his precious blood was shed to save me from the punishment I so richly deserved. The result of this prayer was that Christ transformed my life. He called me out of the 'tomb' of spiritual darkness and brought me into a living experience and knowledge of himself.

The secret of true spiritual reality is to have a personal meeting with Christ through a sincere and vibrant faith. When Christ takes over a heart, every other spiritual blessing is assured.

35

Bruno Bottesin

I Was Not Antagonistic to the Truth

I was born in Vicenza, Italy, in 1917. At the age of eleven I entered the Franciscan College to study for the priesthood. After my ordination I became the pastor of a small mountain parish of Castagnaro. In 1954 I was transferred to a larger parish in the city of Chieti. Then Bishop Piasentini invited me to teach in the seminary in Chioggia and also assigned me to a church there.

Unchanged Lives

At last I thought I had found the right place for my ministry. I was a teacher in the seminary, pastor of a good parish, and had gained the favour of the bishop. I organized a very fine Catholic Action group. I worked

day and night for my people with great zeal, but very soon
I began to realize that all my activities and teaching of the
catechism and Roman dogma were not able to change the
lives of my people. They came to church every Sunday, to
the sacraments, and even to confession but they refused to
follow the teachings of the gospel of Christ. How could I
continue to give the sacraments to people who did not
want to give up their sins? They pretended to be Christians
but they did the opposite of what Christ told us to do in his
gospel. Most of my people who did not want to sacrifice for
Christ and change their sinful lives began to oppose me
and many of them would say, 'What foolish things are
being taught. Why should we change our way of life when
we already do what the Roman Catholic Church asks us?
We receive communion, take our children to the priests to
be baptized and confirmed. We were married by the
priest, we abstain from meat on Friday and we go to
church on Sunday. What more does our new pastor want
from us? We are Christians because we belong to the
Roman Church.'

Christ Only

Someone reported me to the bishop. He called me to his
home and told me that I must give up my position as a
teacher and a pastor because I was not following the
teachings and instructions of the Roman Catholic
Church. He said that I was telling people to go to Christ
and depend upon him instead of telling them to depend
upon the saints of the Roman Church, the sacraments
and the priests who had the same power as Christ had to
forgive sins. I tried in vain to convince my bishop that I
was not teaching heresy but only the gospel, that they
could not be forgiven their sins unless they repented
towards God because there is only 'one Mediator

between God and men, the man Christ Jesus'. The bishop became very irritated and removed me from my position as a pastor and teacher. I told him that I was going to appeal to Rome, to the Pope, and he suggested that I go ahead.

The Grace of God in a Quiet Room

I left for Rome within a few days after preparing my argument, and I went to the Vatican to present my case to Pope Pius XII. For several days I had no answer. Then I was informed that the Pope had no time to hear my case, and I would have to appeal to the Sacred Congregation. At this time I realized that I was left alone, that even the one who calls himself the vicar of Christ and the Holy Father had let me down. In short, I was helpless. I began to realize the difference between the gospel and a church organization. The gospel is for the people, but the organization of the Roman Catholic Church is not set up for the benefit of the individual but for its political and social leaders.

I left Rome and returned to my people, but when I returned I had no church or teaching position. I did not give up but definitely put my trust in the Lord. I remained in town among my people. A friend gave me a room, and there in the quietness of this room, after so many trials and tribulations with the bishop and in Rome, I started to read the New Testament for comfort. Never before had I read any book with such interest. To my surprise, I found the answer to many doubts that I had about some of the teachings of the Roman Church. Very soon, by the grace of God, I began to realize that most of the dogmas and teachings that I as a priest had been urging my people to believe were not in the gospel but were man made, even against the Holy Bible. I began to see that for seventeen years I had not been a servant of Jesus Christ and his priest but the servant of a powerful organization.

Why Seventeen Years to Discover the Truth?

It may seem surprising that it took so long for me to discover the truth. But you must remember that a candidate for the priesthood enters the seminary as just a boy and is an adult when he completes his full training. As a result it is not easy to decide against the Roman Catholic Church. Do you think that all priests believe what they teach? Many of them do not, but they remain in the priesthood because they are afraid to break away. I could not continue to serve two masters, the Pope and Christ.

Christ's Work – Not Ours

I have chosen Christ and received him as my personal Saviour. 'Not by works of righteousness which we have done, but according to his mercy he saved us, by the washing of regeneration, and renewing of the Holy Ghost' (*Titus* 3:5). I am now preaching the true gospel with freedom and without restrictions in the same town where I was a priest. Persecutions are many but the Lord is powerful. Several people have been converted.

My dear priests, if you are reading this, do not be antagonistic to the truth, but seek it in the gospel and preach the truth from the Bible. You must not adapt the gospel to your teachings; but you must be changed according to the gospel. If you do not turn to the gospel truths there will be no hope or happiness for you but only darkness, sorrow and sin. As Christ said to the religious men of his own day, 'If ye believe not that I am he, ye shall die in your sins' (John 8:24).

36

Renato di Lorenzo

A Monk for Twenty Years, Then Born Again

I would never have believed that I would leave the Roman Catholic Church, even less the priesthood. If someone had predicted it, I would have thought it impossible.

I entered the Salesian Order at the age of fifteen and in due time I was ordained to the priesthood. I worked mainly with young people and enjoyed this work very much. Then, after nearly ten years as a priest, my Father Superior imposed a punishment on me, sending me to Rome for one month to perform spiritual exercises. The reason was that I had told him that I had experienced an affection for a young woman. I had broken off the relationship partly because I was not sure that I was truly

in love with her, but also because I had consecrated my
life to God and was not prepared to retract my commitment. There was, of course, much pride and selfishness
in my decision. It would have been somewhat humiliating for me to have to confess that I had been 'unfaithful'
to my priestly calling. I had asked my superior for a
transfer to another monastery, but instead of receiving a
fatherly talk I was duly served with the letter informing
me of my punishment. I knew that for the rest of my life
this blot would stand against me, and I would always be
viewed with suspicion.

Life under the Law of the Church

During my month in Rome desperate and bitter
thoughts surfaced in my mind. Sometimes I wanted to
escape, it did not matter where. Other times I yearned
for my work in Naples. I passed through moments of
very deep depression. I called upon the Lord in prayer,
but everything in and around me remained silent. I felt
completely alone, as if in a prison, constantly aggrieved
and assured of my innocence.

The monastery was situated on Mount Selie, near old
Rome, and commanded a view over the whole of Rome
and the Colosseum. From it I could watch ordinary life
as it flowed beneath me. I saw how people enjoyed one
another's company and loved each other, and I asked
myself whether they really offended God in so doing. I
wanted to mix with these people. I longed to discard my
black robes, my cassock – which made me feel like an
unreal person – and to be a genuine person like everyone
else.

I confided in an old Father and explained my feelings
to him. He suggested that I write to my superior, asking
him to give me permission to return to my former work.

My superior answered that I must bear all these unpleasant experiences as penance for my sin and unfaithfulness. However, he did give me permission to go out in the day.

So I went out. I did not travel about Rome as a pilgrim as he clearly intended, but as a tourist. I bought gaudy newspapers and magazines, yet I was not satisfied. I used the opportunity to ask advice of many other priests. Their reasoning always ended at the same point: I should never have put my problem before my superior but should have kept quiet. My superior had acted in accordance with church law, even though he had interpreted it in the strictest manner.

I returned to Naples, not to continue my work there, but rather to go back to my parents.

Rome's Teaching Contrary to Scripture

During my time in Rome I had spent some time retracing my steps through the teaching of the Roman Catholic Church and comparing it with the teaching of the Bible. I began to see that the Bible was wrongly and unfairly quoted merely to substantiate church teaching.

I had been taught to believe in the Roman Catholic Church on the grounds that I could only find Christ through the Church. Obedience to Christ, according to Roman Catholic teaching, meant subjection to Christ's substitute on earth, namely the Pope. However, as I read through the Gospels in my 'punishment-cell', I saw that this teaching was contrary to what was written there.

Searching for Truth

In Rome I frequently consulted the telephone directory for the address of a Protestant church, although at that point Protestantism did not exactly fill me with confidence. The only reason I was inclined to contact Protestants was for help in leaving my Church and beginning a new life. I never thought they could help me in my struggles of faith.

During my stay with my family in Naples the thought about contacting Protestants came back to me, and I began to wonder whether they might be right after all. During this time I was allowed to fulfil all my priestly functions, but during a period of seven months I only read Mass twenty times, heard confession on even fewer occasions, and never wanted to preach.

One Sunday, I avoided Mass and went for a walk. During that walk I noticed a building displaying literature about the Bible. It was the entrance of an evangelical church. I did not venture in as I thought I might cause a commotion by going in dressed in my Roman Catholic clerical garments, so I phoned the minister and visited him privately to explain my case.

He put me in touch with several ex-Roman Catholic priests who helped me very much, but I was not yet willing to leave my Church. I was afraid of making a decision which might be influenced by my recent punishment. I therefore resumed my duties as a priest and spiritual leader among young people and, though I threw myself into all manner of religious work with great energy, I found that I developed an increasing repugnance for it.

I no longer believed in the Mass, nor in the priestly hearing of confession. I had several conversations with my new superior, who was very alarmed at how near I had drifted to Protestantism. He advised me to pray very much to Mary, saying that she would help me find my faith again.

'Ye Must Be Born Again'

My departure from the priesthood was now inevitable, and within a short time I left Naples and made my way to the well known 'refuge' for ex-priests in Velp, Holland. In this home, as a result of reading the Bible and praying to God for forgiveness and help, I came to find Christ in a personal way. I underwent that experience of conversion which Christ declares as necessary: 'Ye must be born again' (*John* 3:7). 'And as Moses lifted up the serpent in the wilderness, even so must the Son of man be lifted up: that whosoever believeth in him should not perish, but have eternal life. For God so loved the world, that he gave his only begotten Son, that whosoever believeth in him should not perish, but have everlasting life' (*John* 3:14–16).

Every birth involves effort and pain. Twenty years of monastic life, coupled with my Roman Catholic theological training and my obstinate character, provided great hindrances to my seeking and finding God. But finally I yielded to the Lord in childlike surrender and said simply, 'Lord, I believe.'

Since then the Lord has never forsaken me. He has strengthened my faith through both joy and sorrow and has truly made himself known to me as a living and personal Friend and Saviour.

37

Franco Maggiotto

Saved while Officiating at Mass

During my teens I was very active in the Roman Catholic Church. I was studying for a degree in philosophy and working in an organization called Roman Catholic Action. But none of this activity gave meaning to my life, nor could it suffocate the sense of sin that I had in my heart. My soul was full of the uselessness of everything. I was in despair.

I had everything that a young man could have. My family was well-established, with feet on the ground, as we say in Italy. They had money, so I had everything that human power could provide, but I did not have that which a man must have to live before God.

Reaching for God

So I went to my bishop to tell him this. He said that I was
a very nice boy, but I did not need to have this kind of
problem. Jesus Christ, before going up to heaven, gave
up all his own authority into the hand of Peter, into the
hand of the Pope and the apostles. Therefore I would
find the kingdom of God in the Church. I would learn
how to deal with sin. The Church had all the means to
cleanse souls in the sacraments. I could use the sacraments
to cleanse my soul, to reach through the sacrament a
sure way to meet God. And so I chose, as many young
people do with enthusiasm, the hardest way that the
Roman Catholic Church had to offer, and became a
hermit. I went into a hermitage on a hill near Rome. I
could see Rome from there. I shaved only twice a week
and dressed in one big robe made from wool, the same in
winter and summer. In summer the heat was terrible and
in the winter it was very cold. I was doing all these things
with all my heart to try to destroy my sin through earthly
power, through the human will. I had to reach God and I
was almost killing myself trying to reach him.

Into the Priesthood

After I had been a hermit for almost a year, I had to
leave for medical reasons. I planned to come back later.
However, I decided to go to a seminary to study
theology. I became a priest and was sent into a big parish
with another priest. He was over eighty years old, so I
had to do everything.

I tried to be very nice to the people even though I was
sad. I enjoyed being a priest but I was not happy in
my soul; and, notwithstanding everything I did, I had
nothing with which to meet God. I did not have any

sense of assurance; my sin was still there. When I sought help about this I was told to read the Gospel of Luke. One verse was really a stumbling block for me. It was this sentence: 'He that heareth you heareth me; and he that despiseth you despiseth me; and he that despiseth me despiseth him that sent me' (*Luke* 10:16).

My bishop told me that before going up to heaven, Jesus Christ gave up all his authority to the bishops. Therefore if someone did not listen to them, he did not listen to Jesus. If we despised Jesus we despised God, and so I was even afraid of thinking. I did not need to think. I just needed to trust my bishop.

What Jesus Commanded

One day, almost in desperation, some young people and I began to translate the New Testament from the Greek. It was enjoyable at first, but the more we went on, the more we saw the gap between the Church's teaching and the Bible. The biggest gap I could see was that Jesus Christ sought to bring men to God, while the Church was always trying to bring men to itself.

When we finished the first translation of the Gospel of Matthew, my parish priest was really upset because I was teaching the Bible. 'If they know what we know they will never come back; they will never come to the Church,' he said. But when we came to the end of the last chapter something became clear. Jesus said to his apostles, 'Go ye therefore, and teach all nations, baptizing them in the name of the Father, and of the Son, and of the Holy Ghost: teaching them to observe all things whatsoever I have commanded you: and, lo, I am with you alway, even unto the end of the world. Amen' (Matthew 28:19–20).

So, yes, Jesus Christ did say to his followers, 'He who

hears you, hears me; he who despises you, despises me.'
But Jesus never told them to teach whatever they liked;
whatever would make them important; whatever would
build a big, powerful, earthly Church; whatever would
make the people happy, and if the people despised them
they despised him. He said, 'Go and teach whatsoever I
have commanded you, everything I have already said to
you. And, of course, if you go, and if you say whatsoever
I have commanded you, no more and no less, then, if
they despise you they despise me.' I had to learn more
about this gap between Church and Bible.

Trouble with the Church

So I read the Scriptures more; and the more I read, the
more I discovered. I found myself preaching some things
that were against myself as a Roman Catholic priest. I
was not using my sermon on Sunday mornings to build
up my authority any more, but I was using my sermon
against myself. This brought me into trouble. At first,
they had me conduct Mass at six o'clock in the morning.
There were very few people, just a few ladies saying
their rosaries. I could cry and shout there. But after a
few weeks, the Mass was packed. The authorities knew
that something was going to happen, so the bishop called
me in. He was very upset, and he told me he was going to
send me to another parish. I was promoted to a big
parish of fifty-five thousand people in the town of
Imperia with a new church and a priest under me.

There I found myself in a good position for one so
young. I was a senior priest and I liked to be there with
all the other priests around me listening to me and
saying, 'Oh, he is so young, he has a good career before
him, what a good looking man.' When I look back on it
now I am ashamed. But at that time I was unhappy. I

tried to find out something from the Scriptures and when
I did that I always drew people. Sometimes the people
were coming by busloads, and again I got into trouble
with the authorities. The cardinal told me that there was
no truth outside the Church, and that when Jesus went
up to heaven he gave up his authority into the hands of
the apostles, so the Christian should seek from the
apostle, which is the Pope, guidance, preaching, teaching, rebuking, and so on.

Salvation in Christ Alone

I told the young people of my parish that in our meetings
we would see what the Lord would say to us through the
Bible. One day I read Galatians 1. When I reached verse
8, I could read no further: 'But though we, or an angel
from heaven, preach any other gospel unto you than that
which we have preached unto you, let him be accursed.'
I was shocked. The apostle Paul was saying, 'If I, or the
other apostles, or even an angel, preach to you any other
gospel than the one we have preached, may a curse rest
on us, because there is no salvation in the apostles.
Salvation is in Christ alone.'

The Holy Spirit is the Teacher

I continued to teach my people. The bishop said, 'You
are very proud. Who do you think you are? Do you think
that you can understand the Scriptures better than I,
better than the Pope?' I knew that I had been proud. I
knew that I liked my position, but now I knew where to
look to find the answer – the Scriptures. I knew that I
was a poor sinner and sin was still there to destroy me.

I searched the Old and New Testaments to find where
God had given to the prophets or apostles the power to

interpret Scripture. Nowhere did I find that he had done so. What I did find were the words of Jesus in John 14:26. Before going up to heaven, he told the apostles, 'But the Comforter, which is the Holy Ghost, whom the Father will send in my name, he shall teach you all things, and bring all things to your remembrance, whatsoever I have said unto you.' The Holy Spirit is the teacher, the interpreter of Scripture.

This gave me a lot of courage. Of course I had trouble. I was transferred to another parish, an old parish with nine churches. They thought that going round them all would take up all my energy and leave no time to study, but I went and I managed to preach. Still, most of the time, I was not happy because of my sin. Now I knew where to find out the truth, but what about my sin? What about my soul? I was spending nights kneeling in front of the altar; and, sometimes the caretaker was helping me in the morning, because I had been kneeling there until morning. But the Lord had pity on me while I was conducting the Mass.

The Victory of the Cross

One Sunday I was leading the singing of Mass. Two priests were with me and the choir was singing beautifully. One of the young men read Hebrews 10:10: 'By the which will we are sanctified through the offering of the body of Jesus Christ once for all.' Verse 11 continues: 'And every priest standeth daily ministering and offering oftentimes the same sacrifices, which can never take away sins' (*Heb.* 10:11).

I said to the priests who were with me, 'Do you hear him? Look what is written here.' I was looking at them, and they were staring at me. 'His sacrifice is finished. Our Mass is useless.'

I was looking around the big church. The people there were groaning and crying, and I said, 'He has finished the sacrifice. He did the work, we are useless.' I was so happy, I was crying. Finally something was clear in my mind. Once for ever, once for all, he did the work. The Lord's sacrifice is all-sufficient and complete.

God Alone Forgives Sin

The people said that I was ill; that all this responsibility for a young man like me was too much. Anyway, I was so happy. I told my bishop the same thing when he came to see me. He did not want me to resign, but I could not say the Mass any more. He sent me to a college with eight hundred young students and teachers. I went but I did not want to attend the Mass. I tried to teach others, even the nuns. They were very attentive.

On Saturday evenings the people came to confession. I asked them, 'Why are you here?'; 'To confess my sin,' they replied. 'Do you love Jesus?'; 'Yes.' 'Why do you love him?'; 'Because he died for my sins.' 'So, if he died for your sins, go and praise him. Why do you come to tell your sins to me? What have I got to do with your sin?' And so the confession was very quick. But the nuns went to the bishop, and finally I saw that they could not understand what I taught. So I left the Roman Catholic Church forever, with some people following me. I had studied in the University of Rome and in England and Holland. I met many born-again Christians, people of whom I could say, 'Thy God is my God, thy people are my people.' Now I have plenty of Christian fellowship. I am in contact with many priests and two years ago I preached to three thousand priests in Rome. Christian communities are growing up all over Italy. It is my desire to lead Roman Catholics to Christ, and if at all possible, to see even the Pope converted. 'Therefore being justified by faith, we have peace with God through our Lord Jesus Christ' (*Rom.* 5:1).

38

Edoardo Labanchi

I Received Mercy

The only religion of which I had any knowledge was that of the Roman Catholic Church. So I decided to become a priest and joined the Jesuit Order. My superiors seemed to be quite satisfied with me, and I was admitted to take the vows which are usually taken only after two years of probation. This gave me a certain satisfaction, I must admit, but it was only a human satisfaction. I felt that I was doing something different from other people; and, like the Pharisee standing in the temple before the altar looking down at the publican, I felt I was not like the rest. I was in the Roman Catholic Church and considered as one who was going to be perfect. Indeed, I was so ambitious that I asked to be sent as a missionary, feeling that in this way I might be able to lead an ever higher spiritual life. So it happened that I was sent from my homeland of Italy to Ceylon (now called Sri Lanka).

Ceylon

When I arrived in Ceylon, not yet an ordained priest, I was sent to work in a college before starting my theological studies. The Jesuits have a long period of training. Very soon I became greatly disillusioned at the lack of any zeal on the part of the Roman Catholic missionaries to convert the heathen. I saw them engaged in teaching in schools. I saw their elaborate churches, but I saw very little real 'evangelism' as I understood it at that time. I realized that the atmosphere was quite dead.

India

In due course I was sent to India for my theological studies and, eventually, was ordained as a priest. During my studies I came face to face with the heathen religions of Hinduism, Buddhism and Islam, and I began to be challenged deeply about my own religion and to ask myself what, essentially, was the difference between Christianity and these heathen religions. They had their holy books and writings. They had high ideals and commandments and tried to live up to them. A Hindu would readily put a picture or image of Christ among his other gods and still remain a devout Hindu. Was there any basic difference between these religions and Christianity, or were all religions really the same?

Some Light

It was at this time that I began, little by little, to see the light, and I must admit that I began to do so in spite of

being in the Roman Catholic Church. I was nearing the
end of my theological studies, but it was certainly not
from them that I was getting the light, nor was it from my
professors, nor from my devotions, nor from my obedience to the Pope. I can assure you of that. The means
that God was using was the reading and the study of the
Bible, of his Word. Even before this, I had felt a certain
attraction to the Bible, to something pure and real that
spoke to the heart and could be understood, something
that was more than merely human. I now continued to
read and study the Bible with close attention, and as I
did so I began to realize that the basic difference
between Christianity and the heathen religions lay, not
principally in commandments or doctrines, but in the
person of Jesus Christ. I began to meditate on what the
Bible said about him and about his redemptive work,
and as I did so he began to become more and more real
to me. Little by little, Christ became like the sun
beginning to rise on the horizon of my life. Although I
still held a great many Roman Catholic doctrines,
something wonderful was happening to me.

After Ordination

In 1964, after my ordination, I was sent to Ceylon again.
Now I went as a priest, and it was at this time that I was
sent to a town in the centre of the island to give a series of
lectures on the Bible to some Roman Catholic cate-
chists, because my superiors knew that I had made a
special study of it. On one occasion I visited the
evangelical church of the town. I had, of course, seen
this small evangelical church before, but always despised it. Nearby was a large, imposing Roman Catholic
church, and I used to think, 'What do these puny
Protestants think they can do? If the heathen are to be

converted, it will be through the great Roman Catholic Church.' On this particular day, however, I had an impulse to go inside. Perhaps it was the new ecumenical movement that made me feel that we now had to be kind and friendly to the 'separated brethren'. Evidently they were surprised to see me enter, but they received me very kindly and gave me some leaflets and literature. I could not help being impressed by the zeal and devotion of these people. Some of them were Swedish missionaries and others were Ceylonese Christians and workers. They were holding an evangelistic campaign, distributing leaflets and invitations in the streets and even the children among them were enthusiastically helping in this task. I had not seen such zeal in the Roman Catholic Church. I also saw that they were trying to convert me.

Personal Fellowship with Christ?

One of the papers they gave me interested me greatly. It was a devotional journal called the *Herald of His Coming* which is now published in a number of languages, including an edition in Italian, published in Rome. The articles in this paper constantly referred to the new birth, to a personal surrender to Christ, and to a new life lived in fellowship with him. I already knew these things in theory, but here they seemed alive, real and personal. 'After all,' I thought, 'this is what the gospel is all about and what it should be.' I continued to meet these evangelicals on a number of occasions, and they gave me other gospel leaflets and booklets, some published by the Scripture Gift Mission, as well as subsequent numbers of the *Herald of His Coming*. This literature helped to bring me closer to the Lord. I then returned to India for some months to complete my theological studies, and here, too, I had contact with other evangelicals.

God Continues to Work

It was at this point in my life that God's work became more noticeable than before. Increasingly, I felt that I ought to go back to Italy. At the same time, another development took place. The Ceylonese government decided that all foreign missionaries should gradually be sent out of the country and, as a start, they refused re-entry to Ceylon to those who were already outside. I was also unable to stay in India since my residence permit allowed me to stay there only until the completion of my studies. Our superiors therefore decided to send us back to our own countries and I was told to prepare to return to Italy. Before leaving, I wrote to the director of the Italian edition of the *Herald of His Coming* in Rome, saying that, although a Roman Catholic priest, in the spirit of the ecumenical movement, I had read the paper and liked it very much; and I should like to co-operate with them when I got back to Italy, as far as might be possible and compatible with my office and function as a priest.

A Bible Professor

After about two months in my native city of Naples, my superiors sent me to Rome to become a specialist in the Bible. They knew that in India I had been very interested in the Bible and that I was keen to know still more about it; and the Roman Catholic authorities seemed to think that the Bible might form a bridge to the Protestant churches in the ecumenical movement. I was accordingly sent to the highest Roman Catholic Biblical

Institute in Rome. Realizing that this was a great privilege and honour, I decided when I got to Rome to have nothing further to do with these evangelicals or Protestants. I had no further wish to collaborate with them nor with the *Herald of His Coming.* I now intended to devote myself entirely to the study of the Bible and to prepare myself for my future ministry. I had absolutely no time to have anything further to do with the Protestants. Looking back, I can see that I felt deep in my heart that if I met them I might have to come to a decision and take a step, the prospect of which made me afraid.

I Try to Give the Gospel

So I went on with my studies and assisted as a priest in a church in Rome where I preached on Sundays and holy days to perhaps a thousand people. I listened to confessions and did the things a Roman Catholic priest can do. In my sermons I tried to give the gospel message, and in the confessional I tried to give real spiritual help and advice to tell people about the new birth. I felt the responsibility and importance of these intimate personal contacts, and I thought that besides speaking to them it would be a good thing to give them something to take away and read. It was clear that it would need to be a small booklet, something in simple Italian. It was also important that it should be something I could give them free of charge, so that people could accept it without any difficulty. My problem was where to obtain such booklets.

I then thought of the booklets that I had received in India and Ceylon which were published by the Scripture Gift Mission and others. Someone told me of an evangelical book room in Rome. At first I was a little hesitant to go, but I did so, thinking that after all it was only a book room and that I could go in, do my business, and come out again quickly. Entering the book room I was received very kindly by the man in charge. There was a good range of pamphlets, and I chose those that I thought would be suitable. While the man was wrapping them up, we chatted and I mentioned that I had been a missionary in India and Ceylon. I then noticed that something strange seemed to be taking place. The man and his wife were looking first at me and then at one another. They were exchanging glances and a few words, and I thought that there must be something wrong with my black gown. Then he asked me, 'By the way, what is your name?' I answered, 'Edoardo Labanchi.' 'Have you ever written a letter to the director of the *Herald of His Coming* here in Rome?' he asked, and went on, 'You see, your letter was sent here. I am the editor, and I have your letter here.' Then he actually showed me the letter and said, 'Look, you say here that you would like to collaborate with us.'

God Corners Me

There are, I think, moments in our lives when we feel as if God is cornering us. In one way it was just a sequence of human events; but, at that moment, I felt that something unusual had happened in my life. I felt that God wanted me to have contact with these people, and from that day onwards I continued to meet the friends in the book room which is also the premises of the Christian Service Centre from which various evangelistic activities are carried on. They also invited me, very kindly, to their meetings held in homes. I attended regularly and got to know other believers. This greatly enriched my own spiritual experience but, what is still more important, they began to pray for me, and not only in Italy but also in Britain. They had friends everywhere, and the news went around that a Roman Catholic priest was meeting with them in their centre in Rome and that prayer was asked for him.

Already Founded on the Bible and Christ

By 1966, in my heart and mind, I was already an evangelical, or rather, Christ was becoming more and more the foundation of my life. I began to discard all those Roman Catholic doctrines and practices which have little or nothing to do with the gospel. At the same time I was helping to translate articles for the Italian *Herald of His Coming*, but I had not yet gone all the way in my conversion. At that time the Vatican Council was very much to the fore, and there was more and more talk about the ecumenical movement. I thought, 'Why should I leave the Roman Catholic Church, because we are practically all the same now. We shall all get together and now I can work in the Roman Catholic Church and help to spread the gospel while still following the Roman Catholic Church.' That was my idea, but after a time I became very disappointed with the Vatican Council and the ecumenical movement and wondered what to do. My position, as you will see, was very difficult. I was not what a Roman Catholic would call an ordinary layman. I was an ordained priest. I belonged to the greatest order in the Roman Catholic Church. I had been sent to Rome for special studies, and, of course, my superiors had a special eye on me. At the same time I felt in bondage on account of all the regulations and official doctrines, and I began to realize that it was impossible for me to remain in it for very long without revealing what I really thought in the depths of my heart and without compromise with my conscience. For a time I tried to adapt myself to circumstances thinking that I could do good by remaining where I was. I used to speak about Christ and salvation, referring to Mary only as an example to follow, but my position as a priest compelled me to compromise with what I knew to be right. I knew the decision I ought to make but still tried to put it off. Then the Lord himself made me see that I must act and do so at once. I remembered what Elijah said to the people in the Bible, 'How long halt ye between two opinions?' (*1 Kings* 18:21). It was in fact at this point that God himself took control and gave me the strength. Almost in spite of myself I said to my friends in the book room, 'I have decided to leave the Roman Catholic Church, and, if you think I should do so, I would like to help you with your work here in the centre in Rome.' They were taken unawares by my decision and yet had really been expecting it for some time. Some days later I left the Jesuit Order.

New Life in Christ

The point I want to emphasize very strongly as my final word is that the important thing in my story and in the story of others who have come along a similar path to mine is not that we have left the Roman Catholic Church, left an organization, or a religion. The important thing is that we have found a new life in Jesus Christ. I have yet a long way to go and I say with Paul, 'Not as though I had already attained, either were already perfect' (*Phil.* 3:12), but I know that at the moment when I received Christ as my Saviour and Lord, the Christ who died for my sins, something happened within me. I became a new creature. Paul desired to be 'found in him, not having mine own righteousness, which is of the law, but that which is through the faith of Christ, the righteousness which is of God by faith' (*Phil.* 3:9). I have willingly laid aside all the material benefits and honours I might have had in the Jesuit Order. Any such crowns I gladly lay at Jesus' feet, together with my life, my time, and such talents as I have, that he may use me just as he wills. I thank Jesus Christ my Lord that, though formerly I blasphemed, persecuted and insulted him, I received mercy because I did it ignorantly in unbelief.

39

Anthony Pezzotta

I Found Everything When I Found Christ

I was born in northern Italy and entered a Roman
Catholic seminary at the age of eleven. My ambition was to become a missionary priest. After
theological studies in England, Germany, Spain and
Rome I was ordained a priest in Rome and went immediately to the Philippines where I taught theology in
Roman Catholic seminaries.

While in England I had begun to have serious doubts
concerning certain doctrines of my Church which I
found difficult to reconcile with Scripture. These
doubts continued to trouble me even after my ordination, but I endeavoured to smother them by plunging
into my studies and teaching assignments. My schedule

was so heavy that there was little time for research or prayer.

After ten years of such hard work I had to return to my home in Italy for a year of rest and recuperation. But now my doubts revived and increased in number, as did my determination to find satisfactory solutions to the doctrines troubling my spirit. I read incessantly and pondered deeply the words of our great theologians, but all my doubts persisted.

From Books to the Book

Upon returning to the Philippines I laid aside all my books of theology, determined to focus all my attention on a single Book, the Bible, particularly the New Testament. The Word of God became my only source of wisdom for preaching, teaching, meditation and reading. In a relatively short time, my doubts began to disappear, as one after another they were solved by my study of the Scriptures.

My Suffering Begins

At the end of January 1974 I was in Santa Cruz, south of Manila, where an attractive Baptist church had just been built. I had never been in a Protestant church, so one day I walked quietly into the sanctuary to look around. Almost immediately I was greeted by a friendly Christian believer who introduced me to the pastor, Ernesto Montalegre.

We talked together for a couple of hours; I did all I could to make him a good Roman Catholic, while he was quietly answering all my questions. Of course I did not succeed in converting him to Roman Catholicism but neither did he convert me to Protestantism. Nevertheless, many of his answers struck me with great force, so

that at the end of two hours I left with multiplied doubts
in my heart. From that day on, a period of suffering
started for me, a time of sleepless nights, agonizing
indecision and a frightening lack of courage to profess
the truth of Scripture. Gradually I began to see what the
truth was, but I did not know what I was to do until the
night of 20 February 1974.

The Night of God's Grace

That night I was alone in my room and for the first
time in my life I really prayed. I asked Christ to take
over because I did not know what to do. I felt I was
the chief of sinners. You may ask, 'What kind of
sinner?' I never smoked, drank strong liquor or broke
my vows of celibacy throughout all the years I was
active in the priesthood. I left no bad record behind
me and in fact was rather proud of my achievements
as a parish priest. Pride was my sin. It was my pride
that tried to stop Christ from coming into my life because of what my bishop might think or say. I kept
asking myself, 'If you take Christ as your Saviour,
what will your superiors say? What will your colleagues think, or your students? They esteem you;
how can you betray them?' I lacked the courage to be
honest with these people; the esteem of men meant
more to me than love for the truth. But then, as I was
praying, my eyes fell upon this text in John's Gospel:
'Nevertheless among the chief rulers also many believed on him; but because of the Pharisees they did
not confess him, lest they should be put out of the
synagogue' (*John* 12:42).

Those last words penetrated my heart like a sharp
two-edged sword, but they also filled me with strength
and courage. I was set free. That night I slept without the

pain and agonizing indecision of the previous terrible weeks. The following morning, as I awoke, the picture of that kindly Baptist pastor came to my mind. I dressed hastily and drove to his church where we talked together for some time and I gladly accepted some tracts and pamphlets. As we were parting, I asked, 'In case I leave my Church, can I come to stay with you? Will you accept me?' Smiling he said, 'We have a room here and the believers will take care of you.'

Truth Wins

It took five days of prayer and more reading before I yielded to God's grace. Then, on 26 February, I received Christ as my personal Saviour and Lord. I asked him to take over the direction of my life, as I was leaving everything behind me: my car, my library, all my possessions. I wrote my letter of resignation to the bishop and went to live with my new-found spiritual friends in Santa Cruz.

On 3 March I publicly confessed my evangelical faith and was baptized in the Santa Cruz river which flows behind the church. The important thing is that from the day I came to know Christ to this very moment I have not had one single second of remorse, nostalgia or homesickness for my previous life. I was literally filled with joy and knew a freedom from doubt beyond all description. I remember one priest who visited me a few days later asking, 'Tony, how did you dare in just five days to make such a decision? You have left the Roman Catholic Church, twenty centuries of culture, popes, saints, all that you have learned and loved for so long.' I gave him the answer which came from my heart, 'I don't think I really left anything; rather, I found everything when I found Christ.'

No Longer a Roman Catholic

If you believe that you are saved because of your faith in Christ, and accept his Word as final authority, you are not a Roman Catholic but a Protestant, even if you do not like the word Protestant. Salvation by faith and the sole authority of Scripture are the very foundation of biblical faith, as against salvation by works and sacraments and the authority of Roman Catholic tradition.

Many Roman Catholics simply have a sentimental attachment to their Church, which they were trained to call 'Holy Mother Church'. This common expression reflects their belief that they owe their spiritual life to the Church, for it made them Christians through baptism, and keeps them spiritually alive through the other sacraments. The Bible teaches that it is not the church that makes us, but believers who make up the church. And since it is by grace through faith that we become lively stones of his church, Christ is the true builder. On the authority of the Bible alone, one must believe only on him!

40

Salvatore Gargiulo

I Was a Blind Leader of the Blind

I was converted to the gospel of the Lord Jesus in 1977, and I am now serving him in the same place where I previously followed the calling of a Roman Catholic priest. My conversion came about slowly, step by step, over a number of years and it was one of those great miracles that only God can bring about.

I was ordained as a priest in 1951 and it was my firm intention to be a devoted son of the Pope all the days of my life. I was fully convinced that he was the successor of Peter, the visible head of the whole church and the vicar or authoritative representative of Jesus Christ on earth.

Signs and Lying Wonders

The Roman Catholic Church really follows Mary rather than Christ. I never stopped urging people to recite the holy rosary (monotonous repetition of prayers to Mary). I enthusiastically passed on to others the stories about miracles she is supposed to have performed, which are nothing but the work of the powers of darkness, intended to lead millions of souls astray and to prevent them coming into contact with the truth.

The Apostle Paul foretells the appearance of a Wicked One, 'whose coming is after the working of Satan with all power and signs and lying wonders. And with all deceivableness of unrighteousness in them that perish; because they received not the love of the truth, that they might be saved. And for this cause God shall send them strong delusion, that they should believe a lie: that they all might be damned who believed not the truth, but had pleasure in unrighteousness' (2 Thess. 2:9–12). Again he tells us that 'Satan himself is transformed into an angel of light' (2 Cor. 11:14).

However, my life had been moulded in this system of errors and I had only a superficial knowledge of the Holy Scriptures. I was deceived myself and deceived others (2 Tim. 3:13). In fact my theological studies were really based on scholastic philosophy and not on the Bible.

Broken Cisterns

In my religious fanaticism and faithfulness to the provisions of the official code setting out the rights of priests, I one day burned a 'Protestant' Bible because it did not have the *imprimatur* of the Roman Catholic Church which I thought was needed to allow it to be read.

Nevertheless, all my certainty and faith in the Roman Catholic institution did not prevent me from being deeply unsatisfied at heart. I administered the sacraments as my turn came around to do so, but I lacked the greatest gift that God desires to give to man, that of knowing that he has been accepted by God because his sins have been forgiven through Christ's work at Calvary. 'Therefore being justified by faith, we have peace with God through our Lord Jesus Christ: by whom also we have access by faith into this grace wherein we stand, and rejoice in hope of the glory of God' (*Rom.* 5:1–2). I also had a great fear of death and of the judgment of God. My religion spurred me on to do things in order to get merit. I celebrated Mass, observed the Sacraments, recited the rosary, paid money for indulgences and practised acts of self-denial, but at heart I felt that I was lost. Sadly, in spite of having a degree in theology, I knew nothing of the peace and simplicity which salvation by grace provides. The broken cisterns of the sacraments were unable to give me the living water which my soul so desperately needed.

An Appeal to My Heart

In the 1960s, I became interested in the ecumenical movement. Naturally my great hope was that this movement would cause the 'separated brethren' to acknowledge the Roman Catholic Church and accept that it was the will of Jesus that the Pope should be the supreme shepherd of all the sheep. In this I thought God's desire would be fulfilled that there should be one flock and one shepherd.

This made it necessary for me to know what Christians who were separated from Rome actually thought. I therefore started to listen to evangelical broadcasts on the radio and television. I particularly remember a series of morning messages given by a German evangelical Christian, Werner Euchelbach, which were broadcast by Radio Luxembourg. These never failed to finish with a heartfelt appeal as he said, 'What you really need is Jesus.' To me he was merely the representative of a sect, a heretic, but the earnestness in his voice touched me. The centre of his message was Jesus. 'Verily, verily, I say unto you, he that believeth on me hath everlasting life' (*John* 6:47).

The Light of Scripture

One day in 1975, as I was walking along a street in Florence, I was attracted by an evangelical bookshop. I went in just to look around. I was struck by the title of one of the books, *Roman Catholicism in the Light of Scripture*, and bought a copy. It was not easy to rid my mind in a moment of all the false doctrines that were so deeply rooted there, but little by little the Holy Spirit caused the light of the truth to penetrate my darkened mind.

Another two years of uncertainty, hesitation and seeking went by. In the end, it was nothing but the Bible, which is the real sword of the Spirit, which finally broke the chains of error which had held me for so many years, 'for by grace are ye saved through faith; and that not of yourselves: it is the gift of God: not of works, lest any man should boast' (*Eph.* 2:8–9); 'Believe on the Lord Jesus Christ, and thou shalt be saved, and thy house' (*Acts* 16:30–31); 'And this is the record, that God hath given to us eternal life, and this life is in his Son' (*1 John* 5:11).

Has the Roman Catholic Church Changed?

Some evangelicals think that times have changed and that it is now possible to hold a dialogue and to collaborate with the Roman Catholic Church to achieve Christian unity. This is a deception of Satan. The doctrines of this ecclesiastical organization have in no way changed. In fact they are now adding new errors to the old ones, and in particular they are working towards bringing in all the other religions. The Vatican Council II document *Nostra Aetate* (1965), for example, says in Paragraph 2:

'Buddhism in its various forms testifies to the essential inadequacy of this changing world. It proposes a way of life by which man can, with confidence and trust, attain a state of perfect liberation and reach supreme illumination either through his own efforts or by the aid of divine help . . . The Catholic Church rejects nothing of what is true and holy in these religions.'

It is therefore of the utmost importance for us at the present time to obey the exhortation of the Word of God, 'Be ye not unequally yoked together with unbelievers: for what fellowship hath righteousness with unrighteousness? and what communion hath light with darkness? And what concord hath Christ with Belial? or what part hath he that believeth with an infidel? And what agreement hath the temple of God with idols? for ye are the temple of the living God; as God hath said, I will dwell in them, and walk in them; and I will be their God, and they shall be my people. Wherefore come out from among them, and be ye separate, saith the Lord, and touch not the unclean thing; and I will receive you, and will be a Father unto you, and ye shall be my sons and daughters, saith the Lord Almighty' (*2 Cor.* 6:14–18).

Walk as Children of Light

As I look back over the many years during which I lived under the power of lies and error, I can only thank my heavenly Father with deep joy and gratitude that he delivered me from the power of darkness and brought me into the kingdom of his beloved Son. 'For ye were sometimes darkness, but now are ye light in the Lord: walk as children of light' (*Eph.* 5:8).

41

Carlo Fumagalli

From Death to Life

My life was tossed about by different opinions and driven here and there by every wind of doctrine (*Eph.* 4:14) until I found Jesus the Rock and Cornerstone (*Matt.* 21:42, *Acts* 4:11, *Eph.* 2:20, *1 Pet.* 2:6–7), or rather until Jesus, my glorious Lord and Saviour, found me. I can now say with David, 'He brought me up also out of an horrible pit, out of the miry clay, and set my feet upon a rock, and established my goings. And he hath put a new song in my mouth, even praise unto our God: many shall see it, and fear, and shall trust in the LORD' (*Psa.* 40:2–3).

Born in Italy

I was born at Olgate Molgara near Como in 1934. When I was nine years of age I went into the Archbishop's Seminary of Milan at Masnago in the province of Varese. Five years later I joined the high school of the Missionaries of the Consolata of Turin, then the novitiate. Afterwards I did a two-year course of philosophy and four years of theology.

In the Higher Seminary of the Consolata at Turin (as in every other Roman Catholic seminary and college) the study was based on Aristotle's philosophy which, with theology, was a prerequisite for all the higher academic grades in Holy Scripture. Roman Catholic theology is thus built up around pagan philosophy. The Bible in turn is influenced and pervaded by an adulterated theology. This approach to the Bible is obviously wrong since the Word of God cannot be linked to or influenced by any human philosophy or doctrine. Paul says, 'Beware lest any man spoil you through philosophy and vain deceit, after the tradition of men, after the rudiments of the world, and not after Christ' (*Col.* 2:8).

Ordination and the USA

After my ordination as a priest in 1961 I was assigned to teach in the Seminary of the Consolata of Bevera (Brianza Castle). In 1966 I was nominated as the spiritual director of the seminary and I continued in this office until 1968 when I was offered the opportunity of going to the United States for further studies. Prior to doing so, however, I went to London for a few months where I attended a theological college.

In September 1969 I started to attend the department of anthropology of the State University of New York in

Buffalo. Faced with new spheres of study and research which included customs, cultures, beliefs, social structures and differing systems of economics, politics and religion, as well as archaeology and evolution, my mind became full of fresh questions and problems. My study of various societies and cultures suggested that the Roman Catholic sacraments and magic have substantially the same characteristics. Both of these, by using a certain rite and formula, guarantee a specific result.

Yoga, Africa and Beyond

Finding it difficult to get into fruitful discussion with other priests to deal with new questions which arose in my mind, I began to explore other areas of thought. I started to attend a course on 'mind control'. This opened the door to the fascinating and unexplored world of the occult which in pseudo-scientific terms is today called 'parapsychology'. I was at the same time practising yoga and doing research into oriental religions. In spite of having many reservations in these areas of study I hoped to find at least some of the answers to the many questions in my mind. I followed two academic courses to get my B.A. and M.A. degrees and then took the difficult and demanding examinations for my Ph.D., in which I was successful. I then proposed to do research in Africa, but before going I spent several months in Italy where I asked my superiors in Rome for a period of release from my duties as a priest so that I could have time for reflection. My superiors tried to convince me that my present crisis was only a passing one and that everything would soon be back to normal for me.

It was while I was in this state of mind that I went to Africa where, in November 1974, I began my research among the Samburu tribe of northern Kenya. My aim was to carry out complex research into the culture, social life and economic system of the tribe. At the same time I studied the history and lifestyle of the area to identify crucial factors causing social and economic change in tribal society, as influenced by colonial and national governments.

Out of Africa and Roman Catholicism

Away from outward pressure and enforced routine I had time to think about my own problems and to take account of the disturbance in my own heart, since I was very dissatisfied with the life I had been living. I knew in my heart that my only honest decision would be to leave my religious institute and the priesthood. I decided to do so early in 1975. I then felt a great peace and a real sense of liberation. I understood that I had been liberated from one of the greatest bondages and types of slavery that exist – that of the Roman Catholic religion and the institutional Church.

In February 1976 at the close of my research in Africa I returned to the United States. Having got free from the yoke of the Roman Catholic Church and all my obligations to it, I decided to follow my own way, which made me an agnostic. I planned to become a university professor.

In September 1977 I received a doctorate in anthropology (Ph.D.) and in November of the same year the Roman Church released me from all my duties as a priest.

I Study the Occult and the New Testament

I continued my research, especially with regard to the occult and oriental religions. In my heart I felt, however, a great emptiness that nothing could fill and there was a great hunger and thirst for truth, love and righteousness which nothing could satisfy. I had separated myself almost entirely from every form and practice of traditional religion. Every day, however, I read a short passage from the New Testament.

Early in March 1979 I started to read an Italian translation of *The Late Great Planet Earth* by Hal Lindsey which I had bought quite casually a day or two previously in a shop in Buffalo.

I started to read the book with great scepticism and with a critical mind. Soon I came face to face with various Bible prophecies which were being actually fulfilled before my eyes. In my years at the university I had learned that not even the greatest scientist in the world could foresee with certainty what might happen tomorrow. I suddenly came to the conclusion that the Bible must be true and that it could have come only from God. In those few minutes I became convinced that I was a sinner and that I could never save myself. I understood vividly that Jesus died on the cross for sinners and that the only way to be saved was to ask him definitely to forgive my sins and to be my Lord and Saviour. This I did.

I Find Life in Christ

Jesus' response to my cry was immediate and very wonderful. In that very moment I had the experience of divine grace purifying me from all my sins, filthiness and wickedness. Weeping for joy I just had to kneel down as I experienced the power of the love and redemptive sacrifice of Jesus who had saved so great a sinner as myself. I had become a child of God (*John* 1:11–13), born anew into the life of the Spirit (*John* 3:3–7) by the incorruptible seed of the Word of God (*1 Pet.* 1:23). I had received the certainty that I was saved by grace through faith (*Eph.* 2:8), and I had a taste of the wonderful spiritual banquet that Jesus promised to all who receive him (*Rev.* 3:20).

The great question I asked myself was, 'Since the message of salvation is so easy, how is it that no one has ever told me about it?' Nothing of all my years of study, the sacraments I had taken and confessions I had made had served in the slightest to save me, but Jesus had saved me when I recognized that I was a lost sinner and called on him: 'And it shall come to pass, that whosoever shall call on the name of the Lord shall be saved' (*Acts* 2:21).

From that day I have felt as if a fire were burning within me and the Lord has given me a great hunger and thirst for his Word, which I now know to be the only fountain of truth. Thus the greater part of my time since has been devoted to studying the Bible.

I started to witness about my salvation to American friends and to Italian relatives but most of them did not want to know anything about it. I realized that henceforth my only course was to follow Jesus and obey his Word. I gave up my career as a university professor and decided to give the whole of my life to the service of the Lord. Three months later, in obedience to the Word, I asked to be baptized in water. 'And he said unto them, Go ye into all the world, and preach the gospel to every creature. He that believeth and is baptized shall be saved; but he that believeth not shall be damned' (*Mark* 16:15–16). Early in 1981 the Lord made it clear to me that I was to go to Italy to take the gospel of salvation, especially to Roman Catholics and to priests. I therefore went to Italy in the middle of March 1981.

42

Gregor Dalliard

Not Ashamed of Christ

I was born on 10 November 1947 in the vine-growing village of Salgesch in Switzerland, the seventh in a family of twelve children. In most Roman Catholic areas there was at that time no real alternative to the Roman Catholic Church and from our early days, from the age of seven, the priests spared no effort to drive into us that Roman Catholic teaching was basic truth and that outside the Roman Catholic Church there was no salvation. Deeply respecting my religious leaders, I gave serious attention to what they taught and made every effort to obey their instructions and to carry out the many Roman Catholic practices demanded of us. I attended the daily Mass and used to repeat the prayers of the rosary regularly. I attended Vespers and took the sacraments and also went on pilgrimages. I faithfully did all the religious exercises recommended by the Church, including voluntary sacrifices and penances, nine-day prayer sessions, and prayers and works that were awarded indulgences by the Church. By doing all these things faithfully I hoped I would one day be canonized a saint by the Church. I also wanted to become a priest. 'Could anything be better', I thought, 'than to be a mediator between God and man and thus be able to administer the sacraments without which no one can be saved?'

My father died in 1967 and my mother, a very devout woman, in 1973 after a brief illness.

The Charismatic Renewal Movement

From 1972–5 I studied in the theological seminary of the Benedictine Monastery of the Black Madonna in Einsiedeln, Switzerland. Then, during my studies in a theological college in Freiburg, I came to know about the charismatic renewal movement. This movement, from which I dissociated myself in 1986, had been introduced into the Roman Catholic Church by the Second Vatican Council, held in the years 1962–5. It created uncertainty in the minds of millions of Pope-conscious Roman Catholics who felt that the movement had the smell of Protestant influence.

Everyone brought his Bible to the meetings arranged by this movement. I personally was sceptical about the Bible which I regarded as fertile ground for the numerous Protestant sects. The teachings of the Church prompted me to be cautious but at the same time I wanted to understand the line that the movement was following and how it could form an integral part of the Roman Catholic Church. I did realize that it might serve as an important bridge for reaching other non-Roman churches and groups and help to bring them back under the supreme control of the Pope. The new development was seen by some as having been foreshadowed in the eschatological messages given at Fatima in Portugal in 1917. These thoughts produced in me a new fire of enthusiasm for the Pope and the Church. At the same time the weekly Bible studies that I was attending awoke a deep and growing love for the Word of God whereas previously this had been of no importance whatsoever to me and in no way binding.

I Disobey the Bishop

The fact of young people reading the Bible began to disturb other priests and nuns and, under the surface, opposition began to spread. Indeed sometimes it came out in the open.

In 1983 the bishop appointed me to be priest in the parish of Grächen. I was told that for at least a year I was to go forward quietly and not to start any new Bible groups. This was contrary to the declared aims of the Second Vatican Council and of the new canon law of 1983 which stated explicitly that it should be the foremost duty of a priest to make known the Word of God. We had experienced how the promises of the Bible were fulfilled and noted in Acts 4:19–20 that the apostles, when opposed by the high priests and teachers of the law, replied, 'Whether it be right in the sight of God to hearken unto you more than unto God, judge ye. For we cannot but speak the things which we have seen and heard.' We felt that we must do the same. Only a few months later evening Bible study and prayer meetings were started.

I Query Roman Catholic Doctrines

It was during this period that I became aware of how many of the Church's teachings concerning the way of salvation contradicted the teachings of the Bible. This led to distressing difficulties. In our Bible study groups clarity on many basic subjects was sought as never before. These subjects included the following: What were the divinity and authority of Jesus? What does the inspiration of the Holy Scriptures mean and what is the inspired canon? What does it mean to fear God and what does our obedience to him involve? What is the significance of baptism and the sacraments? We also considered what the Bible teaches about Mary, about prayer to and the veneration of the saints, and about the place of the deceased in the Christian life. We also studied the meaning and purpose of the ecumenical movement in view of the fact that the Second Vatican Council had unequivocally declared that it was the Catholic Church of Christ alone that held the power of salvation and that all who were in any way part of the people of God must be fully reintegrated into the Catholic Church (*Decree on Ecumenism*, 1964, chapter 1 section 3).

God's Grace in Salvation

In the summer of 1988 I came to see that according to the Word of God in 1 Timothy 2:4, God 'will have all men to be saved'. I knew by this time that all the practices of the Roman Catholic Church could not give me salvation but I saw that the Lord Jesus had paid the price of my sins on the cross and that he offered me forgiveness and eternal life if I asked him for them. I therefore asked him to forgive my sins and to give me new life. This he did. Then I personally gave my life fully over to him.

I then saw that Jesus said, 'For whosoever shall be ashamed of me and of my words, of him shall the Son of man be ashamed, when he shall come in his own glory, and in his Father's, and of the holy angels' (*Luke* 9:26). I did not want to be ashamed of him and of his words any longer, nor did I wish to keep them back from others. I therefore preached his message openly.

I Stand for Truth and Pay the Price

On 15 August 1988, the occasion of the big Roman Catholic feast of the Assumption of the Blessed Virgin as declared in the dogma of 1950, I spoke in public and pointed out the difference between Mary the mother of the Lord and the classical Queen of Heaven and the black goddesses. In consequence I was summoned by the diocesan authorities to appear before the ecclesiastical court where I was asked to revoke certain statements I had made. In my response, although I loved the bishop and my colleagues in the priesthood very much, I could no longer deny the Lord Jesus and his Word nor the testimonies of the apostles by revoking what I had said. I was accordingly excommunicated immediately and stripped of all my clerical functions. The diocesan authorities and the clergy then tried to silence me by making false statements, saying in a circular letter that according to the Canon Law, Section 1044, paragraph 2, I was mentally unbalanced and psychologically ill. In a second letter this charge was withdrawn as being an error but by then the affirmations made in the first letter were already on everybody's lips. About thirty people, however, some from the local area and others from further away, decided to be faithful to Scripture and to take a stand for the Lord and they handed in their notices of withdrawal from the Church.

Nevertheless this campaign of harassment on the part of the clergy encouraged others to take action against us, the nature of which we could not predict. There were threats of death by stabbing and attempts to subject us to psychological terror, isolation and cursing. Most difficult were those days for us but the Lord was faithful to sustain us.

Family Life

Some time later I had a serious illness. Some of the believers recommended a sister in the Lord, Marianne, who might be able to give me some help. Eventually we were married, on 28 October 1989, and now the Lord has given us three children, Nathanael, Josiah and Tabea. Since January 1995 my wife and I have been serving the Lord in fellowship with two organizations: The Help Line for Seeking Catholics (HISKIA) and the Information Service about Catholicism (INFOKA).

'Sanctify the Lord God in your hearts: and be ready always to give an answer to every man that asketh you a reason of the hope that is in you with meekness and fear' (*1 Pet.* 3:15).

43

Toon Vanhuysse

The Truth Set Me Free

I was born in Zwevegem, Belgium, on 13 October 1940, at the beginning of the war years. My parents were very pious Roman Catholics. Father was an extremely strict man, but at the same time very affable. Despite family problems (there were ten children) and his daily work, father found time for all kinds of 'parochial works'. Something I have taken from my father is his deep feeling for righteousness. He also had a great heart for sending out development aid.

My dear mother – she died some years ago – was such a good woman. She was very gentle and quiet. Is not this the most beautiful ornament with which a woman can adorn herself? (*1 Pet.* 3:3–4). She was also a zealous woman and skilful in family ways, supervising the running of the household. She was slightly handicapped and endured much pain in silence. A woman who never complained and accepted everything that was difficult in her life, she considered others more, and we benefited from this.

Mother was not someone who was greatly concerned about the external practice of being a believer, but she had a hidden, upright relationship with God.

The Power of Tradition

The Bible was always a forbidden book for my parents, but God is sovereign and he breaks through much of the resistance which Roman Catholicism has built into the thoughts and hearts of men. Therefore I believe my mother knew the fear of the Lord. So I grew up with a deep awe of God, an awe that was strongly characterized by fear of his anger towards sin.

I remember so well going to the confessional for I failed repeatedly and sinned against God and suffered remorse. It did not leave me, and peace did not come until I had received absolution from a priest in the confessional. The confessional was repeatedly a liberation and a relief for me. We never had any knowledge of the gospel of grace, of the joyful message that through believing in Jesus' work of reconciliation we receive forgiveness of sins and eternal life. Such is the power of tradition in the Roman Catholic system.

Look, for example, at confession. The Bible says, 'To him give all the prophets witness, that through his name whosoever believeth in him shall receive remission of sins' (*Acts* 10:43). Yet Rome pronounces excommunication to all those who testify to the Bible. The Council of Trent declares this, and tradition usually pushes Scripture aside. We must beware of this. The Word of

God warns us of it! People are quicker to accept what the Church teaches than what the Bible says. This is the problem with tradition.

A Call to Missions

I began my secondary studies at a college in Waregem. There I passed a Greek-Latin humanities course. It was still the time of strong discipline. We obeyed and we also learned. It was certainly no easy time throughout my boarding school experience. We could go home for around two to three weeks each year.

I had a desire to do something for poor people. In my study time I had read many accounts about great missionaries, and I felt I had to follow in their footsteps. So in 1959 or 1960 I entered the Order of Oblatory Missionary Fathers of Mary in Korbecklo, near Leuven, where the novitiate of the Order was. It was actually a trial year, when we were tested and trained for the cloistered life. It was a difficult time for me.

Spiritual Exercise without Value

Every day we had a prayer meeting. It began early in the morning with the breviary, meditation, Mass and devotion to Mary. In the course of the day we had our 'spiritual reading', the rosary, and a period of Bible reading. In the afternoon, we usually did handicraft work in silence. On some Friday afternoons we had a short time of 'flogging'. Every novice had his whip and had to scourge his back. It was as if one could whip out the uncleanness of the past week.

So we were trained for a year for cloister life. We did not realize that all those so-called spiritual exercises and all our efforts to serve God were without any value, as

Paul taught in the letter to the Colossians. They only served to satisfy the flesh! All those so-called 'holy' methods chip away at Jesus as Mediator. 'So then they that are in the flesh cannot please God' (*Rom.* 8:8). What grace it is to be able to rest in Jesus' accomplished work of salvation! I want to say this to every priest and everyone in a cloister, 'Repent and believe the gospel!'

I find it so sad that Roman Catholics usually do not know the difference between truth and lies in regard to spiritual things. Lies have acquired a strong foothold in the thoughts and hearts of the people. This is expressed in so many doctrines of Rome. A lie does not yield easily. I experience this now when I evangelize door-to-door, which I am doing with a congregation of born-again Christians in Munsterbilzen. People have a deep-rooted aversion to the truth. The truth of the Word deals with sinful people and shows clearly how wretched and lost they are. Everybody prefers to listen to the suggestions of their hearts, which the Bible calls 'deceitful' and 'desperately wicked': 'The heart is deceitful above all things, and desperately wicked: who can know it?' (*Jer.* 17:9).

A Priest in the Church of Rome

We then moved to the Students' Centre in Gijzegem, a village between Aalst and Dendermonde. After two years of study in philosophy and four years of theology, I was ordained as a priest on 20 February 1966. It was, of course, an enormous event for me, the crowning event of my study and education.

There was not a higher calling. To be a priest in the Church of Rome! We were chosen to carry out again the sacrifice of Jesus Christ in the present. We had become offerers of God's grace; that was my conviction. We had the coveted pretension of being a kind of 'maker of blessings'. How I had diverted from the Scriptures! It is dishonouring to God to weaken Jesus' perfect and all-sufficient sacrifice through the 'Mass offering' and to fail to recognize its depth and eternal saving power. The letter to the Hebrews is very clear about this.

I had a year's preparation in the junior seminary of the Fathers at Waregem, a middle school with the option of going on to a cloistered life. I was then asked to go to Antwerp to engage in parochial work with a team of priests. My assignment was specifically working with youth.

After a year I had to leave Antwerp-Kiel, because my Order called me up for a similar assignment, this time to start a new parish in Houthalen-East. With three Fathers we formed a team and worked there. I wondered about their position and their idealism. It was yet more human power, a human building not erected on the rock but on sand. God's Word was not the basis for our life, with the result that this self-made structure was very shaky and its fall was great, as the Bible says. How we need to accept the Word of God as the steady foundation for our lives!

After my ten years of priestly service, I was spiritually extinguished. I could not help seeing my official service in the Roman Catholic Church as a fiasco, particularly when I was confronted with fundamental human needs. To people who were truly sick, I could not give the comfort of God's Word. To people with guilty feelings about wrong steps in their lives, I could not present the forgiveness or reconciliation found in Jesus Christ. I myself needed to know God and to receive forgiveness for my sins. As a result of this fundamental lack, my life had become a spiritual rubbish heap. The deepest cause of my failure was not knowing the Lord Jesus Christ or the Scriptures. People ask with astonishment how it is possible that someone who is a priest does not know the gospel and lacks the right knowledge of Christ. It is deeply humiliating to have to admit that this was indeed the case. Jesus, for us Roman Catholics, was above all the great example, the example of a moral upright life, the example of social and economic justice. That was why I was involved in welfare work, trying to be like him and somehow achieve salvation.

New Spiritual Birth

But by God's grace I was led to true spiritual new birth in Christ Jesus and to the written Scriptures of God. This had natural consequences, actually painful consequences. In the light of the truth of the gospel, I have discovered who I actually am, namely a thoroughly sinful being, incapable of any good and inclined to evil. There is nothing good in me! This is the testimony of the Bible! The Bible itself taught me also that I was excluded from all hope of salvation and was destined for dreadful destruction, as Paul clearly writes in the letter to the Ephesians. God could find nothing good in me! Who could have thought that, after ten diligent years as a priest in the Church of Rome? Yet Paul used a word that describes the value of all the diligence, namely dirt; it is of no value in the eyes of God (*Phil.* 3:8). I thought that my works could be grounds to stand before God in a good light, but on the contrary, they were harmful. 'For I know that in me (that is, in my flesh,) dwelleth no good thing' (*Rom.* 7:18), Paul exclaims. Outside Jesus Christ, salvation is impossible. We all need to be pointed to the grace of God. There is no other way.

The Bible makes no compromise on this point. There is no middle path between truth and falsehood. It is either truth or lie! There is a great temptation to consider people who are pious and faithfully attending services as righteous. God has broken in me the deep-rooted but pernicious inclination to self-redemption, which runs so deep in a man. We are born with it. I do not believe that there is a man who wants to live by 'grace alone'. We hope in secret that there will still be something good in us. We are too proud to admit the contrary. The Bible breathes an atmosphere of sovereign grace. The sinner is justified by grace, through faith. The co-operation of people is totally excluded. I am glad that God has revealed this truth to me. 'And ye shall know the truth, and the truth shall make you free' (*John* 8:32).

44

Herman Hegger

Light and Life in Christ

During my childhood I often heard it said that one of the best ways to escape from eternal hell was to enter a monastery. I decided to follow that advice.

My Efforts in the Monastery

Monastic life is meant to cultivate strong will-power and make one capable of controlling all passions and lusts. In my monastery, various forms of bodily torture were employed to achieve such will-power. We scourged ourselves several times a week, lashing our naked bodies with knotted cords. Despite the great pain, we were told that if we could endure such whipping calmly, we would receive strength to resist every kind of sensual and sexual urge. We were also told that by scourging ourselves we could atone for sins we had already committed and so shorten future punishment in purgatory. Around our waists, thighs and arms we wore penitence chains on which were spikes which dug into our flesh. There were also many other kinds of bodily chastisements.

Along with self-inflicted punishments we had other kinds of humbling exercises designed to extinguish our pride and vanity. In one of these routines a priest had to lie on the floor across a doorway so that other priests would tread on him as they went by. Whenever I did this I felt like a worm upon which people trod, but I thought that God must be very pleased with me for such a voluntary self-humiliation.

The worst humiliation included licking an area of the floor clean with our tongues. Doing this made me feel like an animal, like a pig wallowing in the mire or a dog sniffing around. Sometimes I even felt like an insect creeping in the dust.

But however I punished and humiliated myself, I could not detect any change or improvement in my character or behaviour. I only discovered that my weak and sinful nature was very much alive. For example, when I licked the floor clean with my tongue, it was just then that the strongest feelings of vanity and pride rose up in me. What a wonderful chap you are, I would think. What will-power you must have. You inflict such painful humiliations upon yourself. How wonderful! I realized that by these absurd practices I was only inflating myself with pride. The monastery is a sublime effort that is doomed to fail. Why? Because the priest or monk takes his sinful nature along with him into the cell.

My Attempt to Reach God by Mysticism

During the novitiate years, in addition to our attempt to
gain the victory over the body with its passions by means
of asceticism, we also applied ourselves to the practice of
prayer. This was called the cultivation of the spiritual or
inner life. Its purpose was to bring about an increasing
intensity in our uninterrupted contact with God, Jesus
Christ and Mary. Our highest goal was the attainment of
true mysticism.

During my novitiate I never experienced this desired
mysticism. Consequently I thought the practice of prayer
very difficult. We were shown a few methods to pass the
time of meditation well. In the evenings pious reflections
on our Lord's passion by various authors were read aloud
to us. We were to ask questions such as the following: Who
is suffering? What does he suffer? Why? For whom? The
answers to these questions were intended to induce acts of
repentance for our sins and acts of faith, hope and love, as
we were to make up our minds to lead better lives.

Usually I was prompt with the answers to these questions, and then my imagination wandered away out of
the chapel. Also I thought the reflections of Roman
Catholic authors upon Christ's suffering quite poor.
They were thoughts that had been worked out by men
who had coloured and moulded them in conformity to
their own emotional life. They never could hold my
attention for long.

One day in 1940 the idea occurred to me: Why not
take the Bible? In it you will not find the thoughts of
men, but of God himself. Our monastic rules, however,
required us to listen to what was being read to us during
meditations. We were not to read the Bible on those
occasions unless granted permission. That permission
was given me.

My Provisional Use of the Bible

From that time everything became quite different.
Meditation no longer caused me mental fatigue as
before. I began to enjoy it; the very thought that I now
had to do with the infallible Word of God made me
happy. I knew I entered holy ground. My imagination
would lovingly rejoice in the biblical text. I would turn it
about again and again, and tremble before the blazing
fire of God's presence in its sentences. And I would be
profoundly moved by the love of the Father who
revealed himself to me in his words. I preferred above all
else to meditate on the story of the passion. Every
sentence revealed something of the greatness of the
suffering soul of Jesus. He rose before me in his glory,
his mercy, his purity and his peace.

Jesus was no longer a coldly intellectual idea, no
longer the effeminate and characterless doll at which for
so long I had been obliged to look in countless pictures.
There was now a bond between him and me, though I
did not yet know Jesus through the pure gospel as my
personal, perfect and only Saviour.

Obstacles to My Goal of Union with God

There were several hindrances to the personal union I
sought. One was the fear that God would finally reject
me on account of my sins. Another was the Roman
Catholic worship of Mary. I never succeeded in developing great affection for Mary and this troubled me. I had
been taught that a child of Mary will never be lost. When
in my meditation I surrendered wholly to the contem-
plation of Jesus Christ, it would suddenly occur to me
that I rarely prayed to Mary. Then turning nervously to
the mediatrix of all grace, I implored her to save me from

eternal damnation. And when I thought that I had paid enough attention to her, I returned at once to Christ, as he had revealed himself in the holy Word of God.

But my greatest stumbling block was the doctrine declaring that the pronouncements of the Roman Catholic Church are the highest and the ultimate source of the knowledge of God's revelation. Whichever way one views it, this doctrine reduces the Bible to a second-rate book in Roman Catholic eyes. No papal admonitions to believers to read their Bibles often can alter that fact. A Roman Catholic, therefore, never can devote himself fully to meditating upon the Bible. The deeper meanings of the divine Word, which he is convinced he must infer from it, are always surrounded by a multitude of questions. If the Church has made some pronouncements on the matter, the Roman Catholic must relinquish his own conviction as to what the Scriptures say and conform to the view of the Church. The Bible never can have the central and prominent position which it has with biblical Christians. Who will continue to read a second-rate book which cannot give absolute certainty, and do so day after day and year after year? Besides, it is a book that brings along with it the risk of doubting the doctrines of one's own Church, which doubt amounts to a capital sin and might spell eternal damnation.

My Promotion and Doubts

After seven years as a priest I was promoted to be professor of philosophy in a Roman Catholic seminary in Brazil. However, serious doubts had already begun to assail me. We were forbidden to have any real doubts about the doctrine of the Church. This absolute prohibition against doubting or questioning the doctrine of the Roman Church is the source of her great strength.

Protestants wonder how it is possible for Roman Catholic scholars to study the Scriptures without discovering the pure gospel. The answer lies in the simple fact that the mind of the Roman Catholic is not free; it is ever under the threat of fire unquenchable should it deviate from Rome. The very instant he even considers as a genuine possibility the idea that the Reformation view of the Bible might be correct, the abyss of rejection opens at his feet. We were allowed to have a methodological doubt. Such a doubt was often indulged for didactic purposes. Thomas Aquinas makes a systematic use of it in his *Summa Theologica*. It consists of positing the correctness of the opposite view for the time being, to understand it better and afterwards to refute it more effectively. The same method also is applied to discussions with non-Roman Catholics. A Roman Catholic may pretend to believe that his opponent could be right, but that such an admission might be genuine is really impossible.

As a priest, the first power given me was the daily celebration of the Mass, and this occasioned my first doubt. The doctrine of the magical presence of Christ after transubstantiation frightened me. I felt as if I were standing before a fire which seared me, not a glow that warmed me. There was no question of love. Afterwards there often remained a sense of frightening emptiness.

My second important function as a priest was to administer confession, and this occasioned my second doubt. Confession holds a very important place in the structure of Rome's power. To Rome it is a strategic basis of the highest importance. It emphasizes the subjection of the layman to the clergy. In the confessional, the priest is sitting in his judgment seat. The penitent is confessing his weaknesses. He divulges secrets that he would not reveal to anyone else. And it depends upon the priest whether or not the penitent will be absolved from his sins. The priest decides for him between heaven and hell. I would only ask: Is this the 'glorious liberty of the children of God'? Is this the blissful salvation of which the Bible speaks in rapturous praise? Is there anything here of the picture of the Good Shepherd who goes to seek the lost sheep in the wilderness and carries it on his shoulders back to the fold? Are not the sheep rather kicked along the path of auricular confession to the so-called sheepfold with the threat of eternal death?

I Am Pressed by Truth

At various times I read the Bible and asked myself, 'Is my Church really in accord with this book?' In the Bible it is clearly stated that the only mediator between God and man is Jesus Christ, who took away the punishment of sin on Calvary's cross. My Church, however, taught that there were several mediators, especially Mary, the 'mediatrix of all grace'. I also began to doubt that God had given to the Pope infallible authority and power to interpret the Bible and that it was the duty of every Christian to accept the Pope's view. Could it be right that the Pope had absolute authority to overrule and restate the plain words of the Bible?

Since it is especially through fear that one's mind is paralysed and one's thoughts are blurred, how can the intellect work properly if, behind it, there is the threat of deadly sin and hell and if the flames of eternal reprobation force one to a particular conclusion? Critically speaking, the conclusions of an understanding that is forced to operate in such a way are manifestly unreliable. Do what I would, I could not attain to any degree of certainty about Roman Catholic doctrine. At best, I could grant the probability of its truth, but nothing more. I should be lying to myself were I to assert anything beyond that. My subconscious could now no longer succeed in projecting an irrational conviction upon my intellectual uncertainty. I had observed too long the workings of the subconscious. I knew that my conscience would always reproach me with being guilty of self-deceit. And, holding such a view, I could no longer be called a Roman Catholic. The doctrine of my own Church drove me out.

It was a terrible moment when, in all sincerity, I felt obliged to refuse to submit my mind to the doctrinal pronouncements of Rome. Until then the Roman Catholic Church had been my support, the rock on which I had built my convictions. Now I saw that I had built my house on sand. The waves of honest self-analysis had washed away the sand from under its foundations, the house collapsed, and I was carried along by the flood of despair. Nowhere could I find a support on which to lean. Alone I had to push my way through the undergrowth of many views of life.

With such doubts in my heart I could obviously not remain a priest in the Roman Catholic Church. For me the living death of the monastery came to an end. I left the life of semblances and shadows for a world of fascinating reality in which I was free to breathe at last. I surrendered my office as professor and left the Roman Catholic Church. I laid aside my priestly cassock, which in tropical Brazil just soaked up the heat, and walked lightly and free in my shirt sleeves. But deep within I still carried the burden of my guilt.

Saved by Grace Alone, through Faith

Outwardly I was free, but inwardly I was not at rest, for I had lost sight of God completely. I received much help from an evangelical church in Rio de Janeiro – a local church where the congregation based their faith only on the teachings of the Bible. The sympathy of the people there helped me very much, for they provided me with civilian clothing which I had no money to buy, and food and shelter. I shall always be grateful to them. But most of all the preaching of their minister gripped me. It was completely new to me to hear such explanations of the Bible. But could I be helped by a non-Roman Catholic preacher?

Certainly in my seminary training and as a priest I had heard regularly about the alleged false teaching of such churches, but I had never understood what they taught. In Rio de Janeiro I heard the minister explain that a man cannot save himself, or deserve entrance into heaven by any of his own efforts because he is utterly lost and hopeless. With all this I could heartily agree, for I had all too clearly experienced my inability to change myself. In spite of the greatest efforts and every kind of penitence, I had not succeeded in becoming a different kind of person. The preacher went even further and showed that there is only one way to be set free from sin, and that is to be given by God a completely free pardon and a new life. He showed how this experience must be obtained directly from Jesus Christ, who gives it freely and unmistakably to all who hand themselves over to him in complete trust in his perfect sacrifice.

Light and Life

At first I found this difficult to believe. It was like a fairy story – too good to be true. I could see the beauty of yielding to Christ. It sounded wonderful, and yet at the same time it seemed too easy, too cheap. As a Roman Catholic I believed that salvation was the hardest battle in life, a matter of struggling for and deserving God's favour. But now I began to understand the true teaching of the Bible. Yes, salvation is indeed the hardest thing in the world and must be deserved by perfect obedience to all the demands of God's law, in other words, perfect sinlessness. But the amazing fact is that the Lord Jesus Christ, God's Son, has fulfilled all these demands for us and on our behalf, if we trust him. 'Being justified freely by his grace through the redemption that is in Christ Jesus: whom God hath set forth to be a propitiation through faith in his blood, to declare his righteousness for the remission of sins that are past, through the forbearance of God; To declare, I say, at this time his righteousness: that he might be just, and the justifier of him which believeth in Jesus' (*Rom.* 3:24–26).

At last the wonderful breakthrough came. My soul opened itself wholly to Christ in complete trust. I could see that it was not the Jews who had crucified Christ – I had done it. My sins were taken by him. A blinding flash of light illuminated the rubbish heap of my former life.

My soul lay like a bombed-out city before me, and I was filled with anguish at seeing the sin which had permeated my whole being. But, over the rubbish heap I realized and knew that Christ had forgiven me and made me a true Christian. I had become a new creature.

Jesus spoke of the relationship between himself and true Christians in these words, 'I am the good shepherd, and know my sheep, and am known of mine' (*John* 10:14). I had begun a new life, with all the feeling of close fellowship with God which I had never known in all my days as a Roman Catholic priest. The dead legalism of the Church of Rome was behind me and the future was a living personal relationship with our wonderful God.

45

J. M. A. Hendriksen

From Priest to Preacher

While I was a priest in Rotterdam I met a rough
Roman Catholic sailor who joked with me about
eating meat or fish on a Friday. Nearly a year later I was
called to see the same sailor. He was very ill; the doctor
had said that he had incurable cancer. When I saw him,
he asked me, to my surprise, if he were allowed to
confess. Obviously I let him. I was even pleased he
asked me.

Then followed an appalling life-story, one of the worst
I have ever heard. This man had wasted his life. But the
environment in which he had to live during his youth and
later years had been particularly bad and corrupt. When
in the middle of his story he asked me if I did not think
him to be terribly bad, I could only answer, 'No, for if I

had lived in your circumstances, I would have been far worse.'

In the meantime, I discovered with surprise as well as with emotion that there was not much left of the devil-may-care sailor of the previous year. Seeing his sorrow and repentance was heart-rending. Jesus Christ seemingly laid hold of this rough fellow at the end of his life, just as he had with the malefactor on the cross.

Because the doctor told me the sick sailor had not much longer to live, I went to visit him again a few days later. He was dying. During the conversation I asked him if perhaps together we would again ask for forgiveness for all the wrong he had committed during his life. 'I have already done that', was the response. And when I sat looking at him quietly awhile, he said: 'Listen please, Reverend. If a son who had insulted me asked me for forgiveness and I had told him all is well, he need not ask me again after a few days. That is how even I would act, as a father. And the dear God in heaven is a better Father than I.' 'I will greatly rejoice in the LORD, my soul shall be joyful in my God; for he hath clothed me with the garments of salvation, he hath covered me with the robe of righteousness' (*Isa.* 61:10).

What a faith! How was it that this tough lump of a fellow at the end of his life was a true believer with assurance of salvation? The next day he died in peace. He did not have a religious funeral; his family did not want it. But I know for sure that at the end of my life, I would much rather be in the shoes of this sailor than in those of many to whom I had given a solemn church funeral!

I Leave the Roman Catholic Church

Shortly afterwards, many big changes came into my life. I was transferred from Rotterdam to Amsterdam. In

itself this was a promotion, but in the meantime my
inner conflict with the Roman doctrine and life had
become so great that I felt compelled to leave the
Dominican Order and the Roman Catholic Church. On
top of that, through my almost purely earthbound
philosophy of life, there was not much faith left within
me. For that reason I left in November 1955. For leaving
the order I requested and received 'dispensation'. Not,
of course, for leaving the Roman Catholic Church!

I went to live in The Hague, where I started a
completely different life. Through the intercession of an
influential man of the world, I became the administrator
of a hotel in Rotterdam. This certainly was different
from being a priest. Mentally and spiritually I felt
completely empty. I wanted to get away from a religious
atmosphere. I tried to free myself completely from the
past and to think about it as little as possible. I nearly
succeeded. But that sailor I could not forget.

My Roman Catholic belief was at a low ebb. I seldom
went to a place of worship. The Roman Catholic Church
had left me disillusioned and Protestant churches left me
often bored by the dull, fixed, dry, uninspiring, traditional sermons, behind which one could not detect much
personal conviction or enthusiasm. With some exceptions, the few Protestant sermons I listened to gave the
impression of being more or less successful as a personal
or theological essay about the gospel, but not one was
charged with conviction and proclamation of the gospel.
Especially the reading from papers and the very style of
the sermon was foreign to me. Besides, on two occasions
the preacher was a modernist whose vague talk put
me off even more quickly. I lost interest in church
altogether. But that sailor I could not forget.

After three years of hotel life, for which I was totally
inadequate, I became a teacher in classical languages at

a couple of high schools. The third and last one of these was a Christian high school in The Hague. As a matter of course I had to mix with Christian colleagues. Now I would not say that they were all examples of a living Christianity, but there were some who lived their lives out of a conscious religious conviction and in whom the freedom and gladness of God's children were obviously present. Involuntarily, I began to watch them, and it became an attractive experience for me.

The Bible Begins to Fascinate Me

I had to begin classes each morning by reading a small portion of Scripture. To my surprise, I gradually began to enjoy this. The Word of God began to take hold of me and to fascinate me as never before, and of my own accord I began to read far more from the Scriptures than the small portion I had to read at school. I also read commentaries by learned men. At times it was enlightening and inspiring, but most of the time I found it dull and arid. It annoyed me, as I did not feel one needed the help of scholars to understand the Scriptures. The Ethiopian eunuch did not learn to understand his reading from Isaiah through a professor or minister but through the deacon Philip. 'Then Philip opened his mouth, and began at the same scripture, and preached unto him Jesus' (*Acts* 8:35). And Philip preached in such a way that the man believed, was baptized and went on his way rejoicing.

After reading some commentaries, I could not possibly say that I went on my way rejoicing. On the contrary, very often the joy I had already in the wonderful message of God's love and mercy was dampened and hindered. Therefore, of all the learned writings about the Scriptures which I read there was not much that remained with me. But that sailor I could not forget.

The more I read the Scriptures, the more it became clear to me why I could not forget that sailor. That man was a true believer. Personally I was not and never really had been, in spite of the fact that in earlier days I had accepted a great number of theological theses as 'religious truths' and in spite of the fact that I held a leading position within the Church.

That is the conclusion to which I came through reading the Scriptures. At one time I thought that to believe was to accept the authority of someone else (for instance, the Church), and to accept with the intellect a certain number of truths (for example, that God exists, that there is a heaven and a hell, that there are sacraments, etc.). The Scriptures, however, taught me that this is not faith. If that were so, the devil himself would also be a believer. The devil accepts these truths! But that is not faith.

Abraham Believed God

According to the Scriptures, believing is the same as trusting. The Scriptures call Abraham the father of all believers because he trusted in God and in God's Word, even when he did not understand it intellectually. 'And he received the sign of circumcision, a seal of the righteousness of the faith which he had yet being uncircumcised: that he might be the father of all them that believe, though they be not circumcised; that righteousness might be imputed unto them also' (*Rom.* 4:11).

When Abraham and his wife were nearly a combined 200 years of age, God said that they would have a child. Biologically this was completely unbelievable, yet

Abraham trusted that what God had said would come to pass.

That sailor was like that. He knew no formal theology at all and had rarely been to church, yet he was a believer at the end of his life. He knew that God was his Father, that his sins were forgiven and that he was one of God's children. That steadfast trust made him cry from his death-bed, 'Abba Father'.

I Believe God

A short time after it had become clear to me through reading the Scriptures what faith really is, the Bible became an entirely different book to me. I could do no other than submit to Scripture and trust in the Lord. Then I also could, in an unforgettable moment, cry out with all my heart, 'Abba Father'. I also now belonged to the children of God. All that the Holy Scriptures tell about believers and the promises to believers could be wholly trusted. I could also have 'everlasting life', not only much later, but *now!* 'Verily, verily, I say unto you, He that believeth on me hath everlasting life' (*John* 6:47).

Sorrow and Joy

Feelings of sorrow and repentance over my many terrible sins surged up and were not to be restrained. But they were mingled in a wondrous way with the abundant joy of the sure knowledge that I was saved by the precious blood of Jesus from eternal rejection and that now I was forever one of God's children. It is indescribable what this means to someone who has never known such certainty before. After that complete spiritual change in my life, I felt unspeakably happy. And I still feel that way. That is why I would wish nothing less than that many, many others would experience the same happiness; for that I pray daily.

'And you hath he quickened, who were dead in trespasses and sins' (*Eph.* 2:1). The ones sentenced to eternal death are you, and I! Upon the cross at Golgotha, where you and I had deserved to hang before our eternal rejection, Jesus suffered. He took our place and died to save us from eternal death and to sanctify and bless us now and forever! This immensely impressive message of God's endless love is the heart of the Scripture, that unique book with its unique contents. To tell without distortion this wonderful, hopeful message of redemption, of deliverance and everlasting life, is why I became a minister.

Only Christ

For more than fifteen years I was a friar but, however important that was in the eyes of people, it was impossible for me to find peace and happiness. I could not, nor can I, live happily and in peace without knowing for certain that my sins are forgiven and that I am a child of God. The Roman Catholic Church has never been able to give me that assurance, not even when I was a priest and friar. The Roman Church did not teach me rightly what is necessary. The Roman Church did not teach me that only God's mercy is necessary, and from the human side, only faith, and the way thereto is only to be found in the Scriptures.

46

Jacob Van der Velden

God's Grace in New Guinea

I made the decision to become a priest out of a
deep conviction. I wanted to go as a missionary
to the unexplored islands of New Guinea to bring
them the message of God, the gospel of Jesus Christ. I
thought that I was well-acquainted with all the difficulties which were waiting for me there. With the slogan
'I go because I must' I went to that part of New
Guinea which was formerly a Dutch colony, only to
find out after five years that even though I had started
out enthusiastically my mission had become a great
disaster. I became aware of how my fellow-workers
and others completely ignored me. My burden was
heavy because of that. Disappointed, angry and
wounded, I did not want to pray any more. I wanted

nothing more to do with God. I had to face my utter failure.

I Learn of My Sinful Nature

Just when my spiritual crisis was at its height, I met a Reformed missionary. I did not at all desire to talk with him, but still I did and found out that the man was a truly joyful Christian. He listened to my story, and that alone was a comfort and an encouragement to me. He could understand my disappointments and also my anger. Out of my conversation with him, it became clear to me that I had listened to myself and to my own foolish convictions. I had not been listening to the Word of God, or praying to God or trusting in God. Slowly but surely I began to see what a useless servant I was as long as I continued to lean upon my own strength, but that I could also be a useful instrument in God's hand if in all things I would let myself be led by him. It was as if a new world opened to me. I learned from God's Word, came to see the greatness of God and the deep depravity of men because of sin.

It was humiliating to me to discover two truths. The first was that I did not know the Scriptures. Those with whom I discussed spiritual matters would say to me, 'What you say is unscriptural. The Word of God teaches differently.' The second was that men are totally corrupt, unable to do any good thing towards God. I had believed that the good works of our meritorious lives brought salvation to us and even to others. I came to see God as the God of wrath who does not leave sin unpunished.

God's Rich Grace

When God in his infinite mercy had convinced me, I had no more claims. When his light was thus cast upon me, I understood the seriousness of Paul's word: 'O wretched man that I am', and then I could understand Romans 3:9–20. The Lord there held up a mirror in front of me and I knew it was I. But I have to add this in the same breath: great was my joy in salvation in Jesus Christ. Then I was able to taste the richness and depth of that Scripture verse, 'For God so loved the world, that he gave his only begotten Son, that whosoever believeth in him should not perish, but have everlasting life' (*John* 3:16).

So I was able to call for help at the throne of the merciful Father in heaven who, in Jesus Christ, saved me, made me a new creature by the new birth, and filled and renewed me with the Holy Spirit. I could now live a life of thankfulness to my God and my Lord. I learned to know and to worship the God who calls and chooses. I was made to understand that one stands before God with empty hands, letting them be filled by him alone. And all this has, by God's grace, whereby I came to believe, allowed me to go forward in the power of that belief. Being a hopeless failure, I was unexpectedly made able to succeed. God led me in a wonderful way. It is in his grace that I now openly boast, for he took me by the hand and I have become joyful in his service.

Having become his property, re-created according to his image, I lived in him with a new heart. I was enabled to love God and my neighbour and to keep his commandments. I not only felt myself another person, I really became a completely new creature, renewed in his image by his Spirit. The new creature only wants to be thankful to him and to praise him who has regarded our misery and has made us so rich.

When I hear that once in a while a converted Roman Catholic has returned to the bosom of the 'Mother Church', it makes me reflect in silence on the many things I have received, being called and seized by the Lord inescapably. I had to hear innumerable times, 'What a change, what an enormous transformation, from a Roman Catholic priest to a Reformed minister!' Yet it was a change, a transformation I had not brought to pass – rather quite the contrary! David was still able to thank God while singing, 'In my distress I called upon the Lord, and cried unto my God' (*Psa.* 18:6). Such was my foolishness that I did not call upon the Lord at that time; no, I did not even ask him for help, but he simply took what he wanted. He took and placed the unwilling one where he knew it was good: in his church, where his Word is soundly preached, his sacraments are administered faithfully, and his discipline is maintained.

Ecumenism Hurts

It hurts me when Christians witness to Roman Catholics while at the same time accepting Roman doctrine and practices. The practice of smoothing over Roman Catholic sinful doctrines and practices should be another warning to us of the false ecumenical movement which causes such great damage to the work of the Lord!

I am thankful to be chosen to experience the rich thoughts which are readily described in the Bible, God's own written Word. Through his written Word, we learn to understand what is our eternal peace. It is by the sound preaching of the Word through the operation of the Holy Spirit that the hardest hearts become soft. 'I will praise thee forever, because thou hast done it' (*Psa.* 52:9).

Often while on the mission field in New Guinea I had to meditate upon this Scripture: 'So then faith cometh by hearing, and hearing by the Word of God' (*Rom.* 10:17). In the same way that I had been saved by God's grace alone, salvation has come also to others here. Heathen who did not have the slightest desire for righteousness have become righteous in Jesus Christ. He, the Lord, sent us to make the heathen his disciples through the preaching of his Word.

The Light Shines in the Darkness

God in his love, mercy and forgiveness came into my life and a miracle happened. A Roman Catholic priest in his late fifties would never naturally have begun a conversation with a Reformed missionary. The priest that I was would surely not! I had never seen a Reformed missionary, had never spoken to one, and yet I somehow did talk to one. An invisible hand intervened. At first I resisted, but when the Reformed missionary asked me to sit next to him by the river, the Spirit of God was at work. In that first conversation (and in many that followed) we together found God's face, and we were among the most joyful people on earth. His grace was victorious. My eyes were opened to the light that shineth in darkness and I found the truth of the Scriptures. By this truth, I came from being a priest to being saved, from being a missionary to being a minister, from the busy do-it-yourself man to a servant who learned to ask his Lord for obedience to his Word. Since I came to see that salvation is by grace only (*Eph.* 2:8–9), I am a different person, living because of God's grace in Christ, a witness that Jesus Christ is the only Saviour. When I look back at my life, I can do nothing else but rejoice as a thankful, joyful man. I would let the whole world know that I did not earn this, but God was merciful, and unexpectedly he saved me by free grace alone.

May the Lord call you in his grace that you may know Christ and the power of his resurrection (*Phil.* 3:10). To God alone be the glory!

47

Charles A. Bolton

My Path into Christ's Joy

I remember on one occasion working in a hayfield from morning until evening under a burning sun. Then, weary and with my skin feeling as if it were on fire, I went off to a clear blue pool in a shaded woodland to throw off my sweaty clothes and bathe in the refreshing waters, which were like a miracle of healing and made me feel a new man. That is how I have felt after leaving the Roman Catholic Church, after working like a slave for her and sweating in her service. Now divested of the clammy superstitions and false trappings of servility, I have been cleansed in the living waters of Christ's love. Thanks be to God for his saving mercy. I now repeat with a greater understanding the words which were printed on the souvenir card of my ordination: 'Whom

having not seen, ye love; in whom, though now ye see
him not, yet believing, ye rejoice with joy unspeakable
and full of glory' (*1 Pet.* 1:8).

Priest and Professor

I was born in the county of Lancashire in northern
England and educated there at a Jesuit high school.
Some of my studies were at Oxford University, where I
qualified as Master of Arts and Bachelor of Letters
through historical research. I was also awarded the
Oxford Diploma of Education as a qualified teacher.
As a preparation for the priesthood, I studied at the
Catholic Institute in Paris and at the University of
Louvain in Belgium, a famous Roman Catholic centre of
learning. There I received the degree of Bachelor
of Theology. I was ordained priest by the rector of
Louvain, Bishop Paulinus Ladeuze, on 30 April 1930.
At this time I hoped to be a missionary priest and apostle
of the Roman Catholic Church to the people of Russia,
but this was always a vain hope because the Soviet
government was never willing to admit such missionary
priests.

So it came about that for the next twenty years I was a
professor at St Bede's College in Manchester, England,
where I became senior history master, although I also
taught some modern languages. I thus became known
over the years to many hundreds of students, and I also
travelled all over the north of England as a special
preacher for charitable causes. Later I was in charge of a
rural parish so that I could pursue my studies. Among
my published works are studies on St Patrick and other
early saints of the British Isles and the official history of
my diocese.

Vain Repetitions

Later my historical research made a deep impression on my mind and outlook, in particular when I studied the Jansenist reformers inside the Roman Church during the seventeenth and eighteenth centuries. I shared their love for the Bible and for the primitive church, and I deplored the developments in theology and popular devotions since the Middle Ages. As a result, when I preached, I could never extol the power, the primacy and the infallibility of the popes, which I found had already been denounced in the third century after Christ by the great Christian martyr, Cyprian of Carthage. I was never able to exhort congregations to go through the monotonous repetitions of the rosary contrary to Christ's precept: 'But when ye pray, use not vain repetitions, as the heathen do: for they think that they shall be heard for their much speaking' (*Matt.* 6:7).

Another Gospel

I discovered that several of the fourteen stations of the cross which are displayed on the walls of Roman Catholic Churches are not mentioned in the Gospels, for instance, 'Veronica wipes the face of Jesus'. Veronica is a character of fiction, yet is venerated in nearly every Roman church. I could find no value in indulgences, which are distributed like an inflated currency. One short prayer equals so many days or months of penance. I found that medals, statuettes and scapulars were used like pagan amulets and totems. The burning of votive lamps and candles and the sprinkling of holy water seemed acts without any relation to true religion.

While we treasure communion as instituted by Christ at the Last Supper as the memorial of his passion and of his offering of himself on the cross, there is surely no justification in Scripture or the early church for making the communion bread into a white wafer to be adored like an idol, to be incensed and carried in public processions, as at the Feast of Corpus Christi. Christ used bread and wine as the sign of his body and blood, but for centuries the Roman Church has substituted a piece of dried biscuit which not even a starving man would recognize as food. Thus does Rome maintain the tradition of Christ's institution, the tradition of which she claims to be the only rightful guardian.

Salvation in Christ Alone

My studies showed me that there is no true authority for doctrines such as the immaculate conception or the bodily assumption of Mary into heaven. The Roman Catholic Church has in recent years been yielding to a popular craze, fostered greatly by the so-called appearances at Lourdes and Fatima, which make Mary more and more into a supreme goddess, ruling heaven and earth. Many Roman bishops and self-styled Marian theologians are hoping to promote the doctrine that Mary redeemed the world – in spite of Paul's declaration: 'For there is one God, and one mediator between God and men, the man Christ Jesus; who gave himself a ransom for all, to be testified in due time' (*1 Tim.* 2:5–6). This declaration is also at variance with the attempt of some debased Roman theology to prove that all graces must come to us through Mary. The Scriptures, however, make it abundantly plain that through Christ alone we have our salvation: 'Neither is there salvation in any other: for there is none other name under heaven given among men, whereby we must be saved' (*Acts* 4:12).

Roman Catholic Censorship

As a student of the Bible and of the history of the Church, I saw many things which are ignored by most Christians and by many Roman Catholic priests. I could not publish such things because of the Roman laws of censorship. When you see a book with an *imprimatur*, there is no certainty that this represents the original thought of the author and that it has not been tampered with by Roman censors, eager to play safe. If any book escapes the censors, it can be put on the index of prohibited books by decree of the Inquisition or Holy Office, against which there is no appeal. The implacable dictatorship of the Inquisition, which still maintains supreme power in church government, is only one example of the totalitarian and eminently un-Christian methods of Rome. Nobody is safe from its spies, who are in every diocese, and who are commissioned to denounce anybody suspected of disobedience to Rome.

Abuse of Power

What has turned my soul against Roman abuse of power is the way in which it has tortured and burned such people as Joan of Arc, hundreds of the Albigensian martyrs in France in the twelfth century, the Knights Templar, John Hus, the Dominicans Savanarola and Giordano Bruno, and the Anglican bishops, Cranmer, Ridley and Latimer. The Inquisition has promoted at least two wholesale massacres, that of thousands of Protestant Waldensians in northern Italy, and that of thousands of Protestant Huguenots in France. More than thirty thousand of the most cultured Protestants of France were put to the sword on the night of St Bartholomew, 24 August 1572. At the news, the Pope had cannons fired, proclaimed a jubilee, ordered a *Te Deum* of thanksgiving to be sung, and struck a special medal to commemorate the glorious 'victory'. For a long time I observed the Feast of St Bartholomew as a day of special prayer and intercession for Protestants, as an act of love and reparation. 'And I saw the woman drunken with the blood of the saints, and with the blood of the martyrs of Jesus: and when I saw her, I wondered with great admiration' (*Rev.* 17:6).

Grace Alone

I thank God for having brought me to read the great Lutheran teacher Professor F. Heiler, a converted Roman Catholic priest, who taught me the value of faith in Jesus and of salvation through his grace alone. Heiler's *Mysterium Caritatis*, a wonderful book of sermons, was the subject of my meditations for many years before the Spirit gave me the final courage to act on that teaching for my own salvation. To leave the Church of one's birth and of one's accustomed labour, to turn away from family and friends, is a hard struggle, only possible through the wonderful grace of God.

Some of my friends, who had already left the Roman Catholic priesthood and had found a welcome from others in the brotherhood of Jesus Christ, had told me how different is the atmosphere of a Christian church that does not know intrigues, spying, informing on others and condemnations as practised under the Roman Catholic system: 'Wherefore by their fruits ye shall know them.' Rome must bear the responsibility before the tribunal of history in this world, and before the judgment seat of God hereafter, for founding, promoting, and maintaining even today the iniquitous

Holy Inquisition, and later the Jesuits, suppressed once but, sad to relate, only restored to greater power later.

My path to Christ's joy has been long and sometimes difficult, but it has been a pilgrimage well worthwhile. I must record my gratitude that after teaching in Washington, D.C. and elsewhere in the USA, I have been led into the fullness of joy in Christ as my personal Saviour and everlasting Redeemer, and into the company of truly Christian friends, ministers of the gospel and their faithful people both young and old, who have been a great source of strength, help and understanding. Among evangelical Christians, born again in Christ's redeeming love through his one perfect sacrifice, I have found charity, joy, peace, patience, meekness, mildness and mutual trust. I have found that simplicity spoken of by Jesus Christ: 'The light of the body is the eye: if therefore thine eye be single, thy whole body shall be full of light' (*Matt.* 6:22). That light, which is from Christ, is the gladsome light of truth which fills us, the redeemed and enlightened, with unspeakable and most glorious joy.

For all these reasons I have committed myself to Jesus Christ as my all-sufficient Saviour and through him have passed from the death of sin to life: 'Therefore being justified by faith, we have peace with God through our Lord Jesus Christ: by whom also we have access by faith into this grace wherein we stand, and rejoice in hope of the glory of God' (*Rom.* 5:1–2).

48

Leo Lehmann

The Soul of a Priest

I have seen Roman Catholicism at work on three
continents. I have ridden with cardinals in their
luxurious limousines past the saluting Swiss Guards and
through the Damascus gate of the Vatican, leading to
the Pontiff's private apartments. I have watched while a
pope died, seen him buried and his successor elected and
crowned. I stood beside the late Pope Pius XI while
Pope Benedict XV made him a cardinal by placing the
quaint pancake hat on his head, I myself holding up the
long crimson train of another newly made cardinal. I
have ministered as a priest not only in magnificent
cathedrals of Europe, but also in Dutch farmhouses on
the wide African veldt and in tumble-down shacks of
churches in the backwoods of Florida.

I was born in 1895 in Dublin. I have no joyous memories of my boyhood years. A sense of constant fear overshadowed everything. Fear is bound up with every act of religion with the priest – whether confession, attendance at Sunday Mass, what to eat on fast days and days of abstinence, hell, heaven, purgatory, or death and the judgment of an angry God.

The Bible was a closed book to us in the classroom, in church and in the home. We had not the money to buy a Roman Catholic version, usually high-priced, and did not have the courage to accept a free Bible from a Protestant society. It was principally the fear connected with everything in the Roman Catholic religion that helped me with my decision to become a priest. I applied for admission and was accepted into the missionary college of Mungret, near Limerick.

Doubts

It was during my seminary years in Rome that doubt and distrust of the papal practice of Christianity first assailed me. Some of my thoughts at that time were: If Rome be the only centre of the true faith, how is it that true religion is so lacking in its own citizens? Why so much atheism, indecency, lawlessness? Common courtesy was denied us from the Roman rabble as we passed along the streets; obscene insults were shouted after us even by the children of Rome. Also, why was there so much clamour for priests from Ireland and elsewhere to exile themselves in China, India and Africa as missionaries of papal propaganda, when Rome itself swarmed with ten thousand priests lolling lazily in the Vatican offices and scarcely finding sufficient altars in its four hundred churches to say Mass? Again I asked myself why the boasted three hundred million Roman Catholics throughout the world should be represented in Rome by a body of cardinals nearly two-thirds of whom are Italians. Italy's forty million people were Roman Catholics in name only and not at all religiously minded. But the twenty million Roman Catholics in the United States, for instance, were not only faithful Mass-goers but contributed a lot of money to the coffers of the Vatican. Yet only three Americans were allowed to be cardinals – mediocre but loyal servants of Rome, men who would never venture to express any disagreement with its dictates. I got to know of the intrigues among the ecclesiastics in Rome to gain the favour of those in power at the Vatican, of their greed for papal honours and advancement to high positions, for we found that there were bitter factions among high church dignitaries. Daily I passed many landmarks of the subversive doings of greedy, ambitious warrior popes and their vile politics. There was a Castel di Sant'Angelo, or Hadrian's Mole, with its walls scarred from the cannon of one pope in the Vatican fortress bombarding a rival pope defying his anathemas.

At last the day of my ordination came. It is a long drawn out ceremony. I was bewildered by the countless rituals, by the many prayers and endless chantings. My fingers were consecrated to say Mass and then wrapped in rich linen cloths. My head was anointed and likewise wrapped in linen bandages. I was given the golden chalice to touch. I was given the power to hear confessions and to forgive sin, to anoint the dying and to bury the dead. For the first time I tasted from the Mass chalice the wine which, according to Roman Catholic belief, I had just helped to transubstantiate into Christ's blood by the formula of consecration. The ordaining prelate was Cardinal Basilio Pompilj, and the ceremony took place in St John Lateran.

Repetitious Prayers

Any joy which I experienced on that day was offset by a sad incident which I witnessed late that night. One of my companions became affected in his mind; for the strain of mechanical routine, innumerable petty restrictions, countless repetitions of prayers and formulas often unbalances the mind and brings on a species of religious madness called 'scrupulosity'.

I remember another incident similar to this one. In Florida, as a priest, I used to visit an institution for feeble-minded children outside Gainesville. The doctor in charge brought me a Roman Catholic girl about fourteen years old whose species of insanity consisted in feverishly repeating and counting 'Hail Marys'. Her mind was deranged by the idea that she was obliged to say this prayer a hundred times each day, and to make sure of having them said on time, she was over a thousand ahead. Some priest, doubtless, had imposed the saying of these 'Hail Marys' as a penance in confession.

After three and a half years of working as a priest in South Africa, I was recalled to Rome to work in the Vatican. As time went by, doubts kept recurring to me concerning the origins of the papacy. Growing distrust of Roman Catholic practice as truly Christian, intimate knowledge of the wrecked lives of my brother-priests, and a waning hope of any possibility of Christian church betterment under papal supremacy had already caused me grave disquiet. Spiritually, doctrinally, juridically and personally, the Roman papacy, as the divinely appointed guardian of Christianity, was rapidly crumbling to pieces within me. I was faced with the bitter realization that I must completely break with it if I were to retain my faith in Christianity.

From Rome I was transferred to America. New as I was in this strange country, I thought to save myself from total disillusionment by taking a keen interest in the humble work of ministering to the spiritual needs of the simple people.

A Boy Condemned to Die

One instance will illustrate the sense of failure which I experienced. Once I had the sad ordeal of assisting a young man condemned to die in the electric chair in the Florida state prison at Raiford, which came within the confines of my parish in Gainesville. He was from a city in the east, born and baptized a Roman Catholic and a product of a Roman Catholic parochial school. In his youth he was taught all the Roman Catholic practice deemed essential for a God-fearing life. He was convicted in Tampa as accessory to first-degree murder during the hold-up of a restaurant in which the proprietor was killed. I did all I could to prepare this young man for the 'last mile'. I administered to him in full every rite which the Roman Church has ordained and by which divine grace and strength are said to be poured into needy souls. Even as he lay limp and dead in the electric chair the moment after the fatal current had done its work, I anointed his forehead with oil as prescribed for the administration of the sacrament of 'extreme unction'. Yet I knew I had failed to carry any real consolation to the sin-scarred soul of that poor lad.

I had visited him in his death-cell during his week of fearful waiting and signed with him the form of absolution many times over. On that last morning I was at the prison gates at dawn, carrying with me all the cumbrous instruments necessary to celebrate Mass. These I arranged on a table near the double bars of his cage. I donned

all my shining Mass vestments and proceeded, with all
the dignity which the ominous atmosphere of a condemned cell would permit, to offer the 'sacrifice' of the Mass
in full. The poor lad, in a fever-dread expectation, paced
up and down behind the bars smoking one cigarette after
another. He threw away a cigarette to receive on his
tongue the wafer of holy communion which I passed to
him through the bars of his cell. It produced no effect.
The injection of morphine administered by the doctor
ten minutes before he was led to the chair calmed him
somewhat. It suddenly dawned upon me that the
doctor's single injection of morphine had brought the
boy more external relief than all my administrations of
the Roman Catholic sacraments, which are believed to
soothe both body and soul. We followed him to the
chair.

The Electric Chair

As the full force of the destructive current went through
the boy's body, jerking it up violently and holding it
tense and stiffened almost in the air, my hand went up
and down in repeated signs of the cross, accompanied by
the Latin words of absolution, as if I, too, could send a
current of absolving grace through to his departing soul.
His body fell limp and dead when the current had
ceased, and I stepped forward with my vial of oil poised
in my fingers. I requested the warden to remove the iron
cap from the dead boy's head and smeared his forehead,
damp with the dew of death, with the oil used in the last
rite of the Roman Church. Since none of his relatives
were there, I claimed his body and had it buried with full
Church rites in the Roman Catholic part of the cemetery
– though not without protest on the part of some pious
Roman Catholics in my congregation who objected to a

convicted murderer resting among their departed relatives. I had to remind them that Jesus Christ died between two murderous thieves.

Yet, I confess that in spite of all this elaborate working of the power of Roman Catholic sacramental rites through my consecrated fingers, I felt that I had failed the poor lad in his most needful hour. It might have been all my fault; I had nothing of any real worth to give him, it all seemed empty and pathetic. Nevertheless, I had to accept the praise of Roman Catholic people for having apparently succeeded in doing a true priest's work for the poor condemned boy.

All this ritual has been invented by the Roman theologians to fit in with their basic teaching that salvation can only be gained by 'the works that are worked' by a priest. The grace of salvation is taught as something that can be 'poured' into one's soul through the specially devised channels of the seven sacraments. These in turn are supposed to act as conduits from the great reservoir of grace over which the Pope in Rome has sole monopoly. This engineering of external unrealities, to act with magical force to produce a spiritual effect, runs through the entire system of Roman Catholic theology. The works of a priest's hands must be accepted both as a matter of belief as well as of organization and practice. But of such is not the power of the kingdom of heaven. Paul the apostle declares the true power of the gospel: 'For I am not ashamed of the gospel of Christ: for it is the power of God unto salvation to every one that believeth; to the Jew first, and also to the Greek. For therein is the righteousness of God revealed from faith to faith: as it is written, The just shall live by faith' (*Rom.* 1:16–17).

Along the difficult path from the Church of my childhood and its priesthood I had to travel alone, without any human guidance or sympathy. Jesus Christ was my only companion and guide. Resolutely I grasped his outstretched hand and followed whither he led.

After I broke free from Romanism, the Lord Jesus revealed himself to me as a personal Saviour, through reading God's Word. I saw the many errors of Roman Catholicism. From my sacerdotal eminence I had to come tumbling down upon my knees to confess that, like all other men, I myself was a sinner needing to be saved by the Lord Jesus Christ.

Over against the fearful conditions arrogantly laid down by the papacy as essential for salvation, I now place the sweet, simple invitation of Jesus Christ in Matthew 11:28–30: 'Come unto me, all ye that labour and are heavy laden, and I will give you rest. Take my yoke upon you, and learn of me; for I am meek and lowly in heart: and ye shall find rest unto your souls. For my yoke is easy, and my burden is light.'

49

Vincent O'Shaughnessy

From Dead Religion to New Life in Christ

I was born and raised on a farm in West Limerick, Ireland, and have happy memories of my childhood. The youngest of seven children (three girls and four boys), I had lots of relatives to visit or to receive as visitors on Sundays after Mass. No one ever missed Mass on Sunday in those days in Ireland unless they were seriously ill. Such a lapse was designated a mortal sin, meaning deadly sin, deserving of hell should one die with it unconfessed and unforgiven by a priest. The priests were revered, even idolized. I decided I would like to be a priest myself.

As a very small boy I remember rolling out of bed each morning to my knees to say my morning prayers, beginning with the morning offering which my mother taught me, together with the Our Father and Hail Mary. I still remember the morning offering going like this: 'O Jesus, through the most pure heart of Mary', which meant to me that to get to Jesus I had to go through Mary. I also have a vivid picture of kneeling in the kitchen each evening to pray the rosary with the family, but most of all I remember that the trimmings to the rosary were longer than the rosary itself. Everyone who had any problem in the neighbourhood had to be prayed for with three Hail Marys each time, and all the deceased relatives likewise.

I Become a Priest

I applied to St Patrick's College, a missionary college seminary in Thurles, County Tipperary. I was accepted and began my six years of studies for the priesthood, which consisted of two years of philosophy and four years of dogmatic theology and moral theology, plus canon law and other subjects. We did no real study of God's Word, just an academic smattering about the Bible, but nothing of any depth or consequence. I often regret that no one ever told me to study God's Word during those six long years. However, without being born again it probably would not have interested me. I would have lacked understanding, as the eyes of my understanding had not been opened up to the Word of God.

The long-awaited day of ordination finally came on 15 June 1953. It was a memorable occasion with a big reception for family and friends. The celebration continued through the next day, the day of the first Mass, when most of the parish people came for the young priest's first blessing.

Coming to America

Following three months' vacation in my homeland, I
set sail for New York with several other recently
ordained priests, destined for various places in the
United States. My first assignment was to the cathedral
in downtown Sacramento, California, one block from
the state capitol. I began my priestly duties with much
zeal and commitment to the work of the ministry; I was
determined to do the very best job that I could do and
to be the very best priest I could be. I was assigned a
room on the third floor of the cathedral rectory which
had just been vacated by a man who had a common
problem among Roman Catholic priests, namely
alcoholism. It took me several trips to the garbage
container in the backyard to get rid of all the empty
bottles I found in drawers and closets. I was grieved
because at this time I was a 'teetotaller' and belonged
to an Irish organization called 'The Pioneer Total
Abstinence Association'. (We identified ourselves by
wearing a little red heart-shaped pin. When Irish
people saw someone wearing such an emblem, they
would not offer him alcoholic drinks.)

Humbled in the Confessional

At the cathedral I remember spending long hours in the
confessional, not wanting to walk out of the confessional
while people were still waiting in line. However, when
the allocated time was up, walking out of the 'box' did
not seem to bother the other priests. The result was that
I used to arrive late for scheduled meals and was made
fun of by the others for my service to the latecomers,
especially the Mexican-Americans. God gave me special
love for these humble, unassuming people who in turn

loved their padre as they knelt and kissed my hand. This experience touched me and humbled me.

From the cathedral, I went to fill a vacancy at another parish in the suburbs which had an Irish staff. My new parish priest (in the States we call them 'pastor') was a semi-invalid with three assistants, but I soon found out that the real acting pastor was the Monsignor's sister, who was the housekeeper. She answered all the door calls and phone calls and routed them to her brother whether they asked for him or not. The kitchen was out of bounds and so was the dining room, unless one was invited by the housekeeper to come in for the meals. One day she chased one of the assistant priests out of 'her kitchen' with a carving knife, causing him to grab a chair to keep from being stabbed.

I remained in that environment for five years as the old pastor grew worse in health. This caused me to have more and more responsibility in running the parish and, believe it or not, the housekeeper took a liking to me and we got along well for the rest of my time there.

Heresy of Activism

I soon got caught up in what I call the heresy of activism, which caused my spiritual life to suffer the consequences. I still spent time in prayer before and after Mass and read the breviary (the official prayers for the clergy) daily. I prepared my sermons on Saturday from the outline supplied by the diocese. Preaching I enjoyed, as I had been trained how to appeal to the emotions of the soul. I had no training and no idea how to minister to the spirit of the people. I made the people feel good and on that score I was considered successful.

'Are You Saved?'

When I had been a priest for about five years God spoke to me through a little child, but I did not pay any attention to what this child was saying to me. I was standing in front of the church. I think I may have been waiting for a funeral to arrive. I had the vestments on for the funeral Mass. There was nobody around except a little black boy about three or four years old. He walked up to me and around me, all the while sizing me up with his big eyes. Finally he said, 'Who are you? You a preacher?' Then he walked around me again and looked me right in the eye and said, 'Are you saved?' I don't remember what my response or my reaction was to him, perhaps one of pity or prejudice. That little boy had asked me the all-important question of life and I had no idea what he was talking about. Obviously, he understood what it meant to be saved and God was using him to get my attention, but to no avail. If I only knew then what I found out twelve years later, I would have had to admit honestly to that little boy that I was not saved. I was forty-five years old before I knew what the little boy was saying to me, before I knew what it meant to be saved, to be a born-again Christian.

The Role of a Priest

I had applied for a transfer and found myself out in a farming community. Not long after this I welcomed Sister Yvonne and Sister N. to our parish in August 1968. From the moment we met, there was instant rapport between Sister Yvonne and me, as though we had been long-time friends. Our relationship was kept on a professional level. We both enjoyed conversation and sharing views on various subjects.

One day, in the midst of a discussion about a book, I asked Sister Yvonne, 'Sister, how do you see me functioning in the priesthood? And I want you to be brutally honest with me.' Her response to my question shook me. She said, 'Father, I see you doing all the right things, I hear you saying all the right words from the pulpit, I see you fulfilling the "rôle" of a priest.' In other words, she viewed me in the character of a priest. Although she did not realize the full effect of her words, it was the turning point in my life. To me it spoke of rôle-playing on the stage of life. Shakespeare says, 'All the world is a stage.' I no longer wanted to be a priest performing on the stage of life; now I wanted to get off the stage as quickly as possible. Thus began long months of agonizing.

Sister Yvonne Resigns

In December 1968 Sister Yvonne resigned from the Sisters of the Holy Family. She offered to stay until her year's contract was fulfilled and was reassigned to Mount Shasta. I was very upset that she would not be coming back to my parish and finally had to admit to God and to myself that I was in love with her. Obviously Yvonne did not want that kind of relationship because of her high regard for my calling as a priest. She did not want to be responsible for my leaving the priesthood.

I Leave the Priesthood

I went through a lot of agonizing, crying out to God for direction in my life. I asked the best missioner that I knew to come and hold a mission in an effort to bring a spiritual revival to my life and to the parish. The mission was held the first week of Lent, but the message rang hollow; it was empty, devoid of a heart for God. It had a form of godliness, but denied its power, as Paul says in 2 Timothy 3:5. My mind was made up. I must leave the priesthood.

I wrote to Yvonne to tell her about my final, irrevocable decision. We had dinner together, and I convinced her that I was leaving the priesthood whether or not our relationship developed. She told me I must know it was God's will. I wrote to my bishop and told him of my decision and requested that he apply for a dispensation to Rome so that we could be married in the Roman Catholic Church.

Yvonne and I Marry

Yvonne and I were married and moved to the town of Colusa. The dispensation finally came and our marriage was blessed by the Roman Catholic Church. I got a job with the Probation Department and Yvonne became Director of the Confraternity of Christian Doctrine for the parish. Please remember that we were committed Roman Catholics and that is how we were determined to remain. However, each time we came home from being at Mass, we felt so dry, so thirsty and hungry for the reality of God, for some spiritual food to chew on and digest, but it seemed nowhere to be found. God had given us jobs, a beautiful home and now a precious daughter, Kelly Ann. We were happy and filled with gratitude to God for all his goodness to us, but we were seeking for a deeper and more meaningful relationship with him.

We Are Born Again

One day we obtained a book about a priest who was born again by the Holy Spirit. This was all very new to me. The book was a testimony of his life and his meeting with God. Not long after reading this little book, Yvonne and I were invited to a meeting where a nun shared her testimony of God's power to save, and how she was born again. I felt the Lord had touched my heart and was speaking to me. When the altar call or invitation was given Yvonne and I were the first to go forward. We prayed that Christ would be Lord of every area of our lives, and immediately we began to feel different. It was at this point I believe I was born again and received assurance of salvation. Our prayer life had a new meaning and reality. The Bible, the Word of God, began to come alive and be more meaningful as we began to read and study it.

Saved by Grace, Not by Works

We started attending a Bible study and dipping into the Word of God deeper and deeper. As we did so, we found that many of the things we had been taught as Roman Catholics did not line up with God's Word. Essentially the Roman Catholic Church teaches a gospel of works (that is, salvation through man's own efforts to lead a good life and to do penance for sins, as if Jesus Christ did not pay for it all with his shed blood on Calvary's cross). Ephesians 2:8–9 makes it very clear that salvation is a free gift of God, received by faith; 'For by grace are ye saved through faith; and that not of yourselves; it is the gift of God, not of works, lest any man should boast.'

Jesus Alone Is Saviour

We have come to see the need for Roman Catholics to separate themselves from the errors of Roman

Catholicism, even as we have. The Lord Jesus has really
blessed our lives as we have sought to serve Him. We
have never been so happy. The Lord has blessed us with
two beautiful daughters and has opened many doors to
minister God's Word and to pray for people. Our prayer
for all who read this testimony is that they may know
Christ and the power of his resurrection. Why not seek
the Lord Jesus with all your heart?

50

Richard Peter Bennett

From Tradition to Truth

Born in Ireland, in a family of eight, my early childhood was fulfilled and happy. My father was a colonel in the Irish Army until he retired when I was about nine. As a family, we loved to play, sing and act, all within a military camp in Dublin.

We were a typical Irish Roman Catholic family. My father sometimes knelt down to pray at his bedside in a solemn manner. My mother would talk to Jesus while sewing, washing dishes or even smoking a cigarette. Most evenings we would kneel in the living room to say the rosary together. No one ever missed Mass on Sundays unless he was seriously ill. By the time I was about five or six years of age, Jesus Christ was a very real person to me, but so also were Mary and the saints. I can identify easily with others in traditional Roman Catholic nations in Europe and with Hispanics and Filipinos who put Jesus, Mary, Joseph and other saints all on a par with one another.

The catechism was drilled into me at the Jesuit School of Belvedere, where I had all my elementary and secondary education. Like every boy who studies under the Jesuits, I could recite before the age of ten five reasons why God existed and why the Pope was head of the only true Church. Getting souls out of purgatory was a serious matter. We memorized the words, 'It is a holy and a wholesome thought to pray for the dead that they may be loosed from sins', even though we did not know what these words meant. We were told that the Pope as head of the Church was the most important man on earth. What he said was law and the Jesuits were his right-hand men. Even though the Mass was in Latin, I tried to attend daily because I was intrigued by the deep sense of mystery which surrounded it. We were told it was the most important way to please God. Praying to saints was encouraged, and we had patron saints for most aspects of life. I did not make a practice of that, with one exception: I prayed to St Anthony, the patron of lost objects, since I seemed to lose so many things.

When I was fourteen years old I sensed a call to be a missionary. This call, however, did not affect the way in which I conducted my life at that time. The years from sixteen to eighteen were the most fulfilled and enjoyable years a youth could have. During this time, I did quite well both academically and athletically.

I often had to drive my mother to hospital for treatments. While waiting for her, I found quoted in a book these verses from Mark 10:29–30, 'And Jesus answered and said, Verily I say unto you, There is no man that hath left house, or brethren, or sisters, or father, or mother, or wife, or children, or lands, for my sake, and the gospel's, but he shall receive an hundredfold now in this time, houses, and brethren, and sisters, and mothers, and children, and lands, with persecutions; and in the world to come eternal life.' Not having any idea of the true salvation message, I decided that I truly did have a call to be a missionary.

Trying to Earn Salvation

I left my family and friends in 1956 to join the Dominican Order. I spent eight years studying what it is to be a monk, the traditions of the Church, philosophy, the theology of Thomas Aquinas, and some of the Bible from a Roman Catholic standpoint. Whatever personal faith I had was institutionalized and ritualized in the Dominican religious system. Obedience to the law, both Church and Dominican, was put before me as the means of sanctification. In addition to becoming 'holy' I wanted to be sure of eternal salvation. I memorized part of the teaching of Pope Pius XII in which he said, 'The salvation of many depends on the prayers and sacrifices of the mystical body of Christ offered for this intention.' This idea of gaining salvation through suffering and prayer is also the basic message of Fatima and Lourdes, and I sought to win my own salvation as well as the salvation of others by such suffering and prayer. In the Dominican monastery in Tallaght, Dublin, I performed many difficult feats to win souls, such as taking cold showers in the middle of winter and beating my back with a small steel chain. The Master of Students, Ambrose Duffy, knew what I was doing, his own austere life being part of the inspiration that I had received from the Pope's words. With rigour and determination, I studied, prayed, did penance and tried to keep the Ten

Commandments and the multitude of Dominican rules and traditions.

Outward Pomp – Inner Emptiness

In 1963 at the age of twenty-five I was ordained a Roman Catholic priest and went on to finish my course of studies of Thomas Aquinas at the Angelicum University in Rome. But there I had difficulty with both the outward pomp and the inner emptiness. Over the years I had formed, from books, pictures in my mind of the holy see and the holy city. Could this be the same city? At the Angelicum University I was also shocked that hundreds of others who poured into our morning classes seemed quite uninterested in theology. I noticed *Time* and *Newsweek* magazines being read during classes. Those who were interested in what was being taught seemed only to be looking for degrees or positions within the Roman Catholic Church in their homelands.

One day I went for a walk in the Colosseum so that my feet might tread the ground where the blood of so many Christians had been poured out. I walked to the arena in the forum. I tried to picture in my mind those men and women who knew Christ so well that they were joyfully willing to be burned at the stake or devoured alive by beasts because of his overpowering love. The joy of this experience was marred, however, for as I went back in the bus I was insulted by jeering youths shouting words meaning 'scum' or 'garbage'. I sensed that they were doing this not because I stood for Christ as the early Christians did but because they saw in me the Roman Catholic system. Quickly I put this contrast out of my mind, yet what I had been taught about the present glories of Rome now seemed very irrelevant and empty.

One night I prayed for two hours in front of the main

altar in the church of San Clemente. Remembering my earlier youthful call to be a missionary and the 'hundred-fold' promise of Mark 10:29–30, I decided not to take the theological degree that had been my ambition since beginning study of the theology of Thomas Aquinas. This was a major decision but after long prayer I was sure I had decided correctly.

The priest who was to direct my thesis did not want to accept my decision. In order to make the degree easier he offered me a thesis written several years earlier. He said I could use it as my own if only I would do the oral defence. This turned my stomach. I held to my decision, finishing at the university at the ordinary academic level, without the degree. Not long afterwards I received orders to go to Trinidad, West Indies, as a missionary.

Pride, Fall and a New Hunger

On 1 October 1964 I arrived in Trinidad and for seven years I was a successful priest, in Roman Catholic terms, doing all my duties and getting many people to come to Mass. By 1972 I had become quite involved in the Roman Catholic Charismatic Movement. At a prayer meeting in March of that year, I thanked the Lord that I was such a good priest and requested that if it were his will he might humble me that I might be even better. Later that same evening I had a freak accident, splitting the back of my head and hurting my spine in many places. Without thus coming close to death, I doubt that I would ever have got out of my self-satisfied state. Rote, set prayer showed its emptiness as I cried out to God in my pain.

In the suffering that I went through in the weeks after the accident, I began to find some comfort in direct personal prayer. I stopped saying the breviary (the

Church's official prayer for the use of clergy) and the rosary and began to pray using parts of the Bible itself. This was a very slow process. I did not know my way through the Bible and the little I had learned over the years had taught me more to distrust it than to trust it. My training in philosophy and in the theology of Thomas Aquinas left me helpless, so that coming into the Bible now to find the Lord was like going into a huge dark wood without a map.

When assigned to a new parish later that year I found that I was to work side-by-side with a Dominican priest who had been a brother to me over the years. For more than two years we were to work together, seeking God as best we knew in the parish of Pointe-á-Pierre. We read, studied, prayed and put into practice what we had been taught in Church teaching. We built up communities in several villages. In a Roman Catholic religious sense we were very successful. Many people attended Mass. The catechism was taught in many schools, including government schools. I continued my personal search into the Bible, but it did not much affect the work we were doing; rather it showed me how little I really knew about the Lord and his Word. It was at this time that Philippians 3:10 became the cry of my heart, 'That I may know him, and the power of his resurrection'. I knew that it could be only through his power that I could live the Christian life. I posted this text on the dashboard of my car and in other places. It became the plea that motivated me, and the Lord who is faithful began to answer.

The Authority of Scripture

First, I discovered that God's Word, the Bible, is absolute and without error. I had been taught that the

Word is relative and that its truthfulness in many areas is
to be questioned. Now I began to understand that the
Bible could, in fact, be trusted. I discovered that the
Bible teaches clearly that it is from God and is absolute
in what it says. It is true in its history, in the promises
God has made, in its prophecies, in the moral commands
it gives, and in its instructions as to how to live the
Christian life. 'All scripture is given by inspiration of
God, and is profitable for doctrine, for reproof, for
correction, for instruction in righteousness: That the
man of God may be perfect, thoroughly furnished unto
all good works' (*2 Tim.* 3:16–17).

This discovery was made while I was visiting Vancouver and Seattle. It was the first time that I had
understood such a truth or talked about it. In a large
parish church in Vancouver, before about four hundred
people, I proclaimed, Bible in hand, that the absolute
and final authority in all matters of faith and morals is
the Bible, God's own Word.

Three days later, the archbishop of Vancouver, James
Carney, called me to his office and officially forbade
me to preach in his archdiocese. I was told that my
punishment would have been more severe, were it not
for the letter of recommendation I had received from
my own archbishop. Soon afterwards I returned to
Trinidad.

Church–Bible Dilemma

While I was still parish priest of Pointe-à-Pierre, Ambrose Duffy, the man who had so strictly taught me
while he was Student Master, was asked to assist me.
The tide had turned. After some initial difficulties we
became close friends. I shared with him what I was
discovering. He listened and commented with great

interest and wanted to find out what was motivating me. I saw in him a channel to my Dominican brothers and even to those in the archbishop's house. When he died suddenly of a heart attack, I was stricken with grief. I had seen Ambrose as the one who could make sense out of the Church–Bible dilemma with which I so struggled. I had hoped that he would be able to explain to me and then to my Dominican brothers the truths with which I wrestled. I preached at his funeral and my despair was very deep.

I continued to pray Philippians 3:10, 'That I may know him, and the power of his resurrection', but to learn more about him, I had first to learn about myself as a sinner. I saw from the Bible (*1 Tim.* 2:5) that the role I was playing as a priestly mediator – exactly what the Roman Catholic Church teaches but exactly opposite to what the Bible teaches – was wrong. I really enjoyed being looked up to by the people and, in a certain sense, being idolized by them. I rationalized my sin by saying that after all, if this is what the biggest Church in the world teaches, who am I to question it? Still, I struggled with the conflict within. I began to see the worship of Mary, the saints and the priests for the sin that it is. But while I was willing to renounce Mary and the saints as mediators, I could not renounce the priesthood, for in that I had invested my whole life.

Tug-of-War Years

Mary, the saints and the priesthood were just a small part of the huge struggle with which I was working. Who was Lord of my life, Jesus Christ in his Word or the Roman Church? This ultimate question raged inside me especially during my last six years as parish priest of

Sangre Grande (1979–85). That the Roman Catholic Church was supreme in all matters of faith and morals had been dyed into my brain since I was a child. It looked impossible ever to change. Rome was not only supreme but always called 'Holy Mother'. How could I ever go against 'Holy Mother', all the more so since I had an official part in dispensing her sacraments and keeping people faithful to her?

In 1981 I actually rededicated myself to serving the Roman Catholic Church while attending a parish re-newal seminar in New Orleans. Yet when I returned to Trinidad and again became involved in real-life prob-lems I began to return to the authority of God's Word. Finally the tension became like a tug-of-war inside me. Sometimes I looked to the Roman Church as being absolute, sometimes to the authority of the Bible as being final. My stomach suffered much during those years; my emotions were being torn. I ought to have known the simple truth that one cannot serve two masters. My working position was to place the absolute authority of the Word of God under the supreme authority of the Roman Church.

This contradiction was symbolized in what I did with the four statues in the Sangre Grande church. I removed and broke the statues of St Francis and St Martin because the second commandment of God's law dec-lares in Exodus 20:4, 'Thou shalt not make unto thee any graven image'. But when some of the people objected to my removal of the statues of the Sacred Heart and of Mary, I left them standing because the higher authority, that is, the Roman Catholic Church, said in its law (Canon 1188), 'The practice of displaying sacred images in the churches for the veneration of the faithful is to remain in force.' I did not see that what I was trying to do was to make God's Word subject to man's word.

The Turning Point

In October 1985 God's grace was greater than the lie that I was trying to live. I went to Barbados to pray over the compromise that I was forcing myself to live. I felt truly trapped. The Word of God is absolute indeed. I ought to obey it alone; yet to the very same God I had vowed obedience to the supreme authority of the Roman Catholic Church. In Barbados I read a book in which was explained the biblical meaning of the church as 'the fellowship of believers'. In the New Testament there is no hint of a hierarchy; the 'clergy' lording it over the 'laity' is unknown. Rather, as the Lord himself declared, 'one is your Master, even Christ; and all ye are brethren' (*Matt.* 23:8). Now to see and to understand the meaning of 'church' as 'fellowship' left me free to let go of the Roman Catholic Church as supreme authority and depend on Jesus Christ as Lord. It began to dawn on me that in biblical terms the bishops I knew in the Roman Catholic Church were not believers. They were for the most part pious men taken up with devotion to Mary and the rosary and loyal to Rome, but not one had any idea of the finished work of salvation, that Christ's work is done, that salvation is personal and complete. They all preached penance for sin, human suffering, religious deeds, 'the way of man' rather than the gospel of grace. But by God's grace I saw that it was not through the Roman Church nor by any kind of works that one is saved, 'For by grace are ye saved through faith; and that not of yourselves: it is the gift of God: not of works, lest any man should boast' (*Eph.* 2:8–9).

New Birth at Age Forty-Eight

I left the Roman Catholic Church when I saw that life in Jesus Christ was not possible while remaining true to

Roman Catholic doctrine. When I left Trinidad in November 1985 I only reached neighbouring Barbados. Staying with an elderly couple I prayed to the Lord for a suit and necessary money to reach Canada, for I had only tropical clothing and a few hundred dollars to my name. Both prayers were answered without my making my needs known to anyone except the Lord.

From a tropical temperature of ninety degrees I landed in snow and ice in Canada. After one month in Vancouver, I came to the United States of America. I now trusted that the Lord would take care of my many needs, since I was beginning life anew at forty-eight years of age, practically penniless, without an alien resident card, without a driver's licence, without a recommendation of any kind, having only the Lord and his Word.

I spent six months with a Christian couple on a farm in Washington State. I explained to my hosts that I had left the Roman Catholic Church and that I had accepted Jesus Christ and his Word in the Bible as all-sufficient. I had done this, I said, 'absolutely, finally, definitively and resolutely'. Yet, far from being impressed by these four adverbs, they wanted to know if there was any bitterness or hurt inside me. In prayer and in great compassion they ministered to me, for they themselves had made the transition and knew how easily one can become embittered. Four days after I arrived in their home, by God's grace, I began to see in repentance the fruit of salvation. This meant being able not only to ask the Lord's pardon for my many years of compromising but also to accept his healing where I had been so deeply hurt. Finally, at age forty-eight, on the authority of God's Word alone, by grace alone, I accepted Christ's substitutionary death on the cross alone. To him alone be the glory.

Having been refurbished both physically and spiritually

by this Christian couple together with their family, I was given a wife by the Lord, Lynn, born-again in faith, lovely in manner, intelligent in mind. Together we set out for Atlanta, Georgia, where we both got jobs.

A Real Missionary with a Real Message

In September 1988 we left Atlanta to go as missionaries to Asia. It was a year of deep fruitfulness in the Lord that once I would never have thought was possible. Men and women came to know the authority of the Bible and the power of Christ's death and resurrection. I was amazed at how easy it is for the Lord's grace to be effective when only the Bible is used to present Jesus Christ. This contrasted with the cobwebs of church tradition that had so clouded my twenty-one years as a missionary in Trinidad, twenty-one years without the real message.

To explain the abundant life of which Jesus spoke and which I now enjoy, no better words could be used than those of Romans 8:1–2: 'There is therefore now no condemnation to them which are in Christ Jesus, who walk not after the flesh, but after the Spirit. For the law of the Spirit of life in Christ Jesus hath made me free from the law of sin and death.' It is not just that I have been freed from the Roman Catholic system, but that I have become a new creature in Christ. It is by the grace of God, and nothing but his grace, that I have gone from dead works into new life.

The Present Day

My present task, the good work that the Lord has prepared for me to do, is as an evangelist situated in the Pacific Northwest of the USA. What Paul said about his fellow Jews I say about my dearly loved Roman Catholic brothers: my heart's desire and prayer to God for them is that they may be saved. I can testify about them that they are zealous for God, but their zeal is based in their church tradition rather than in the Word of God. If you understand the devotion and agony that some of our brothers and sisters in the Philippines and South America have put into their religion, you may understand my heart's cry: 'Lord, give us a compassion to understand the pain and torment of the search our brothers and sisters have made to please you. In understanding pain inside the Roman Catholic hearts, we will have the desire to show them the good news of Christ's finished work on the cross.'

My testimony shows how difficult it was for me as a Roman Catholic to give up church tradition, but when the Lord demands it in his Word, we must do it. The 'form of godliness' that the Roman Catholic Church has makes it most difficult for a Roman Catholic to see where the real problem lies. Everyone must determine by what authority we know truth. Rome claims that it is only by her own authority that truth is known. In her own words (Canon 212, Section 1), 'The Christian faithful, conscious of their own responsibility, are bound by Christian obedience to follow what the sacred pastors, as representatives of Christ, declare as teachers of the faith or determine as leaders of the Church' (*Code of Canon Law,* based on Vatican Council II, promulgated by Pope John Paul II, 1983). Yet according to the Bible, it is God's Word itself which is the authority by which truth is known. It was man-made traditions which caused the Reformers to take as their watchword, 'The Bible alone, faith alone, grace alone, in Christ alone, and to God alone be the glory.'

The most difficult step for us dyed-in-the-wool Roman Catholics is repenting from thoughts of 'meriting', 'earning', 'being good enough', to accepting simply, with empty hands, the gift of righteousness in Christ Jesus. To refuse to accept what God commands is the same sin as that of the religious Jews of Paul's time, 'For they being ignorant of God's righteousness, and going about to establish their own righteousness, have not submitted themselves unto the righteousness of God' (*Rom.* 10:3).

Repent and believe the gospel!

Epilogue

The testimonies in this book illustrate five principles of the Reformation of the sixteenth century, also confirmed in all subsequent heaven-sent revivals. These are that, under the final authority of the Bible alone *(Sola Scriptura)*, an individual is saved by grace alone *(Sola Gratia)*, through faith alone *(Sola Fide),* in Christ alone *(Solo Christo)*, and that, in consequence, all glory and praise belong to God alone *(Soli Deo Gloria)*. A brief consideration of these principles in relation to present-day Roman Catholicism will form a fitting epilogue.

The Final Authority of the Bible Alone *(Sola Scriptura)*

The Scriptures are full of statements showing that God's written Word is the ultimate authority on all matters with which it deals. From hundreds of references in the Old Testament we might cite Isaiah 8:20, 'To the law and to the testimony: if they speak not according to this word, it is because there is no light in them.' Likewise, in the New Testament, it is the written Word of God alone to which the Lord Jesus Christ and his apostles refer as final authority. 'The Scripture cannot be broken' *(John* 10:35) because it expresses the very mind of God, and therefore 'Man shall not live by bread alone, but by every word that proceedeth out of the mouth of God' (*Matt.* 4:4).

It is the conflict between the final authority of Scripture alone and the rival authority represented by the Roman Catholic Church which gives poignancy to many of the testimonies in this book. Finding that they could not serve two masters, the Bible and tradition, Christ and the Pope, after many struggles the men concerned chose Christ and his Word.

Salvation by Grace Alone *(Sola Gratia)*

God's Word declares that all who believe are justified freely by God's grace through the redemption that is in Christ Jesus (*Rom.* 3:24). Through the substitutionary death of Christ, God can be 'just and the justifier of him which believeth in Jesus' (*Rom.* 3:26). But current Roman Catholic teaching on grace contradicts biblical teaching, affirming that 'Grace is the help God gives us to respond to our vocation of becoming his adopted sons.'[1] By these words, not only is the power of God unto salvation reduced to a 'help', but God's 'adoption of children by Jesus Christ to himself, according to the good pleasure of his will' (*Eph.* 1:5) is made the result of man's response to his own vocation. If this definition of grace is true, those responding in this way can, with God's help, justify themselves. If so, then 'grace is no more grace' (*Rom.* 11:6).

Under the same general heading, 'Grace and Justification', the new Catechism attributes merit to man's 'collaboration' with the grace of God: 'Merit is to be ascribed in the first place to the grace of God, and

---

[1]*Catechism of the Catholic Church* (Liguori Publications: Liguori, Mo., 1994), Para. 2021, p. 489.

secondly to man's collaboration.'[2] The same false hope of attaining merit by 'collaboration' with the work of God is held out under the heading 'Our Participation in Christ's Sacrifice': 'The possibility of being made partners, in a way known to God, in the paschal mystery is offered to all men . . . In fact Jesus desires to associate with his redeeming sacrifice those who were to be its first beneficiaries. This is achieved supremely in the case of his mother, who was associated more intimately than any other person in the mystery of his redemptive suffering.'[3] There is no scriptural basis for the idea of being made partners with Christ in the paschal mystery. Christ 'by himself purged our sins' (*Heb.* 1:3). The gospel excludes meritorious works on the part of man: 'Not by works of righteousness which we have done, but according to his mercy he saved us' (*Titus* 3:5).

Salvation through Faith Alone *(Sola Fide)*

The Bible teaches clearly that it is through faith alone that the believer is justified: 'Therefore being justified by faith, we have peace with God through our Lord Jesus Christ' (*Rom.* 5:1). The Reformers held to this biblical principle over against all concepts of attaining eventual union with God by mysticism, works or 'the treasury of the saints'. According to the new Catechism, 'This treasury includes . . . the prayers and good works of the Blessed Virgin Mary. They are truly immense, unfathomable, and even pristine in their value before God. In the treasury, too, are the prayers and good works of all the saints, all those who have followed in the footsteps of Christ the Lord and by his grace have made

---

[2]*Catechism of the Catholic Church* (Liguori Publications: Liguori, Mo., 1994), Para. 2025, p. 490.

[3]ibid., Para. 618, pp. 160–1.

their lives holy and carried out the mission the Father entrusted to them. In this way they attained their own salvation and at the same time co-operated in saving their brothers in the unity of the Mystical Body'.[4] The Catechism also teaches Roman Catholics to place their faith in the clergy and substitutes the sacramental system, including penances and indulgences, for the biblical truth that Christ's perfect righteousness is imputed to the believer through faith alone.[5] 'But to him that worketh not, but believeth on him that justifieth the ungodly, his faith is counted for righteousness' (*Rom.* 4:5).

Salvation in Christ Alone *(Solo Christo)*

All the blessings of salvation are in Christ alone. There is no other mediator, 'For there is one God, and one mediator between God and men, the man Christ Jesus' (*1 Tim.* 2:5). Nevertheless Rome points to other mediators, especially Mary and the saints. According to the new Catechism, 'The witnesses who have preceded us into the kingdom, especially those whom the church recognizes as saints, share in the living tradition of prayer by the example of their lives, the transmission of their writings, and their prayer today. They contemplate God, praise him and constantly care for those whom they have left on earth ... Their intercession is their most exalted service to God's plan. We can and should ask them to intercede for us and for the whole world'.[6] But Scripture leaves no room for any other heavenly intercessor than Christ: 'It is Christ that died, yea rather, that is risen again, who is even at the right hand of God, who also maketh intercession for us' (*Rom.* 8:34).

[4]*Catechism of the Catholic Church* (Liguori Publications: Liguori, M., 1994), Para. 1477, p. 371.
[5]ibid., Para. 976–87, pp. 254–7, and Para. 1434–98, pp. 360–74.
[6]ibid., Para. 2683, p. 645.

In Roman Catholic teaching, Mary, too, is a mediator, and the source of holiness: 'From the Church he [the baptized Roman Catholic] learns the example of holiness and recognizes its model and source in the all-holy Virgin Mary'.[7] In the light of Scripture, however, all calling on Mary and the saints is idolatrous. All the blessings sought through them, God alone can bestow. Christ, at the right hand of God, is made to the believer 'wisdom, and righteousness, and sanctification, and redemption' (*1 Cor.* 1:30). 'Neither is there salvation in any other: for there is none other name under heaven given among men, whereby we must be saved' (*Acts* 4:12).

To God Alone be the Glory (*Soli Deo Gloria*)

Because salvation is by grace alone, through faith alone and in Christ alone, on the sole authority of God's written Word, all the glory must be to God alone! This principle excludes all idolatry and summarizes the content of the second commandment. The Roman Catholic Church, however, sanctions the making and use of images. The new Catechism teaches that the incarnation of Christ brought in 'a new economy of images'.[8] The reason given is that 'the honour rendered to the images passes on to the prototype'.[9] This is to elevate human rationalization above God's written Word. Any attempt to make a similitude or likeness of what is divine is expressly forbidden (see Deuteronomy 4:12–16). Let us also beware of giving any of the glory of salvation to anyone or anything other than the triune God: 'They have no knowledge that set up the wood of their graven image, and pray unto a god that cannot

[7]*Catechism of the Catholic Church* (Liguori Publications: Liguori, Mo., 1994), Para. 2030, p. 490.

[8]ibid., Para. 2131, p. 515.

[9]ibid., Para. 2132, p. 517.

save . . . there is no God else beside me; a just God and a Saviour; there is none beside me. Look unto me, and be ye saved, all the ends of the earth: for I am God, and there is none else' (*Isa.* 45:20–22).